CHINA'S ECONOMIC REFORMS

CHINA'S ECONOMIC REFORMS

Edited by
Lin Wei & Arnold Chao

University of Pennsylvania Press
Philadelphia · 1982

Design by Patricia Pennington

Copyright © 1982 by the University of Pennsylvania Press

Library of Congress Cataloging in Publication Data
Main entry under title:

China's economic reforms.

Includes bibliographical references and index.
1. China—Economic policy—1976–   —Addresses,
essays, lectures. 2. China—Economic conditions—
1949–   —Addresses, essays, lectures. I. Wei, Lin,
1916–   . II. Chao, Arnold, 1923–   .
HC427.92.C4647   1982   338.951   82-60262
ISBN 0-8122-7857-7

Printed in the United States of America

Contents

v

Foreword

THERE ARE PERHAPS two reasons why the economic readjustment and reform in China have attracted world attention. First, China has a large population and an abundance of natural resources, and the state of its economy is of vital concern to many people, particularly those who desire economic cooperation and exchange with China. Second, China is a socialist country, and its search for an economic pattern and a system of economic management suited to actual conditions, for better ways to build up the economy, may provide a fresh example of what socialism means or what it should be like.

The economic achievements of the People's Republic of China are clear. But errors in economic guidelines, plus the drawbacks of the managerial system, have retarded progress and prevented a fast enough rise in the people's living standard. By decision of the Communist Party of China, steps have been taken since 1979 to readjust the economy and change the managerial system in an effort to eliminate the influence of previous mistakes. In the view of most Chinese economists, the country is shifting to a better course of economic development. Neither readjustment nor reform can be accomplished in a short time, but they will have to be accomplished sooner or later if they are to be the answers to China's economic problems.

The present volume, which is drafted but not published in Chinese, is specially written for people abroad who wish to know what is going on under China's present economic policies, including those who have misgivings about these policies. We have, within the limits of our abilities, tried to present the material in a way that is understandable to the foreign reading public. Whether we have achieved that goal is for readers to judge.

The contributors are each responsible for their own views, speaking neither for official quarters nor for the institutions they belong to. The data quoted in the volume are based on those released by the State Statistical Bureau of the People's Republic of China, unless noted otherwise.

THE EDITORS

CHINA'S
ECONOMIC
REFORMS

INTRODUCTION: China's Economy After the "Cultural Revolution"

by Zhang Zhuoyuan

THE ARREST OF THE GANG OF FOUR in October 1976, which ended the ten-year "Cultural Revolution," gave rise to a popular demand for faster economic progress and a better living standard in the People's Republic of China.[1] The Communist Party and government authorities decided to push up production and increase people's income, but this was no easy job. Production had become seriously dislocated during the ten years of turmoil. Chronic disproportions had surfaced among the different sectors of the economy, notably among agriculture, light industry, and heavy industry. The economic setup had proved to be a handicap to both human initiative and material growth. What is more, for two decades the nation had sustained losses because of the rash steps taken to "work miracles," to borrow from the language used in the "Great Leap Forward" years of 1958–60.

Unaware of past mistakes, however, some people wanted to proceed along the old course. Ambitious plans were made, but the unwieldy economy was in no sense ready for a speedy advance.

---

1. The "Gang of Four" refers to four ex-members of the Political Bureau of the Chinese Communist Party Central Committee: Jiang Qing, head of the "gang" and widow of the late Chairman Mao Zedong; Zhang Chunqiao, a vice-premier; Yao Wenyuan, who controlled the media; and Wang Hongwen, a vice-chairman of the Central Committee. They were arrested on October 6, 1976, while making a final bid for supreme power. The trial which started in November 1980 ended with death sentences, each with a reprieve of two years, for Jiang and Zhang, twenty years' imprisonment for Yao, and life imprisonment for Wang.

1

Clearly, no economic endeavor would be successful without a clarification of the issues involved. But the shadow of the Cultural Revolution prevented people from speaking their minds.

The situation lingered on until 1978, when a public debate took place on the *final* or *sole* criterion of truth—should it be practical experience or the statements in books? The debate was more political than academic or philosophical, for it posed the question "What do you do if practical experience proves something different from or contrary to isolated principles or conclusions in Marxist classics or in a few theses advanced by the late Chairman Mao Zedong? One school pointed out that in a case like this the genuine Marxist principle is to go by the truth as proved by practical experience and not automatically follow the books. The opposing camp fought back, insisting that there must not be any departure from the decisions and instructions of the late Chairman on any question. But times had changed, and people had waited long enough for a major political-ideological breakthrough that would enable them to think for themselves and depart from the beaten track whenever necessary so long as they uphold the basic principles of Marxism and the teachings of the late Chairman. This was the reason that most of the politically conscious people accepted the thesis "Practice is the sole criterion of truth."

Following this explosion, economists took a fresh look at the ways socialism had been built in China since 1949. Analyzing the successes and failures, they brought up ideas of changing the pattern of China's economy and reshaping her economic setup. The general orientation was approved at the Third Plenary Session of the Eleventh Central Committee of the Chinese Communist Party in December 1978, followed by the announcement of a policy of readjustment, reform, consolidation, and improvement. *Readjustment* means remedying the disproportions among the different sectors of the economy, primarily among agriculture, light industry, and heavy industry, and also between the allocations of funds for production and construction and those for people's consumption. *Reform* means changing the economic setup, or the system of management, both nationally and within each enterprise. *Consolidation* refers to a revamping of the enterprises, particularly those in a state of confusion, while *improvement* is defined as the attainment of a higher level of production, technology, and managerial skill.

Academically, a whole series of questions have come under discussion in the last few years. For instance, what is the main trouble with China's economy—the unbalanced pattern or the faulty setup? And what is the main trouble with the setup? How should it be changed, and where to begin? Would it be necessary to introduce elements of the Western market economy into the country?

I shall try to answer these questions by outlining economic developments since the end of the Cultural Revolution and discussing some basic questions of economic readjustment and reform.

ECONOMIC RECOVERY SINCE 1976

China's economy has seen some recovery and expansion since the end of the Cultural Revolution in 1976.[2] The main indications are:

1. *A rise in industrial and agricultural production.* Compared with 1976, the year 1980 witnessed an increase of 23.54 percent in agricultural output, of 53.03 percent in industrial output, of 64.37 percent in the output from light industry, and of 44.23 percent in the output from heavy industry (see Table I.1). During the period 1977–80, the nation also did better in terms of growth rates in these four areas than in the Cultural Revolution years of 1966–76 (see Table I.2). It should be noted, however, that the speedy pickup in 1977–78 was followed in the next two years by a slowdown in the growth of industrial output as well as in the combined output from industry and agriculture (see Table I.3).

2. *Faster rises in the output of some major products.* Steel, cotton, cotton cloth, and the three oil-bearing crops (peanuts, sesame, and rapeseeds) increased faster in 1977–80 than in 1966–76 (see Table I.4). However, slower rates of growth were seen in the case of such other important products as coal, crude oil, grain, and pigs (see Table I.5).

3. *A bigger volume of transport.* The total volume of rail, road, water, and air transport, plus the total volume of oil and gas conveyed by pipelines, increased from 1.998 billion tons in 1976 to 2.213 billion tons in 1977, 2.463 billion tons in 1978, and 2.456 billion tons in 1979.

2. Unless otherwise noted, all the economic data used in this book are quoted or calculated from data released by the State Statistical Bureau of the People's Republic of China and data given in *Jingji Nianjian* (Economic Yearbook), 1981, edited by Xue Muqiao and published by the journal *Jingji Guanli* (Economic Management), Beijing, in 1981.

TABLE I.1
INDUSTRIAL AND AGRICULTURAL PRODUCTION, 1976–80
(IN BILLIONS OF YUAN*)

	1976	1977	1978	1979	1980	1980 increase over 1976
Agricultural output	131.7	133.9	145.9	158.4	162.7	23.54%
Industrial output	326.2	372.8	423.1	459.1	499.2	53.03%
Output from light industry	142.6	163.0	180.6	198.0	234.4	64.37%
Output from heavy industry	183.6	209.8	242.5	261.1	264.8	44.23%

*For the exchange rate between the Chinese yuan and the U.S. dollar, which varies from year to year, see note to Table A.18 in Appendix, Tables on the Economic Development of the People's Republic of China, 1949–80, on p. 254 in this book.

TABLE I.2
AVERAGE ANNUAL RATES OF GROWTH, 1966–76 VS. 1977–80

Area	Average Annual Rate of Growth	
	1966–76	1977–80
Agriculture	3.3%	5.5%
Industry	8.4%	11.3%
Light industry	6.8%	13.3%
Heavy industry	9.7%	9.8%

The 1980 figure was a 5.6 percent increase over 1979. This means an increase of 29.83 percent in 1980 over 1976.

4. *Rises in domestic and foreign trade volumes.* Total domestic retail sales went up from 131.74 billion yuan in 1976 to 214 billion yuan in 1980, an average increase of 20.57 billion yuan a year. Imports and exports rose from 27.25 billion yuan in 1977 to 56.3 billion yuan in 1980.

TABLE I.3
GROWTH RATES IN INDUSTRIAL OUTPUT VALUE AND THE COMBINED
OUTPUT VALUE OF INDUSTRY AND AGRICULTURE, 1977–80

	1977	1978	1979	1980
Industrial output value	14.3%	13.5%	8.5%	8.7%
Combined output value of industry and agriculture	10.7%	12.3%	8.5%	7.2%

TABLE I.4
FASTER ANNUAL RISES IN MAJOR PRODUCTS DURING 1977–80 vs.
1966–76

	Steel	Cotton	Cotton Cloth	Three Oil Crops	Electricity
1977–80	16.1%	7.1%	11.1%	22.2%	10.3%
1966–76	2.9%	−1.2%	1.9%	−0.2%	9.4%

TABLE I.5
SLOWER ANNUAL RISES IN MAJOR PRODUCTS DURING 1977–80 vs.
1966–76

	Coal	Crude Oil	Grain	Year-end Stock of Pigs
1977–80	6.4%	5.0%	2.7%	1.5%
1966–76	6.7%	19.6%	2.9%	4.0%

5. *A rising national income.* As Table I.6 shows, national income increased 49.6 percent in four years. On the other hand, there was a financial deficit in 1979 and in 1980, and the growth in capital construction investment by 49.9 percent in four years is not regarded as a good thing either, because it imposed a great burden on the nation. But like the rising national income, the expanding budget and investment in capital construction are signs of the growth of the economy, not the decline. In this sense, they should also be listed as manifestations of economic recovery.

6. *Wider employment.* Some 27 million people were given jobs in cities and towns during 1977–80. This took care of the great majority of young men and women who had waited for placement since the Cultural Revolution years.

7. *A general rise in people's monetary income.* The annual wages of the workers and staff in state enterprises and institutions averaged 605 yuan in 1976, 602 yuan in 1977, 644 yuan in 1978, 704 yuan in 1979, and 803 yuan in 1980—a rise of 198 yuan, or 32.7 percent, and an average yearly increase of 7.3 percent during 1976–80. In the countryside, each peasant received from his farm collective an average of 62 yuan in 1976, some 65 yuan in 1977, 73.9 yuan in 1978, 83.4 yuan in 1979, and 85.9 yuan in 1980—a rise of 23.9 yuan, or 38.06 percent,

TABLE I.6
RISES IN NATIONAL INCOME, STATE REVENUE AND EXPENDITURE,
AND CAPITAL CONSTRUCTION INVESTMENT, 1976–80
(IN BILLIONS OF YUAN)

	1976	1977	1978	1979	1980	1980 increase over 1976
National income (based on the year's price)	242.70	264.40	301.10	335.00	363.00	49.6%
State revenue	77.66	87.45	112.11	110.30	106.99	37.8%
State expenditure	80.62	84.35	111.09	127.39	119.09	47.7%
Capital construction investment	35.95	36.44	47.90	50.00	53.90	49.9%

during 1976–80. The average total income of each peasant, including earnings from his collective and those from his personal pursuits, rose from 117 yuan in 1977 to 170 yuan in 1980—an annual increase of 17.7 yuan in the four-year period as against an annual increase of only 2 yuan in the twenty years from 1956 to 1976, that is, from the year of agricultural collectivization to the final year of the Cultural Revolution. Are people actually faring better? I shall answer the question below by showing the complexity of the situation.

8. *Advances in education, science, culture, and public health.* State investment in these fields and in urban construction other than housing amounted to 8.8 percent of total investment in capital construction in 1976, some 9.8 percent in 1977, 9.6 percent in 1978, and 12.2 percent in 1979. University enrollment reached 1,144,000 in 1980, more than double the 1976 figure of 565,000. Enrollment in secondary technical schools almost doubled, increasing from 690,000 in 1976 to 1,243,000 in 1980. Professional medical workers numbered 2,790,000 in 1980, 26.6 percent more than the 1976 figure of 2,210,000.

However, the achievements could have been greater without the mistakes made in 1977–78.

THE MISTAKES OF 1977–78[3]

In the days immediately after the Cultural Revolution, the nation had not yet drawn proper lessons from previous mistakes in economic construction, particularly the "Great Leap Forward" of 1958–60. The initial successes in economic rehabilitation turned some people's heads, and once again impetuosity won the day in economic planning. As China was opening its gate to foreign investment, there arose the illusion that the country could do a speedy job of modernization by relying on foreign loans and imported equipment and technology. The results were the following:

- Instead of remedying the economic disproportions which were becoming ever more obvious, it was stressed that the time had

3. For a full discussion of these mistakes, see "Correct the Guidelines in Economic Work," part 2, "Old Mistakes in a New Form," *People's Daily,* April 9, 1981.

come for "quickening the pace of economic construction with a free hand."

• It was announced, without a scientific, realistic basis, that farm mechanization would be basically accomplished by 1980 and that steel production would rise from 23.74 million to 60 million tons and petroleum from 93.94 million to 250 million tons in 1976–85.

• Construction or expansion was planned for 120 major projects in the same period.

• In particular, contracts were signed with foreign companies for the import of twenty-two major projects on loans much too large for China to pay back in a short time, while the building of the infrastructure and ancillary equipment for these projects would cost even more.

• These ambitious targets led inevitably to a high rate of accumulation,[4] which rose from 31.1 percent in 1976 to 32.3 percent in 1977 and then to 36.5 percent in 1978. The 1978 rate was the third highest in the history of the People's Republic. It was higher than the rate in 1958, the first year of the "Great Leap Forward" (33.9 percent), and only next to the rates of 1959 and 1960, the second and third years of the "Great Leap Forward" (43.8 percent and 39.6 percent).

• The high rates of accumulation were accompanied by speedy rises in capital construction investment, which increased from 35.95 billion yuan in 1976 to 36.44 billion yuan in 1977 and 47.95 billion yuan in 1978. The steep rise of 31.59 percent in 1977–78 exceeded the rise in gross industrial-agricultural output value (12.30 percent), in national income (13.24 percent), and in state revenue (28.20 percent).

Although a policy of economic readjustment was officially announced in April 1979, it took time for people to realize the harm of these hasty attempts. No drastic steps were taken to cut down the scale of capital construction or to suspend the giant imported projects. The adventurous undertakings overburdened the economy, aggravated its disproportions, contributed to the country's financial deficits in 1979

4. The percentage of national income used mainly for production and construction. See Glossary.

and 1980, and affected prices and people's life, all of which will be discussed in the next section.

READJUSTMENT: ADVANCES AND PROBLEMS

Briefly, readjustment means remedying the situation where too much stress has been laid on heavy industry and too little on agriculture and light industry, and too much money has been set aside for production and national construction and too little used to raise the living standard of the people. While this remains the basic aim of readjustment, the financial deficits that appeared in 1979 and 1980 have pushed to the foreground the question of balancing the state budget, limiting the issuance of money, and stabilizing prices.

Despite the mistakes of 1977–78 and the financial deficits, the policy of readjustment has proved effective in the following respects:

1. *Greater incentive among the peasants, better farm production, and a more rational pattern of agriculture.* The reason that readjustment had to begin with agriculture was simple: China is a country of one billion people, of whom 80 percent are peasants. The state of agriculture is decisive to the entire economy, and the incentive of the peasants is decisive to agricultural production.

Most Chinese economists and administrators now agree that the enthusiasm of the rural population for farm production was dampened for years by a blind quest for a higher and higher form of socialist ownership in disregard of the low productive level in the countryside. The worst example was the "communist wind" stirred up after the people's communes came into being in 1958. In place of the socialist principle of "to each according to his work" in the distribution of personal income, equalitarianism reigned supreme. Manpower and material resources were requisitioned by commune or county authorities without compensation to the lower collectives, production brigades, and production teams from which they were taken. In violation of the basics of Marxism, things like these were called steps for a "transition to communism." The "communist wind" was stopped after it had wreaked enough havoc. It was officially made clear that in the three-level socialist collective ownership by the commune, the production brigade, and the production team, the last one constitutes the "basic accounting unit," within which the distribution of personal income was to be conducted according to the work done by each peasant for his team. In other words, it was generally considered unsuitable to distribute income on a commune or brigade basis, because the productive level and financial situation varied from one team to another. No human or material resources must go from one collective to another unless they were exchanged at equal value.

While these policies stabilized collective ownership and promoted production in the countryside, people raised this question after the Cultural Revolution: Was distribution within each production team the best way to carry out the principle of "to each according to his work" or "more pay for more work" in the countryside? Could anything be done to link the peasant's contribution to his collective more tangibly with his income?

More flexible policies worked out by the Party Central Committee and much spontaneous action taken at the grass roots, both of which will be discussed in detail in Chapter 6, resulted in a system of production responsibility whereby members of a production team are subdivided into groups for the fulfillment of production quotas and get extra rewards for overfulfillment. A group may be a single family, in which case its working members try their best to increase the family income. The *People's Daily* reported on November 5, 1980, that 20 percent of all production teams in the country had assigned their production quotas to the families. It may be recalled that during the Cultural Revolution one of the charges leveled against the late Liu Shaoqi was that he had "restored capitalism" by "fixing output quotas on the basis of each household." Whether the practice is a capitalist one will also be discussed in Chapter 6.

This new system of production responsibility, coupled with higher prices for state purchase of major farm produce, encouragement of the peasants' sideline production, and the revival of free markets for peasants to sell whatever they produce on their private plots, gives the peasants greater incentive in working for the collective and on their own.

In 1979, the first year when the new rural policies were put into effect, total output value from agriculture showed a rise of 8.6 percent over 1978. Grain increased by 6.1 percent, reaching 332.12 million tons, a record high in the history of the People's Republic of China. Cotton rose by 1.8 percent, and the three oil-bearing crops (peanuts, sesame, and rapeseeds) by 23.5 percent.

The year 1980 saw a serious drought in North China and much waterlogging in the south. Peasant enthusiasm helped to minimize the losses. Grain output amounted to 318.22 million tons, 13.89 million tons less than the 1979 figure but 13.47 million tons more than the 1978 figure, making the year the second best in the history of the People's Republic. The cash crops were much better. Cotton increased by 22.7 percent, the three oil-bearing crops by 10.6 percent, and sugar crops by 12 percent, all breaking previous records.

Readjustment is also bringing changes to the pattern of China's agriculture, which has become abnormal through a lopsided stress on grain production since the late 1950s. Some of the latest developments:

- An end is being put to the artificial shift to farming and particularly to grain production in stockbreeding regions like Inner Mongolia, Tibet, and Qinghai, where animal husbandry is again receiving top priority in economic development.
- A similar shift is also being stopped in North China's cotton belt, where the cotton acreage has been expanded. Thus cotton output rose by 100,000 tons in Hebei in 1980 over 1979, by 200,000 tons in Henan, and by 350,000 tons in Shandong.
- By decision of the State Council (the central people's government), 225,000 tons of grain are being shipped to Hainan Island every year for the 1981–85 period, so that the local people may do a better job of growing rubber, coconut, cocoa, coffee, pepper, aromatic plants, medicinal herbs, and other tropical crops and precious species of trees.
- By decision of the State Council, mechanized bases are being built in Northeast China for the production of marketable grain and soybeans.

A significant sign of the turn for the better in agricultural production has been the abolition of the pork ration in all Chinese cities. Except for the Hui people and a few other ethnic minorities who are Muslims accustomed to beef and mutton, most Chinese use pork as the main meat dish on their dinner tables. Beginning in 1957, the great demand created by the growing industrial and urban population and the short supply caused by incorrect rural policies made it necessary to introduce a ration in most Chinese cities. For twenty years the ration increased or decreased with the ups and downs in production, but it could not be abolished altogether because there was no basic improvement in the supply situation. Its abolition in one city after another in the last few years showed that the peasants were happier and were producing and selling more under the new rural policies. It also meant a major improvement in the food supply for the urban population.

2. *Initial reforms in the economic setup.* Reforms have been carried out along the following lines:

- Over 6,000 industrial enterprises, accounting for some 45 percent of the gross output value from state industries, have been granted the right to retain part of their profit earnings instead of turning over all of them to the state, plus greater powers to make their own decisions. The practice has given the management and the workers of these enterprises an urge to improve production and business operations, resulting in higher income for the workers, the enterprise, and the state. The theory and practice of this experiment will be discussed in Chapter 3.
- Breaking through the conventional lines of division between industries and trades, specialized associations and joint ventures have been established to link raw material bases with processing factories, and producers with marketing agencies. This has enabled industrial enterprises to secure better sources of raw materials, tap their productive potentials, and find a ready market.
- While China's economy remains basically a planned socialist economy, the market mechanism has been brought into play to invigorate the economy. Even such means of production (capital goods) as machine tools and power generation equipment, once considered "noncommodities" in a socialist country, have appeared on the market in large quantities. The relationship between state planning and market operations will be discussed in Chapter 4.
- Some decentralization has taken place in foreign trade. In addition to the import-export corporations under the Ministry of Foreign Trade, which used to monopolize almost all business with other countries, similar institutions have been established by the central ministries and by local authorities to deal with foreign businessmen directly. This is part of China's open-door economic policy, which will be discussed in Chapter 11.

3. *A more appropriate relationship among agriculture, light industry, and heavy industry.* As stated above, the new rural policies carried out in the last few years have quickened the growth in agricultural production. Meanwhile, an effort has been made to lower the excessive rate of accumulation and tone down the emphasis on heavy industry. The growth rate in light industry now exceeds that in heavy industry. In 1979 the output value from light industry grew by 9.6 percent over 1978, while that from heavy industry rose by 7.7 percent. In 1980 the former increased by 18.4 percent and the latter by only 1.4 percent. The output value from light industry accounted for 42.7 percent of gross industrial output value in 1978, some 43.1 percent in 1979, and 46.9 percent in 1980.

4. *More income and a slightly higher living standard for the great majority of people.* By "the great majority of people" we mean, in general, the peasants as well as the industrial workers and all those who earn more than their standard wages, as distinguished from administrative personnel and office workers who have little means of coping with the rising prices by supplementing their regular salaries.

Chinese peasants earn no regular wages but receive their pay from their farm collectives, usually their production teams, on the basis of the work they have done for the collectives. They may supplement their income by selling the handicraft products from their household sidelines and whatever they grow on their private plots.

Provided a peasant does conscientious work for his collective, his income from the latter is determined by two factors: whether the year is a good one and whether the government offers favorable prices for its purchase of farm produce. His income from his household sidelines and private plot is determined by whether government policy encourages or discourages such personal pursuits.

In 1979 the government raised the prices for its purchase of grain, cotton, edible oils, pigs, and fourteen other major types of farm produce, offering even higher prices for sales by the farm collectives beyond the assigned quotas. In addition, special purchases were started by government commercial agencies at floating prices, which were usually higher than the above two kinds of standard prices. During the year, state prices rose by 22.1 percent over 1978 for purchases within the assigned quotas and by 25.7 percent for purchases both within and beyond these quotas. This increased peasant income by a total of 10.8 billion yuan, averaging 13.3 yuan for each person. On the other hand, the peasants had to spend an extra sum of 1.42

billion yuan because of the rises in the retail prices of consumer goods, which meant a net increase of 9.38 billion yuan in peasant income, or a per capita increase of 11.6 yuan. The readjustment narrowed the gap between industrial and farm prices by 18 percent as compared with 1978.

In 1979 wages were increased for 40 percent of all industrial and office workers, who also began to receive a monthly subsidy to offset the rises in the prices of nonstaple foods. Bonuses and other subsidies were issued in all enterprises. Wages paid to the workers and staff in state enterprises and institutions rose by 6 billion yuan in 1979 and by 10 billion yuan in 1980.

Housing construction assumed greater speed. A total floor space of 62,560,000 square meters was completed in cities and industrial and mining areas in 1979, and 82,300,000 square meters, a record figure for the People's Republic, were added by state institutions for their workers and staff in 1980.

While making all these advances, the nation has encountered a series of problems and difficulties in the course of economic readjustment and reform. Readjustment and reform, particularly the effort to introduce the long-overdue improvements in people's livelihood, cost money. On the other hand, the overextended scale of capital construction, inherited through long years of a blind quest for high-speed economic development and made worse through the aforementioned mistakes of 1977–78, could not be cut down all at once. These two factors made it difficult for the nation to make both ends meet. State expenditure exceeded revenue by more than 17 billion yuan in 1979 and by 12.1 billion yuan in 1980. The estimated 1981 deficit of 2.72 billion yuan indicates that the nation is approaching the goal of balancing its budget.[5]

The financial deficits compelled the government to issue more money, and 7.6 billion yuan were put into circulation in 1980 alone. As the money in circulation exceeded market demand, prices rose. The general level of retail prices in December 1979 showed a rise of 5.8 percent over that in December 1978, causing a rise of 6.4 percent

5. The latest official figures for the 1979 and 1980 deficits are 17.06 billion and 12.75 billion yuan. See "Report on the Final State Accounts for 1980 and the Implementation of the Financial Estimates for 1981," by Wang Bingqian, Minister of Finance, in *China's Economy and Development Prospects* (Beijing: Foreign Languages Press, 1982), pp. 84 and 91.

in the living-cost index of industrial and office workers. Average retail prices in 1980 were 6.0 percent higher than in the two previous years. Among them, the prices of nonstaple foods rose by 13.8 percent. Products made from or related to pork, beef, mutton, poultry, eggs, vegetables, aquatic products, and milk all became more expensive, and consumers were annoyed by the illegitimate handling of prices, such as setting them at random, raising them in a disguised form or without government approval, and floating them over too many kinds of goods at frequently changing rates.

The impact of all this varies from person to person. An auto worker or hairdresser may get enough in bonuses to offset the effects of rising prices. A university professor may supplement his income by writing books and articles and fare as well as ever. But a staff member of a government ministry, who receives little more than a small "price subsidy" in addition to his salary, sees an actual drop in his income. This is why the government was considering further pay raises for people in the last category in 1981.

Apart from the financial deficits and rising prices, new problems have cropped up in economic life. First, in 1980 some 720 million mu[6] of farmland, or almost half the country's total, were affected by natural disasters, and 350 million mu were seriously hit. This made it impossible to fulfill the year's agricultural targets. The drops in grain and other crops had an unfavorable influence on the entire economy.

Second, in the energy industries a disparity has surfaced between mining and the actual reserves and between tunneling and extraction to a more serious extent than expected, while the effort to cut down energy consumption has made little progress. Thus the energy industries are falling further and further behind the need in economic development. Energy production dropped by 1.3 percent in 1980 as compared with the previous year. The year's coal output of 620 million tons represented a decrease of 15 million tons, or 2.4 percent from 1979's, while the crude oil output of 105.95 million tons was 0.2 million tons, or 0.2 percent less. Further drops in 1981 affected the economy as a whole.

Third, progress has been slow in the revamping of industrial enterprises. In 1980 the government closed down or suspended the operations of industrial enterprises which had turned out high-cost

6. One mu is one-sixth of an acre or one-fifteenth of a hectare.

and low-quality goods unsuited to actual needs or which had long operated at a loss, but they were outnumbered by newly commissioned enterprises. Statistics from Jiangsu, Hebei, and Jilin provinces and from the cities of Shanghai, Tianjin, Shenyang, Luda, Changchun, and Harbin showed that, while 932 enterprises closed down or suspended operation in the first ten months of the year, 5,724 new enterprises were commissioned. At the same time, some were merged or switched to new lines of products. All in all, there was a net increase of 4,007 enterprises in these provinces and cities by the end of October, compared with the beginning of the year. Of the newly commissioned enterprises, 4,028 (70.4 percent) are run by the rural people's communes and their subdivisions. Among them are: 2,268 factories in the textile and other light industries, which use farm and sideline products as raw materials, including 77 small cotton mills and 109 small breweries and distilleries, accounting for 39.6 percent of the total number of new enterprises; 142 factories making household electrical appliances, or 2.5 percent of the total; and 903 farm machinery and other machine-building plants, including 48 small farm machinery plants and 237 other small machine-building plants, or 15.8 percent of the total. A considerable number of these are redundant enterprises which contend with the bigger enterprises over raw materials and markets. This actually means that the small, new, and technically poor factories are trying to drive out the big, old, and technically advanced ones, causing difficulty in economic readjustment and lowering the efficiency of industrial production.

The consumption of much farm and sideline produce by so many small factories resulted in a poorer supply to textile and other light industries in such large cities as Beijing, Tianjin, and Shanghai. In the first ten months of 1980, Shanghai received 380 million yuan's worth of ten major types of farm and sideline produce from other parts of the country, 70 million yuan (15.5 percent) less than in the corresponding period in 1979. Among these, tung oil decreased by 33.6 percent, jute, hemp, and flax by 19.6 percent, bamboo by 23 percent, and cotton by 5.2 percent. The supply of cured tobacco to the city was 34,600 tons, 13,300 tons (27.8 percent) less than in the same months in 1979. In particular, the proportion of high- and medium-quality tobacco dropped to 48 percent from 70 percent in 1978. Thus the production of top-quality cigarettes plummeted by 40 percent.

At the same time, the overproduction of goods already in excessive supply remains a serious problem. Year after year the government has called for the use of rolled steel in stock, but the inventory keeps increasing.

The foregoing shows that, since 1979, China has put her economy in better shape and has made some progress in economic readjustment and reform. Nonetheless, the economy faces potential dangers, notably continual financial deficits and rising prices. Since 1981 a series of measures have been taken for a further readjustment to help balance the state budget. The long-term objective is to eliminate the disproportions in the national economy and establish a rational economic pattern.

WHAT'S WRONG WITH CHINA'S ECONOMY?

The pattern of China's economy is clearly defective. It is an abnormal, wasteful pattern marked by serious disproportions between the various sectors—the inevitable result of more than twenty years of adventurous steps to achieve spectacular advances, with a lopsided stress on heavy industry and particularly on steel production.

Such an economic pattern has given rise to a glaring contradiction. The pace of China's economic development in the past twenty years and more has not been slow and in fact has been faster than that in a number of countries. From 1950 to 1977, China's gross industrial output value rose by an average of 13.5 percent a year, as against 7.6 percent in the Soviet Union, 4.5 percent in the United States, 12.4 percent in Japan, 6.8 percent in West Germany, 2.3 percent in Britain, and 5.2 percent in France. In the same period, China's gross agricultural output value increased by an average of 4.2 percent a year, as against 2.5 percent in the Soviet Union, 1.9 percent in the United States, 2.7 percent in Japan, 1.8 percent in West Germany, and 2.2 percent in Britain and in France. However, the rate of increase in per capita income was slower in China than in Japan, West Germany, and France between 1951 and 1977, and slower than that in the United States, the Soviet Union, Japan, Britain, France, and West Germany between 1960 and 1976.

How did this happen? China's economic pattern created huge quantities of intermediate or unfinished products. Although the output value seemed impressive, the final products that could meet consumer needs were relatively few. Because of the high rate of consumption in industrial enterprises, an excessive proportion of the intermediate products were used up in the course of production. Much waste and low efficiency further cut down the final output. Thus gross output value increased at a fairly high rate, but the growth in per capita income was slow and the rise in the people's living standard was even more so.

At present the most salient feature of China's economic pattern consists in the serious disproportions among the main sectors of the economy. Agriculture and light industry are underdeveloped, holding back the effort to develop the economy and raise the people's living standard. The energy industries, communications and transport, and developments in culture, science, and education fall far short of the needs in industrial and agricultural production and in other fields of economic endeavor. The accumulation rate is still too high, the scale of capital construction is too big for the nation to cope with, and much has been left undone in the area of improving people's livelihood. The infrastructures are weak, hindering the growth in production. Employment remains a serious problem. All this compels the nation to slow down the pace of economic development and focus its attention on economic readjustment for the establishment of correct proportions among various sectors of the economy. The immediate aim is to balance state revenue and expenditure, which will make it possible to achieve a credit balance, stop the issuance of money for financial purposes, and stabilize prices in the main.

Another problem lies in the economic setup, or the system of economic management. The present setup is a highly centralized one which runs economic affairs chiefly along administrative lines. There are four main drawbacks:

1. The enterprises are regarded as appendages to government organs at various levels and enjoy no independence.

2. Because responsibility is divided among government organs and among administrative regions, the managerial system cuts off the connections between one sector of the economy and another.

3. The many compulsory targets assigned by the government subject the enterprises to rigid control and make it difficult for them to suit production to demand.

4. Financially, the government takes over all the earnings of the

enterprises and pays for all their expenses. Thus every enterprise, as the Chinese saying goes, has an "iron bowl" with which it eats "the rice cooked in a single big pot," meaning that it is assured of full financial backing and equalitarian treatment regardless of its performance. These practices run counter to objective economic laws. They are ill adapted to the needs of a developing commodity economy and of socialized mass production. They lag behind the rising needs of the people. They are not in keeping with the principle of achieving the maximum economic results through a minimum expenditure of labor. They dampen the initiative and creativeness of the enterprises and of the workers and hinder an effective management of economic life by the state. In a word, they hamper China's economic development.

One may ask which is the main obstacle—the economic pattern or the economic setup? Many Chinese economists hold that for a period of three to five years the defective pattern will remain the principal and immediate obstacle to China's economic growth. It is therefore necessary to give top priority to a change of the economic pattern and the elimination of the economic disproportions. This may be complemented with minor reforms in the economic setup which facilitate economic readjustment. From a long-term point of view, however, the fundamental task is to reform the economic setup, which is the root cause of the unsound development of China's economy, including the emergence of an abnormal pattern.

Why is it necessary to give top priority to a change of the economic pattern for the time being? First, economic disproportions are the biggest problem at present. Until the proportions are brought into harmony, the economy cannot function normally, social reproduction cannot go on smoothly, and there can be no economic stability.

Second, the serious disproportions are not inevitable products of the prevailing economic setup but the result of incorrect guidelines and the adventurous "leaps forward." Under the one and same economic setup, correct guidelines helped the nation avoid serious economic disproportions in two periods in the history of the People's Republic, namely, the period of the First Five-Year Plan (1953–57) and the previous period of economic readjustment (1963–65). Some countries have established largely the same economic setup as China, but they have never been bothered by economic disproportions to such a serious extent. This shows that the present disproportions in China are an abnormal phenomenon which is not a necessary concomitant of her economic setup, and that they can be remedied even without a change in the latter.

Third, basically correct economic proportions are a prerequisite of a reform of the economic setup. This is because the principles proposed for a reform of the economic setup, such as a full utilization of the market mechanism, making the enterprises responsible for their own profits or losses, and giving proper material incentive to the workers, can hardly be carried out on the basis of economic disproportions. Only a properly readjusted economy that provides sufficient reserves can stand the difficulties and frictions involved in a reform of the economic setup, so that the contradictions which may arise can be resolved in good time. A hasty reform of the economic setup in an unbalanced economy will create confusion.

Why do we say that, from a long-term point of view, a reform of the economic setup is the most essential task? Why is the present economic setup the root cause of China's unsound economic development?

First, the prevailing setup deprives the economy of vigor and vitality. An intrinsic characteristic of the socialist system lies in the fact that the people are the masters of the country and the builders of a dynamic economy. Under the present setup, however, they must follow the orders of administrative organs in all economic activities. This saps their initiative, and the enterprises cannot move a single step without a push from the authorities. Without a change of the setup, China's economy can hardly liven up and the advantages of the socialist system cannot be fully developed.

Second, China's highly centralized economic setup, which runs the economy chiefly by administrative methods, rules out a mechanism that regulates the economy automatically and maintains harmonious proportions among its various sectors. Instead, it is liable to undermine a proportionate growth. It often happens that, for the sake of high-speed development, heavy industry is built up in isolation while agriculture and light industry remain backward. The rate of accumulation is excessively high and capital construction is undertaken on an overextended scale, while the rise in the people's living standard is very slow. This may be characterized as an inconspicuous but chronic imbalance, something common to nearly all countries that have adopted such a highly centralized economic setup. Of course, not every one of these countries has seen disproportions as serious as those in China.

Third, the serious economic disproportions in China have something to do with the highly centralized setup, which has permitted leaders to carry out ultra-left guidelines for a long time, to set high targets, a high speed, and a high accumulation rate regardless of the country's conditions, and to issue arbitrary orders. When the guidelines were basically correct, as in the period of the First Five-Year Plan and in the previous period of economic readjustment, the same setup was able to maintain relatively proportionate relationships among the various economic sectors or avoid serious disproportions, or to replace disproportionate relationships with proportionate ones. But when the guidelines were wrong they could be highly destructive. That is why the prevailing economic setup should be changed in order to eliminate the disproportions.

A PROPOSAL FOR CHANGING THE ECONOMIC SETUP

The communiqué of the Third Plenary Session of the Eleventh Central Committee of the Chinese Communist Party held in December 1978 pointed out, "We are now, in the light of the new historical conditions and practical experience, adopting a number of major new economic measures, conscientiously transforming the system and methods of economic management."[7]

Animated discussions on the reform took place among Chinese economists. Since the reform means a major reorganization of the system of economic management and an extensive readjustment of the economic rights and interests of various sections of people, it has evoked all over the country debates on its direction and principles. Two years of studies and discussions have resulted in an influential, widely accepted proposal, which may be outlined as follows.

China is a vast socialist country with a huge population, a poor economic base, an underdeveloped commodity economy, a low level of socialized mass production, and an uneven economic development. In view of these circumstances, the reform of her economic setup should follow the following three principles.

1. While public ownership of the means of production should remain predominant and the economy should still be a planned one, things must be done in a way that suits the development of a commod-

7. *Beijing Review*, no. 52, 1978, p. 11.

ity economy and promotes socialized mass production. It is necessary to break down administrative barriers as well as the ideas of a natural economy and change the highly centralized policy-making setup of the state to a policy-making setup that combines the state, the economic institutions, and the workers.

2. Regulation of the economy through state planning alone should be changed to a system under which regulation through state planning is complemented by regulation through the market. In other words, while state planning will remain the chief means of running the economy, the market mechanism will play a big role under state guidance.

3. Management of the economy chiefly by Party and government organs along administrative lines should be changed to management chiefly by economic institutions along economic lines on the basis of economic legislation, so as to arouse everybody's initiative, organize economic activities rationally, achieve the maximum results through a minimum expenditure of labor, and accelerate socialist modernization.

The specific guidelines for the reform are:

A. *Changing the enterprises from appendages to industrial ministries and local administrative organs to relatively independent economic entities.* Within the framework of state planning and state laws, decrees, and policies, each enterprise will enjoy the right to carry out production, exchange, and other economic activities on their own in light of social demand and the law of value. It will conduct independent business accounting and assume responsibility for their profits and losses. It will be able to use its profits, minus taxes, production costs, and payment of bank loans, for the expansion of production, workers' welfare, bonuses, and a reserve fund. Provided it fulfills state targets, an enterprise may, in accordance with market demand, draw up its own plans, select sources of raw and semifinished materials, buy supplies, and sell its products and export them with government approval. Within limits prescribed by the state, an enterprise may decide on the forms of wages, the system of promotion, workers' benefits, and the recruitment of workers and the discharge of surplus ones. The living expenses of the discharged workers will be covered by social insurance. The workers and staff members will have the right to choose their jobs within certain limits.

The rural people's communes, production brigades, and production teams will have the right to engage in farming, forestry, animal husbandry, sideline production, fishery, and other economic activities by giving full play to their favorable local conditions. They may each specialize in a certain line of production and form associations through such a division of labor. Provided they fulfill the quotas of major farm and sideline products for state purchase, they may plan their production and sell their products according to market demand and their financial interests. They have the right to decide on the distribution of their income and to reject equalitarian practices, the arbitrary transfer of resources between collectives, and unreasonable orders.

The forms of ownership are to be multiplied and cooperatives and individual businesses permitted in the retail, food and drink, handicraft, transportation, building, and service trades.

B. *Changing the scattered "big and all-embracing" or "small but all-embracing" enterprises to associations based on rational specialization and cooperation.* All forms of association are to be organized on the basis of voluntary participation and mutual benefit, breaking down the barriers among administrative regions, among economic departments, among military and civilian institutions, and among different forms of ownership. The associations must not practice monopoly in relation to one another and must safeguard the independence and decision-making powers of each participating enterprise. Several associations may be established in each trade to encourage competition.

C. *Changing the closed system of the allocation of products to an open market under unified leadership.* Both the means of production (capital goods) and the means of livelihood (consumer goods) are commodities and should be circulated through the market in line with the principles of a socialist commodity economy. Except for a few commodities that are scarce or vital to the national economy and the people's livelihood and should therefore be distributed largely in a planned way, all goods will be open to free sales and purchases. There should be more channels of circulation, fewer links in the chain of circulation, and no barriers between administrative regions and departments. The circulation of commodities will be conducted among economic zones, and various types of trade centers will appear.

It will be necessary to end the monopoly over foreign trade by a single government ministry, which cuts up the links among departments and regions. Foreign trade should be done by large productive enterprises and foreign trade corporations, while the interests of all enterprises turning out export goods should be taken into account. There should be a pooling of efforts between the productive and foreign trade departments, between interior and coastal areas, and between import and export agencies. Taking a unified international stance and coordinating their action, foreign trade executives should adopt flexible forms of operation to suit the changing international market.

D. *Organization of economic activities through economic centers and not along the lines of government ministries and administrative regions.* Industrial and commercial centers will each be supplemented by banking, market quotation, forecast, and consultation centers. In this way the industrially and commercially developed metropolises will become the country's main centers of economic life, surrounded by medium-size and small ones, that is, the other cities and towns, which are in turn linked with townships and villages. This network must not be confused with the system of administrative affiliations. Economic activities must be based on the natural ties of the economy and the principle of achieving the best possible results. The economic centers may intertwine their activities to form a flexible, organic network.

E. *Combining mandatory plans with general guidelines.* The state will guide the development of the national economy through long-term and medium-term plans, which define the orientation of economic development; the main economic proportions; the scale of capital construction, the investment priorities, and the major projects; the range for a rise in the people's living standard, and so on. The yearly plan should mainly seek to balance the national budget, the bank credits, the demand for and provision of supplies, and the international payments.

Mandatory plans will be worked out for key enterprises and products vital to the national economy and the people's livelihood, the purchase of key farm produce and industrial goods, and key construction projects, while general guidelines will be formulated for all other enterprises and products. The state will use economic means mainly to guide the operations of the enterprises along the lines of national plans and social demand, but may interfere by administrative means according to law when necessary.

F. *Regulating the economy mainly by economic means and not mainly by administrative measures.* The prices of industrial goods will be based on the average production cost and profit margin, to be readjusted from time to time in light of the fluctuations in production cost and the changes in supply and demand. The prices of farm produce will be formulated and readjusted on the principle of narrowing the gap between industrial and farm prices. Price control should be flexible and various forms of pricing adopted: unified state prices for key farm and sideline produce, raw and semifinished materials, fuels, and important consumer goods; floating prices within certain limits for some of the farm and sideline produce, raw and semifinished materials, most processed goods and most consumer goods; and free prices for all other products.

Transfer of profits to the state by the enterprises will be replaced by taxation. Different taxes will be imposed at different rates to regulate the profit levels of various enterprises. The sources of revenue of the central government will be separated from those of the local governments. The banks will play a fuller part in the regulation and control of funds.

G. *Strict enforcement of law and discipline, and better legislation, administration of justice, and public supervision in the economic field.* In addition to the civil law in force, the state will formulate a financial law, a banking law, and laws on planning, statistics, accounting, contracts, patents, metrology, corporations, factories, stores, mines, labor, land, grasslands, aquatic resources, capital construction, taxation, price, and so on, so that all economic activities will be governed by legislation. Economic tribunals will be established to deal with legal cases in the economic field. It is necessary to institute a system of economic supervision at the central and local levels and to give full scope to the supervisory role of the statistical, financial, taxation, banking, and pricing agencies and those in charge of industry and commerce.

H. *Changing the overconcentration of economic managerial powers in the hands of the central government, and enlarging the managerial powers of the localities under central guidance.* The scope of economic management by the central government and by the local governments should be properly defined. The central government will be responsible for the formulation of economic and technical policies, economic laws and decrees, plans for national economic development, and the state budget. It will decide on the layout of economic zones, key construction projects, defense construction, aid to economically backward areas, foreign aid, and so on. The local governments will be responsible for the formulation of local economic laws and decrees, plans for local development, and the local budget and will direct urban construction, the service trades, and the building of local infrastructures, as well as local undertakings in agriculture, forestry, water conservancy, culture, education, public health, and so on.

I. *Reforming the system of leadership in enterprises.* The present system of leadership in enterprises, with the director of the factory executing his duties under the Communist Party committee, often results in the Party organization monopolizing all affairs and prevents the director from performing his proper functions. Such a system of leadership will have to be changed in the long run, but it will continue to operate for the time being, with the exception of a few enterprises where experimental reforms are under way, because an immediate, overall change would cause wider repercussions. When the time comes, a reform should be carried out along the lines of (1) proper leadership by the Party organization, (2) truly democratic management, (3) greater executive power for the director, and, most important, (4) the establishment of the workers' congress as the final authority in an enterprise.

As for Chinese-foreign joint ventures and all types of economic associations, each should be directed by a joint committee or board of directors formed by the participants, which should decide, according to contracts and agreements, on the line of business, the production and marketing plans, the distribution of profits, and so on, as well as the appointment or removal of the chief executive officer.

J. *Changing direct management of the economy by Party and government organs to management mainly through economic agencies.* Party committees at all levels should strengthen their leadership in economic construction while freeing themselves from day-to-day affairs. They should concentrate on the improvement of Party organizations in an ideologically and organizational sense and handle well the orientation, line, and policies of economic construction. Governments at all levels should manage the economy mainly by means of policies, laws and decrees, plans, and various economic levers, but they should not interfere with the internal affairs of economic institutions.

While commissions in charge of economic affairs should be set up at the central and local levels, unnecessary ministries and depart-ments should be abolished. Those chosen as executives of the commis-sions should be competent and be able to ensure that the enterprises act according to state guidelines, policies, laws, and decrees.

It will take a long time to put the above ideas into practice. Once this is done, a fundamental change will take place in China's economic setup. With a motive force within and pressure from without, the enterprises will exhibit great vitality and increase the momentum of economic progress. While drawing on the experience of other coun-tries, this new setup is based on China's actual conditions.

The reform of the economic setup is a highly complicated matter. Taking into consideration the interests of all parties concerned, we will have to guard against rashness and adopt a series of interim measures to ensure an orderly advance.

1

The Policy of Readjustment and Its Application

by Zhou Shulian and Zhang Zhuoyuan

THE WORSENING OF ECONOMIC DISPROPORTIONS IN THE COURSE OF ECONOMIC REVIVAL, 1977–78

After the "Cultural Revolution" came to an end in 1976, China faced three economic tasks:

1. Putting the damaged economy back on its feet.
2. Remedying the economic disproportions that had existed since the "Great Leap Forward" of 1958–60 and that had worsened during the Cultural Revolution.
3. Changing the nation's economic setup, that is, the system of economic management characterized by an overconcentration of power and the handling of economic affairs mainly by administrative means.

In 1977–78 the nation concentrated on the first task, economic rehabilitation, while doing little to tackle the two other tasks, because of an inadequate understanding of the seriousness of the economic disproportions. The result was twofold: a fairly speedy economic revival and a further worsening of the disproportions. The two years witnessed rises in industrial and agricultural production, in national income, in the total volume of retail sales, in state revenue, and in the

28

consumption level[1] of workers and peasants (see Table 1.1). The socialist enthusiasm of the masses, who were happy to see the collapse of the Gang of Four, enabled the nation to extricate itself from the economic crisis arising from the Cultural Revolution.

While these achievements enlivened the economy, many problems surfaced during the two years. As stated in the Introduction, mistakes were made which, if not corrected in time, would have led to another "Great Leap Forward." Overly ambitious targets were announced at a time when the economy had only just turned for the better. This could not but increase economic difficulties and worsen the disproportions.

First, the high rate of accumulation was raised further when it was already out of balance with the consumption rate.[2]

Except for a previous period of economic readjustment (1963–65), China's accumulation rate had always been high in the period from 1958, the first year of the "Great Leap Forward," to the mid-1970s. It rose from 31.1 percent in 1976 to 32.3 percent in 1977 and to 36.5 percent in 1978. The amount of accumulation[3] increased 10.0 percent in 1977 and 30.2 percent in 1978, both exceeding the growth in national income (12.4 percent). In contrast, the growth in the

TABLE 1.1
PERCENTAGES OF ECONOMIC GROWTH, 1977–78

	1977	1978
Gross output value of industry and agriculture	10.07%	12.30%
National income	8.40%	12.40%
Total volume of retail sales	5.30%	8.30%
State revenue	12.60%	28.20%
Consumption level of workers and peasants	2.50%	5.50%

1. The quantity and quality of what people use for food, clothing, housing, transportation, and other purposes in everyday life. In a socialist country the consumption level refers also to a wide range of social benefits, including free medical care, government subsidies for rent, the use of water and electricity, and so on.

2. See "consumption fund" in Glossary.

3. See "accumulation" and "accumulation fund" in Glossary.

amount of consumption[4] was much slower, being 3.9 percent in 1977 and 7.8 percent in 1978, and these percentages would be even smaller if population growth is taken into consideration. The increasing rate of accumulation limited the rise in the people's consumption level, making it difficult to effect long-overdue improvements in their livelihood and almost impossible to balance accumulation with consumption.

The rises in the rate of accumulation were accompanied by an extension of the scale of capital construction, as Table 1.2 shows. A survey made at the end of 1978 showed that 65,000 projects, each with an investment of 50,000 yuan or more, were under construction throughout the country, and the total investment amounted to 370 billion yuan. In addition, 39,000 projects were going through renovation. Among the 65,000 projects, 1,723 were large and medium-size ones, as against 1,400 in 1977, which required a total investment of 280 billion yuan. At the end of 1978 the finished projects among the 1,723 represented 160 billion yuan of investment, while the unfinished projects would require an additional investment of 120 billion yuan. If 12 billion yuan were to be spent on these unfinished projects every year, it would take ten more years to complete them.

Second, the disproportions among agriculture, light industry, and heavy industry grew more serious, while the backwardness of certain branches of heavy industry became more pronounced.

TABLE 1.2
INVESTMENT IN CAPITAL CONSTRUCTION, 1977–78 (IN BILLIONS OF YUAN)

	1977	1978
Total investment	36.44	47.90
Rise over preceding year	1.4%	31.6%
Portion of state investment	29.44	39.59
Rise over preceding year	0.1%	34.5%
Portion of local investment	7.00	8.36
Rise over preceding year	6.9%	19.4%

4. See "consumption fund" in Glossary.

China's agriculture has developed slowly for a long time and particularly during the Cultural Revolution. In terms of per capita output, 1976 saw a drop of 29.0 percent in cotton as compared with 1967, of 20.0 percent in the three oil-bearing crops (peanuts, sesame, and rapeseeds), and of 10.0 percent in sugar. The year's per capita grain output was barely equal to the 1956 level. During 1967–76, however, industrial production rose by an annual average of 8.4 percent, a much higher rate than the average of 3.36 percent registered in agriculture. This was why China had to import much grain, cotton, and sugar during the ten years of the Cultural Revolution and began to import animal and plant oils in 1971. After the end of the Cultural Revolution, a wide gap remained between the growth rates of industrial and agricultural production. Industrial output increased by 14.6 percent in 1977 and by 13.6 percent in 1978, whereas agricultural output rose by 0.5 percent and 8.1 percent, showing a worsening disproportion between the two.

The light and heavy industries were likewise out of balance. The lopsided stress on heavy industry continued in 1977 and 1978. While output from heavy industry grew by 14.3 percent in 1977 and by 15.6 percent in 1978, that from light industry rose by 14.3 percent and 10.8 percent. Although the rates were exceptionally equal in 1977, light industry continued to trail behind heavy industry as a general trend of development.

Within heavy industry, the energy, raw and processed material, and building material industries, as well as the communication and transport services, lagged further behind the needs in economic development. This was particularly true of the energy industries, where a serious imbalance existed between the amount of extraction and the reserves and also between extraction and tunneling. The consequences began to be felt in 1980, when first energy output dropped by 1.3 percent and there was a decrease in both coal and crude oil. The last two continued to drop in 1981.

THE POLICY AND MEASURES OF ECONOMIC READJUSTMENT

In effect, the policy of economic readjustment was advanced at the Third Plenary Session of the Eleventh Central Committee of the

Chinese Communist Party, held in December 1978. The communiqué of the session said:

> Due to sabotage by Lin Biao and the Gang of Four over a long period there are still quite a few problems in the national economy, some major imbalances have not been completely changed, and some disorder in production, construction, circulation, and distribution has not been fully eliminated. A series of problems left hanging for years as regards the people's livelihood in town and country must be appropriately solved. We must conscientiously solve these problems step-by-step in the next few years and effectively achieve a comprehensive balance, so as to lay a solid foundation for rapid development.[5]

This actually raised the question of readjusting the national economy. Acting in this spirit, the Party and the government put forward in April of the next year the principle of readjustment, reform, consolidation, and improvement with the focus on readjustment. The policy involved a drastic curtailment of capital construction and steps to close down enterprises that lacked necessary production conditions, to suspend their operation, to merge them with other enterprises, or to shift them to other lines of production. Administrative spending was to be cut down. On the other hand, the readjustment program provided for the development of agriculture, light industry (particularly the production of articles of daily use), the energy industries, the communication and transport services, science, education, health work, and cultural undertakings.

The Second Session of the Fifth National People's Congress, convened in June 1979, set the following aims of economic readjustment:

- To achieve a relative correspondence between the growth of grain production and other farm and sideline production, on the one hand, and that of population and of industry, on the other hand.
- To achieve a growth rate for the light and textile industries equal to or slightly greater than that of the heavy industry; to

5. *Beijing Review,* no. 52, 1978, p. 11.

bring increases in major products of the light and textile industries into general correspondence with the rise of domestic purchasing power while increasing exports.

• To alleviate the current tense situation in the fuel and power industries and the transport and communication services by increasing production and practicing economy. While increasing production in the metallurgical, machine-building, chemical, and other heavy industries, emphasis will be put on better quality and more variety.

• To narrow the scope of capital construction, concentrate on major projects, improve their quality, reduce cost, and shorten construction periods.

• To bring about, on the basis of rising production, a further increase in the average income of all peasants from the collectives and in the average wages of all nonagricultural workers and staff.[6]

It may be asked, Why was the policy of readjustment not adopted earlier? The economy devastated during the Cultural Revolution first had to be rehabilitated before it could be readjusted. Until it was revived to a certain extent, the question of its imbalances did not come to the fore. For instance, although the shortage of energy and means of transportation had existed for a long time, it was not keenly felt during the ten years of turmoil because many factories and mills were not working anyway. Before production went back to normal, nobody could talk about raising the people's living standard, and the government spent no extra money for this purpose.

Another factor was economic thinking. When the Cultural Revolution came to an end, people were not immediately aware of the extent of the damages to the economy and so could not realize the need for readjustment. Besides, their minds were fettered by ultraleftist conventions on a whole series of questions, such as the aim of socialist production, the relationship between the speed and balance of economic development, and mistakes like overstressing heavy industry, particularly the iron and steel industry. The lack of a correct understanding of these questions prevented people from realizing the economic disproportions.

6. *Main Documents of the Second Session of the Fifth National People's Congress of the People's Republic of China* (Beijing: Foreign Languages Press, 1979), pp. 27–28.

The following measures were adopted to carry out the policy of readjustment:

1. *Readjustment of rural policies and acceleration of agricultural development.* On September 28, 1979, the Fourth Plenary Session of the Eleventh Central Committee of the Party adopted the "Decisions of the Central Committee of the Communist Party of China on Some Questions Concerning the Acceleration of Agricultural Development,"[7] as well as a series of measures to boost farm production. The main measures were:

- While keeping to the socialist orientation, observing state laws and policies, and accepting the guidelines in state plans, a production brigade or production team in a people's commune has the right to grow crops as it sees fit according to the seasons and local conditions. It has the right to decide on the ways to increase production, choose the method of management and operation, and distribute its products and cash income. It has the right to reject any unreasonable order from anyone.
- No organization or individual may seize or appropriate without compensation any labor power, land, draft animal, machinery, money, product, or material belonging to a farm collective, such as a production team.
- The people's communes and their subdivisions may adopt a variety of methods for the distribution of personal income, which may be based on the fulfillment of work quotas or on working time, coupled with an evaluation of one's performance. Provided the production team conducts business accounting and income distribution on a unified basis, it may assign quotas to work groups, which receive extra payment for overfulfillment of these quotas.
- The plots of land and animals owned by commune peasants, their household sidelines, and the country markets are all supplementary to the socialist economy and must not be criticized as "tails of capitalism." While it is necessary to consolidate and expand the collective economy, the peasants should be encouraged and helped to develop household sidelines as a means of increasing their income and invigorating the rural economy.

7. The Decisions were published in the *People's Daily,* October 6, 1979.

• The prices for state purchase of farm produce were raised as proposed by the Third Plenum. Starting from the marketing time of summer grain in 1979, state purchasing prices for grain were raised by 20 percent. These new prices were raised by another 50 percent for purchases beyond state quotas. Purchasing prices for cotton, oil-bearing crops, sugar-bearing crops, animal by-products, aquatic products, and forestry products were also raised. The prices of farm machinery, chemical fertilizers, insecticides, plastics for rural use, and other farm-oriented industrial goods were lowered by 15 to 20 percent in 1979 and 1980 on the basis of lower production costs.

The above measures proved effective. As stated in the Introduction, China gathered a record grain harvest in 1979. The 1980 harvest was the second best in the history of the People's Republic, despite a serious drought and much waterlogging. The cash crops also increased, some substantially, during 1979–80.[8]

2. *Speeding up the growth of light industry and increasing its proportion in the industrial makeup.* In June 1979 the National People's Congress decided on a faster development of the light industries, including the textile industry, which were to receive priority in the supply of fuel, power, and raw and semi-finished materials and to sign contracts with transportation departments for a timely delivery of whatever they needed. These industries were given the right to choose useful materials and equipment from government warehouses. Foreign exchange allocations for them increased by 320 million yuan (17 percent) in 1979 over 1978, primarily for the import of raw and semifinished materials unavailable or in short supply in China. Meanwhile, the heavy industries were called upon to manufacture consumer goods for the domestic and foreign markets.

As a result of all this, light industry grew by 9.6 percent in the value of output in 1979, overtaking the growth in heavy industry (7.7 percent), and by 18.4 percent in 1980, far surpassing the latter (1.4 percent). It accounted for 42.7 percent of the nation's gross industrial output value in 1978, some 43.1 percent in 1979, and 46.9 percent in 1980.

3. *Readjusting the ratio between accumulation and consumption*

8. See above, pp. 10–11.

and effecting the long-overdue improvements in people's livelihood. The rises in peasant income, achieved through the application of new rural policies in 1979, have been shown in the Introduction.[9] The total wage bill for the workers and staff in state enterprises rose by 6 billion yuan in 1979 and by another 10 billion yuan in 1980. The general rises in people's income may be seen from the increases in the retail sales volume, which rose by 180 billion yuan in 1979 and by 214 billion yuan in 1980, as compared with an annual average of 3.9 billion yuan during 1953–57 and of 4.2 billion yuan during 1957–76.

Because of the rising consumption level, the accumulation rate dropped from the post–Cultural Revolution peak of 36.5 percent in 1978 to 33.6 percent in 1979 and 31.0 percent in 1980.

WHY A FURTHER READJUSTMENT?

In early 1981 China announced a policy for a *further* readjustment of her national economy.[10] Why is such a policy necessary? Although the economic situation has been turning for the better since the end of the Cultural Revolution, and the nation has been going into the roots of her economic problems, drastic measures must be taken to stop the mishandling of the relationship between national construction and people's livelihood.

The situation may be illustrated by what happened to the 1979 national economic plan. Financially, the plan provided for a cut in capital construction investment by 9 billion yuan and an outlay of 10 billion yuan for farm price support and wage increases. This would mean a more or less balanced budget. In practice, however, government outlays for increases in farm prices and in wages exceeded 10 billion yuan, while there was no curtailment of capital construction investment, which totaled 50 billion yuan, 2.1 billion (4 percent) more than the 1978 figure.

In 1980 the number of large and medium-size projects under construction was 700 (45 percent) less than in 1979. But there was an

9. See above, pp. 6–7.

10. The policy for a further readjustment was announced by Yao Yilin, vice-premier and minister in charge of the State Planning Commission, at a session of the Standing Committee of the National People's Congress on February 25, 1981.

increase and not a decrease in the total investment in such projects, because less investment was involved in the suspended or canceled projects, and more in the newly initiated ones. Thus the total investment needed for the unfinished large and medium-size projects was 25 percent larger than that in the previous year. At the prevailing rate of investment, it would take eight more years to complete these projects even if not a single one was to be added. Meanwhile, small projects mushroomed. Statistics from Inner Mongolia, Liaoning, Jilin, and Guangdong show that 36.6 percent more projects were started in the first eight months of 1980, compared with the same period in 1979.

The scale of capital construction was beyond the resources of the country. Take rolled steel, cement, and timber, the three main types of building material. In 1980 the total amount of rolled steel available for capital construction through state allocation and other channels was 5.7 million tons. If 1.3 tons were allocated for every 10,000 yuan of investment, the total amount would be enough for only 43.1 billion yuan of investment. The cement that could be obtained for capital construction totaled 15.6 million tons. If 5 tons were allocated for every 10,000 yuan of investment, the total amount would be enough for only 31.2 billion yuan of investment. The timber that could be set aside for the same purpose was 6.66 million cubic meters. If 2 cubic meters were allocated for every 10,000 yuan of investment, the total amount would be enough for only 33.1 billion yuan of investment. But the 1980 investment in capital construction was 50 billion yuan. Thus the nation lacked the supplies for 6.9 billion yuan of investment in terms of rolled steel, for 18.8 billion yuan of investment in terms of cement, and for 16.9 billion yuan of investment in terms of timber.

Meanwhile, much capital construction was carried on in the name of technical renovation to tap production potentials. In the first half of 1980, some 2,621 projects, each with an investment of one million yuan or more, were being constructed for such a professed purpose. This was 64 more than the total number of projects under construction in 1979. Ninety-four of the "technical renovation" projects each received an investment of 10 million yuan or more, and 51 of them were started in 1980. In many places half the funds allocated for technical innovations were actually spent on capital construction. All this worsened the imbalance between the allocation of funds and the supply of materials. It was estimated that the supplies allocated by the state for technical renovation could meet only a little more than half of the need for rolled steel, 42 percent of the need for cement, and less than half of the need for timber. This showed that the "technical renovation" projects also had to be slashed back.

The overextended scale of capital construction was an important factor contributing to the financial deficits of 1979 and 1980. In a socialist country, capital construction funds are allocated from the state treasury instead of being supplied by private investors, and too much investment often creates a deficit. There were many factors accounting for the 17 billion yuan deficit in 1979 and the 12.1 billion yuan deficit in 1980, but overspending on capital construction was the main one. Because there were no other guaranteed sources of revenue, the only way for the government to make both ends meet was an overdraft from the national bank and, consequently, an overissue of paper money. Thus the financial deficits disrupted credit balance and led to inflation. In 1980 the issue of banknotes was planned at 3 billion yuan, but it turned out to be 7.6 billion yuan, 4.6 billion in excess of the plan. As the increase in paper money outstripped the increase in commodities, retail prices rose by 6.0 percent in 1980 over 1979, and the prices of nonstaple foods rose by 13.8 percent.

Chen Yun, vice-chairman of the Chinese Communist Party Central Committee and the Party's leading economic administrator, points out that in a socialist country like China "the scale of national construction must correspond to the financial and material resources of the country. Correspondence or incorrespondence means economic stability or instability." He also says, "When the scale of construction is beyond the financial and material means of the state, we see a sign of rashness, which will lead to economic chaos. When the former is in keeping with the latter, we have economic stability."[11]

An urgent task facing China, therefore, was to slash capital construction investment and take other steps to eliminate the financial deficits. This was why China decided on a further readjustment of the economy beginning in 1981.

The program for a further readjustment has three immediate aims: balancing state revenue and expenditure, balancing the bank credits to check inflation, and stabilizing prices. The long-term objec-

11. Both passages are quoted in "The Scale of Construction Must Conform to the Nation's Capacities," by You Lin in the *Zhongguo Caimaobao* (Chinese Financial and Commercial News), January 6, 1981.

tive of the further readjustment is to eliminate the disproportions of the national economy and to create a more rational economic pattern. This program consists mainly of the following points:

1. *A drastic reduction in the scale of capital construction.* The planned capital construction investment for 1981 is 30 billion yuan, 40 percent less than 1980's.

2. *Changing the distribution of investment among different sectors of the economy.* The twenty-two imported projects contracted in 1978 will be dealt with on the merit of each case. A better distribution of investment will enable various enterprises to carry out technical renovation and will make possible a further development of agriculture and light industry, energy resources, transport and communications, and public utilities and housing construction in cities.

3. *A revamping of existing enterprises.* Construction of blindly started or overlapping projects must be stopped at once. Enterprises that do not suit their production to demand, consume too much material, turn out poor products, or lose too much money must be handled properly, and so must the backward enterprises that contend with the advanced ones over the supply of raw materials, fuels, power, and transportation facilities. Most will have to be merged with other enterprises or change their lines of production, and a few will be closed down or suspended. This is particularly applicable to the great numbers of small, backward enterprises. All enterprises are required to improve their economic performance by eliminating waste and practicing economy.

4. *A drastic cut in state expenditure.* Except for allocations for culture and education, scientific research, and public health, all expenses, including those for national defense and administrative purposes, are to be cut substantially.

5. *Economizing on fuel.* In order to strive for a balance between the mining of coal, oil, and so on, and their storage and between tunneling and mining in coal pits, the 1981 crude oil target was lowered from 106 million to 100 million tons and the target for state-distributed coal from 359 million to 338 million tons. With the fuel output going down, its economic use becomes essential for achieving increases in industrial production.

6. *Ensuring a basic stability of prices.* For this purpose it is necessary to exercise strict control over the issue of banknotes and step up the production of consumer goods, particularly the most popular

items. In order to recover more banknotes from circulation, the commercial, foreign trade, and material supply departments are urged to put some of their inventories on the market. The recovery of paper money is also to be effected through noncommercial channels.

7. *More centralized leadership and government interference in a macroeconomic sense* (with respect to the economy as a whole), coupled with flexible measures to enliven production and marketing in a microeconomic sense (with respect to each enterprise).

8. *The issue of treasury bonds and borrowings from the surpluses of local governments.* Treasury bonds valued at 4 to 5 billion yuan were sold to enterprises, and money was borrowed from the financial surpluses of the local governments to balance the 1981 budget of the central government.

THE RELATIONSHIP BETWEEN READJUSTMENT AND REFORM

For some time to come, China will continue to emphasize economic readjustment. Any reform must be subordinated to and beneficial to readjustment. The pace of reform will be slowed down, but there will be no change in its general orientation.

The serious disproportions of China's economy, which have existed for a long time, are due in no small measure to the country's unsound economic setup. This is why some people believe that economic readjustment cannot be successful without a thoroughgoing reform of the setup. But many Chinese economists, including ourselves, regard such a view as divorced from China's realities. They point out that as long as the economy suffers from serious imbalances it is impossible to carry out a large-scale, all-around reform of the setup. There are four main reasons for this:

First, as long as demand far exceeds supply, the market mechanism cannot play an effective role in promoting production and improving management.

An important link in the reform of the economic setup lies in bringing the market mechanism into play, and this means changing an economy regulated almost entirely by mandatory state plans to an economy in which the market plays a regulatory role under the guidance of state planning. What is meant by the role of the market mechanism? It means to suit production to social demand by utilizing the aberrations in supply and demand through which the law of value asserts itself. This will benefit well-run enterprises, spur the poorly operated ones to better efforts, and compel both to improve their management, adopt the latest techniques, and turn out better products. But the market mechanism cannot play such a role without a normal relationship between supply and demand. When they are out of balance or, as things now stand in China, when demand far exceeds supply, even shoddy products can find ready buyers. In these circumstances, if government interference is abandoned and if the market mechanism is given a free rein, there will be a rush for goods, rocketing prices, much speculation, and a chaotic market. To avoid all this, the state must depend largely on a planned purchase of goods, planned allocation of the goods, and a rationing of some goods, and strictly control the prices of commodities in short supply. Thus the transition from the planned allocation and rationing of goods to a free exchange at market prices agreed upon between buyer and seller can be effected only gradually along with the growth in production and the normalization of the relationship between supply and demand. The market mechanism can play an effective role only when the supply of commodities measures up to or is even somewhat greater than the demand backed by purchasing power.

The second reason is that in a disproportionate economy, in which demand exceeds supply, it is difficult to examine the performance of enterprises and reward or punish them properly by making them responsible for their own profits or losses on the basis of the commodity-money relationship.

A basic requirement of economic reform is to make each enterprise a relatively independent economic entity assuming full responsibility for the results of its operation. A well-run enterprise will get bigger profits and more income, whereas a poorly operated one will earn less. Thus the profit margin, which has a direct bearing on the income of the workers, serves as an automatic yardstick of the performance of an enterprise as well as an automatic means of reward and punishment, making possible a strict application of business accounting. In the conditions of the present serious economic disproportions, however, the environment for the production and management of the enterprises is quite abnormal, and it is often impossible to establish proper links between production, the procurement of the means of production, and the marketing of products. An enterprise may do better or worse in production and earn more or less in profit, but this is frequently determined by external and not internal factors.

Third, as long as the economic disproportions remain serious, an enterprise can hardly make decisions to further its interests, even if it is authorized to do so.

Recognizing the relative independence of the enterprises and giving them more power to make their own decisions is the basis of a reform of the country's economic setup. But an enterprise cannot accomplish its aims in production and marketing when raw materials and fuels are in short supply and when there is no market for some of its products. On the other hand, until the state acquires sufficient economic means for such a reform, hasty steps to grant independence to enterprises would lead to the construction of overlapping projects, the appropriation of raw materials and fuels by smaller, poorer enterprises at the expense of bigger, better ones, and so on. This does mean that the enterprises should not be given decision-making powers, but it is important to avoid rashness in promoting such a reform.

The fourth reason is that since the state has a sizable financial deficit, it is difficult to introduce changes involving people's financial interests.

The economic relationships among people manifest themselves primarily as relationships among their respective interests. An economic reform that involves a major readjustment of people's economic relationships will inevitably affect the interests of different social groupings. A measure that benefits all parties enjoys universal support, whereas one that benefits only some people and encroaches on the interests of others will meet with much opposition. From a long-term point of view, an economic reform may raise the income of the state, the collectives as well as the individual, but it may cause a drop in some people's income within a short period of time. To minimize opposition, the state must spend more money to compensate collectives and individuals for their losses. But this cannot be done in the circumstances of economic imbalances and financial deficits.

In short, as long as the serious economic disproportions exist, a large-scale, all-round economic reform is out of the question. To achieve quick results in economic readjustment, centralized leadership must be duly emphasized and the limited financial, material, and human resources must be used in the most crucial areas. During the period of readjustment, reform must be subordinated to readjustment. A delay in readjustment will also delay the projected reform.

This does not mean that no reform may be undertaken until the completion of readjustment and the elimination of all disproportions. The economic disproportions have not appeared overnight. They have taken shape over a long period of time and cannot be remedied in a short time. Economic reform, a highly complicated task, cannot be accomplished in a short time either. If it has to be delayed until economic readjustment comes to an end, the modernization program will be held up for too long. In many respects a reform of the managerial setup does not run counter to readjustment but rather facilitates it. For example, many commodities badly needed by consumers are in short supply, while many others not needed by them are still being produced and stocked in large quantities. Such an abnormality can be removed if these commodities are channeled into the market and production is based on market demand, that is, on contracts between producers and marketing agencies, and if the prices are floated within certain limits. Another example is the state distribution of capital funds for which the enterprises pay nothing. The system has caused the enterprises to contend over state allocations in Chinese and foreign money. If the use of capital funds is placed on a compensatory basis, the enterprises will have to handle them with meticulous care. These examples show that, even during the period of readjustment, centralized leadership should not be overstressed and efforts should be made to decentralize the power of economic management and change the managerial setup wherever possible. Not only will this be necessary for readjustment, but it will create conditions for a large-scale reform of the managerial setup.

2

Changing the Pattern of China's Economy

by Zhou Shulian

CHANGES IN CHINA'S ECONOMIC PATTERN SINCE 1949

Before the founding of the People's Republic in 1949, the pattern of China's economy was an extremely irrational one peculiar to a semi-feudal, semi-colonial society, and the country's productive forces had remained stagnant for a long period of time. The following changes have taken place in the past three decades:

1. *The rise of an independent, fairly comprehensive system of industry and of national economy.* In old China, agriculture and hand-icraft industries were predominant, modern industry was insignificant, and the whole economy was an appendage to foreign imperialism. Large-scale socialist construction was carried out after 1949 to indus-trialize the country. From 1949 to 1979, total industrial output value went up 42.5 times, and the portion from heavy industry rose 98.6 times. The proportion of industrial output value in gross industrial and agricultural output value rose from 30.0 percent to 70.3 percent. The output value of heavy industry in the gross industrial value of output rose from 26.4 percent to 56.9 percent. Coal increased from 32 million to 635 million tons, electricity from 4.3 billion to 282 billion kilowatt hours, crude oil from 120,000 tons to 106.15 million tons, steel from 158,000 tons to 34.48 million tons, chemical fertilizer from 6,000 tons to 10.65 million tons, cotton cloth from 1.89 billion meters to 12.15 billion meters, and sugar from 200,000 tons to 2.5 million

tons. Between 1952 and 1979, major branches of industry increased their shares in gross industrial value of output—the metallurgical industry from 5.9 percent to 8.9 percent, the oil industry from 0.5 percent to 5.4 percent, the chemical industry from 4.8 percent to 12.2 percent, and the machine-building industry from 11.4 percent to 26.6 percent. Old China made no aircraft, automobiles, or tractors. These are all now being produced in the People's Republic, which has also developed a number of new industries, such as high-grade alloy steel, synthetic fibers, plastics, electronics, and atomic energy. The geographical distribution of industry has changed. In old China, heavy industry was concentrated in the Northeast, and light industry in big coastal cities. Today industrial bases are found in the Northeast, North China, Central China, the Southwest, and the Northwest, which means a better distribution of industry between the coastal regions and the interior. China is adding more and more branches to its industry, which has seen a rising level of modernization. It has changed from an agricultural country to an agroindustrial one.

2. *Growth in agriculture.* Land reform was followed by a gradual process of collectivization. Large-scale farmland improvement and water conservancy construction have been undertaken during the past three decades. Initial successes have been achieved in harnessing the Haihe, Huai, Huanghe (Yellow), and Changjiang (Yangtze) rivers. A total of 164,000 kilometers of river dykes and embankments were erected, enough to encircle the globe four times. Large areas of farmland now afford stable, high yields even in cases of waterlogging or drought. By 1979, some 670 million mu of cultivated land (45 percent of the nation's total) had been brought under irrigation. In old China, farm work was done almost entirely by hand. Certain progress has now been made in the mechanization and modernization of farming. In 1978 China had power-driven irrigation and drainage equipment with a total of 65.58 million horsepower, more than 557,000 tractors, and 1.37 million walking tractors. Some 40.9 percent of all cultivated land was plowed by machinery. An average of 5.95 kilograms of chemical fertilizer was applied to each mu of land (counted on the basis of 100 percent purity). Electricity for rural use amounted to 25.3 billion kilowatt-hours (9.9 percent of the national consumption). By the end of 1978 the rural people's communes had amassed 84.9 billion yuan worth of fixed assets, more than five times the 1957 figure (15.5 billion yuan), representing an annual rise of 7.4 percent. Grain output

reached 332.1 million tons in 1979, an increase of 218.9 million tons over the 1949 figure (113.2 million tons). Per-mu yield was 283 kilograms (197.5 kilograms more than the 1949 figure of 85.5 kilograms). The annual rate of increase in the gross agricultural value of output between 1952 and 1979 was 3.4 percent, and that in grain 2.6 percent, exceeding the rate of population growth (2 percent).

3. *Better communications and transport.* Old China left behind few railroads and highways, a low transport capacity, and an irrational distribution of transport facilities. This has been changed. A fairly comprehensive transport network has taken shape, embracing railroads, highways, water transport, airlines, and pipelines. All provinces, municipalities, and autonomous regions are linked by railroads, except Tibet, and all counties by highways, except Mêdog County in Tibet and Derong County in Sichuan. The railroads open to traffic increased from 22,000 kilometers in 1949 to 51,500 kilometers in 1979, and the freight volume rose 19.6 times. Highways open to traffic increased from 80,700 kilometers in 1949 to 890,200 kilometers in 1978, and the freight volume rose 10.2 times. Navigable inland waterways totaled 136,000 kilometers in 1978, as against 73,600 kilometers in 1949, and the freight volume rose 17 times. The total length of civil aviation lines grew from 11,400 kilometers in 1950 to 160,000 kilometers in 1979, including fifteen international lines totaling 51,500 kilometers and direct services to more than ten countries. The ocean fleets sail to more than one hundred countries and regions.

4. *Expansion of domestic and foreign trade.* Domestically, the value of goods purchased by commercial departments rose from 17.50 billion yuan in 1952 to 199.24 billion yuan in 1979, including a rise from 8.45 billion to 138.92 billion yuan in manufactured goods and from 9.01 billion to 58.68 billion yuan in farm produce. The total value of retail sales went up from 27.68 billion to 180 billion yuan. The year 1980 saw a further increase in the value of goods purchased by commercial departments to 226.3 billion yuan. In foreign trade the total value of imports and exports in 1950 was 4.15 billion yuan, including 2.13 billion yuan for imports and 2.02 billion yuan for exports. The total value of imports and exports reached 45.5 billion yuan in 1979, including 24.3 billion yuan for imports and 21.2 billion yuan for exports. The lineups of imports and exports also changed and no longer showed the features accompanying a semi-colonial economy. Of the total volume of imports in 1979, some 81 percent were capital

goods and 19 percent consumer goods; of the total volume of exports, industrial and mineral products made up 44 percent, processed farm and sideline products 33 percent, and farm and sideline produce 23 percent. Foreign trade accumulated funds for modernization projects and brought in much advanced technology and equipment.

5. *Advances in science and technology.* China's industries are equipped with much mechanized equipment and some automatic equipment. The country's machine-building industry is capable of building complete equipment for the first atomic reactor and diffusion machine; for iron and steel complexes each with an annual capacity of 1.5 million tons; for coal mines each with an annual output of 2.5 million tons, and open-cut coal mines each with an annual output of 7 million tons; for oil refineries each processing 2.5 million tons of crude oil a year; for 300,000 kilowatt hydro-power generating units and 300,000 kilowatt thermal power generating units; for auto plants each making 100,000 vehicles a year; for chemical plants each with an annual capacity of 300,000 tons of synthetic ammonia and 240,000 tons of urea; for 30,000-ton hydraulic presses, 50,000-ton oil tankers, 25,000-ton freighters, and 4,000 horsepower transmission diesel locomotives, and so on. In 1978 the country had a total of 2.67 million machine tools, of which 68,000 were large ones, 22,800 precision machines, and 5,300 numerically controlled machines. Efforts have been made to mechanize and modernize farm production. The technical structure of the economy in old China was characterized by manual work. It has now been replaced by a multiple structure consisting of automation, semi-automation, mechanization, semi-mechanization, and manual work. The successful tests of atomic and hydrogen bombs and guided missiles, the launching and recovery of man-made earth satellites, and the synthesis of bovine insulin indicated the progress in science and technology. Of course, China lags far behind the world's advanced countries in these fields, but it has initially established a number of new branches of science and technology from scratch.

6. *Improvement in the standard of living.* The standard of living in China remains low, but it is already a far cry from that in the semi-colonial days, when millions of people struggled for existence on the starvation line. The per capita consumption level of the urban and rural population was 76 yuan in 1952 and 201 yuan in 1979, an increase of about 90 percent calculated on the basis of rises in prices. In 1979 there was a wristwatch for every ten persons, a sewing ma-

chine for every twenty-five persons, a bicycle for every twelve persons, and a radio set for every eleven persons. Although the people's income has increased slowly in the past two decades, they are generally faring much better than in old China.

FAULTY ASPECTS OF THE PRESENT
ECONOMIC PATTERN

In spite of the aforementioned achievements, serious problems have existed in the economic pattern for a long time. The biggest problem lies in the striking imbalances or disproportions in the national economy, which manifest themselves as follows.

1. *Agriculture lags far behind industry, preventing a speedy economic growth.* Since the founding of the People's Republic, agricultural output value has tended to decrease sharply in proportion to the gross industrial and agricultural value of output, plummeting from 70.0 percent of the latter in 1949 to 29.7 percent in 1979. As agriculture lags increasingly behind industry, there is the danger of industry advancing in isolation from agriculture. Productivity is low in China's agriculture. The rural population accounted for 83.8 percent of the nation's total in 1979, and agricultural producers made up 84.9 percent of the total work force in industry and agriculture. However, farm produce is still far short of the needs in economic development. The 1978 per capita output of main farm produce was: grain, 318 kilograms; cotton, 2.3 kilograms; edible oil, 2.4 kilograms; sugar, 2.35 kilograms; meat, 8.25 kilograms; aquatic products, 4.85 kilograms— all below the average world levels (grain, 437 kilograms; edible oil, 15 kilograms; sugar, 25 kilograms; and meat, 20 kilograms). The pattern of agriculture is an extremely backward one. The lopsided stress on farming, particularly on grain, a legacy from old China, remains basically unchanged. In the output value from farming, forestry, animal husbandry, sideline production, and fishery, that from farming accounts for 70 percent. In the output value of twelve categories of farm produce—grain, oil, jute, cotton, silk, tea, sugar, vegetables, tobacco, fruit, medicinal herbs, and miscellaneous goods—the output value of grain accounts for about 70 percent. The overemphasis on "taking grain as the key link" has prevented the creation of a rational pattern of agriculture. This makes it impossible to make full use of

natural resources and upsets the ecological balance. Only 12.7 percent of China's land area is covered with trees, much below the world level of 22.0 percent. Although there are one billion mu of grass-covered hills and slopes in South China, they have not been used to develop animal husbandry. Less than 15 percent of the nation's shallow sea-shores are used to breed aquatic products, and only two-thirds of the fresh waters are utilized. In 1978 China imported, in terms of net figures, 6.96 million tons of grain, 476,000 tons of cotton, 291,000 tons of animal and plant oils, and 1.328 million tons of sugar. This was something that should not have happened to a big agricultural country like China.

2. *Light industry remains underdeveloped, unable to satisfy the growing needs of the people in urban and rural areas.* The inadequate attention paid to light industry over the years has created a wide gap between its growth rate and that of heavy industry. From 1949 to 1978 the output value of heavy industry increased 91.6 times, while that of light industry went up 20.8 times. The share of light industry in gross industrial output value dropped from 73.6 percent in 1949 to 42.7 percent in 1978. Investment in light industry accounted for 5.9 percent of total investment in capital construction in the First Five-Year Plan period, and the percentage tended to decrease in subsequent years. The ratio between investment in heavy industry and that in light industry was 8 to 1 in the First Five-Year Plan (FYP) period; 11 to 1 in the Second FYP period (1958–62); 13 to 1 in the three years of economic readjustment (1963–65); 14 to 1 in the Third FYP period (1966–70); 10 to 1 in the Fourth FYP period (1971–75); and 8.3 to 1 in the first three years of the Fifth FYP period (1976–78). Raw materials for light industry were chronically in short supply. In terms of value, 87.5 percent of the light industrial products were made from farm produce in 1952, and 12.5 percent from industrial materials. In 1978 the ratio became 68.4 percent and 31.6 percent. The sluggish increase in the supply of agricultural raw materials handicapped the growth of light industry. The proportion of rolled steel allocated to light industry declined: 21.3 percent under the First FYP, 13.7 percent under the Second, 12.7 percent under the Third, 11.3 percent under the Fourth, and 12.4 percent in the first three years of the Fifth. Electricity used by light industry accounted for 28.0 percent of total power consumption in 1952 and dropped to a mere 12.9 percent in 1979. The annual growth rate of the output of cotton yarn and cloth

in the Fourth FYP period was only 0.5 percent. For a long time there has been hardly any improvement in the market supply of such light industrial goods as paper, furniture, soap, detergents, beer, and bicycles. Light industrial goods directly available on the market tended to drop. According to statistics from the second light industrial bureaus[1] in sixteen provinces, the proportion of goods that can be placed directly on the market decreased from 50.8 percent in 1965 to 43.4 percent in 1978, while the goods supplied to big industries rose from 27.7 percent to 34.2 percent. Technology and labor productivity in light industry are poor, and disproportions exist between its various branches. For instance, the dyeing capacity of the textile industry can cover only 60 percent, and its printing capacity only 15 percent, of the blank cloth it produces. The finishing capacity for silks and knitwear is even lower. China's light industry appears quite backward when compared to its counterparts in some other countries. The 1977 per capita output of cotton cloth was less than half of that in the Soviet Union, Japan, and France; sugar was less than one-tenth of the amount in the Soviet Union, United States, France, and West Germany; television sets averaged 5 for every 10,000 persons, far below the levels in advanced countries.

3. *Heavy industry develops in isolation from agriculture and light industry and suffers from internal disproportions.* Because the scale of heavy industry and the speed of its development are both beyond the possibilities of the nation's material and financial resources, much harm is done to agriculture and light industry, and to heavy industry as well. Disproportions have arisen among the different branches of heavy industry, especially between the raw and semi-finished material industries and the processing industries. Machine tools increase much faster than rolled steel. In 1978 there were 3.8 times more machine tools than in 1956, while rolled steel output had grown only 2.5 times. At present the processing capacity of machine tools exceeds the supply of rolled steel by three to four times. In 1978 more than 180,000 machine tools were turned out, equivalent to the output in the United States and the Soviet Union when each produced 80 million tons of steel a year. But many of the machine tools made in China are backward types and far less efficient than those made abroad. China has

---

1. These bureaus in Chinese cities are in charge of industries developed on the basis of former handicraft trades.

34 hydraulic presses of or above the 1,000-ton class. The number is not small, but the ancillary equipment is incomplete, preventing full use of their capacity and making it necessary to import things like large forgings. The lack of ancillary equipment limits the capacity for producing high-tension power transmission and transformation equipment to 4 million kilowatts, and the production of auxiliary machines, pumps, valves, and automatic meters is far from sufficient. The farm machines are often outdated and inefficient, while many badly needed machines are in short supply. The metallurgical industry is affected by its own imbalances. First, iron mining is in a backward state. Six of the 10 iron and steel centers in the country and 16 of the 28 iron-producing provinces, municipalities, and autonomous regions are short of iron ore, which must be imported by millions of tons every year. Second, steel-rolling capacity is low. The ratio between rolling capacity and steel-making capacity in China is 0.65 to 1.0, as against 1 to 1 in some other countries. Third, some nonferrous metals mining is also underdeveloped, and many of the nonferrous metals have to be imported. The building industry and the building material industry are both backward. Between 1953 and 1978, the building material industry increased its output by an annual rate of 11.8 percent, lower than the general rate in heavy industry (13.6 percent), giving rise to a chronic shortage of building materials. All this shows that China's heavy industry has not played a satisfactory leading role in relation to agriculture, light industry, and the national economy as a whole.

4. *Production is affected by an acute shortage of energy.* As the world faces an energy crisis, China too must deal with the energy problem. From 1953 to 1978 China's gross industrial value of output rose by 11.2 percent a year, but energy output increased at an annual rate of 9.6 percent. In 1977 and 1978 about one-quarter of the nation's enterprises had to operate under capacity. According to a survey made by the authorities in charge of power generation in the metallurgical, chemical, light, textile, and machine-building industries, which are the major power consumers, and in the Northeast, East China, and Central-South regions, which are seriously affected by the power shortage, the country needs additional generating equipment with a total capacity of 10 million kilowatts or, in other words, an extra power supply of 30 to 40 billion kilowatt-hours a year, the lack of which is costing China tens of billions of yuan in the value of industrial output every year. While there are prime movers with a capacity of 160 million

horsepower for rural use, the state can supply only 8 million tons of diesel oil a year, averaging a little over 50 kilograms per horsepower, which is enough for only fifty-odd days of operation and seriously affects the utilization of farm machinery. There is also a major shortage of energy for household use. The nation's 170 million peasant households generally lack cooking fuels for three months every year. The overintensified extraction of coal and oil and the overloaded operation of thermal power plants have aggravated the disproportions within the energy industry. Frequent shifts in energy policy and structure in the past few years, with the stress on coal at one time and on oil at another, have resulted in enormous waste within the energy industry. The irrational pattern of industry adds to ·the strain on energy supply. It is estimated that every 100 million yuan of output value from heavy industry costs five times as much energy or three times as much electricity as the same output value from light industry. In terms of the gross industrial value of output in 1978, if the proportion of light industry rises by 1 percent and that of heavy industry drops by 1 percent, energy consumption can be cut by more than 6 million tons of standard coal. If the proportion of light industry in the gross industrial value of output remains at the 1957 level of 51.7 percent, more than 50 million tons of energy (standard coal) can be saved. There is a serious waste of energy too. The average utilization efficiency of energy in China is only 30 percent as against 50 percent in advanced countries. Judging by the energy consumption in industrial production, China produces much less than the United States and Japan by the use of every 10,000 tons of energy. China consumes roughly the same amount of energy as Japan, but the gross value of its social production comes to just about one-quarter of Japan's.

5. *Communications and transport are not keeping pace with the development of production.* Communications and transport are a weak link in China's national economy. The freight volume in one-third of China's 120 railroad sections has already reached the saturation point, while a dozen sections have become bottlenecks in rail transport because they can handle only 45 to 70 percent of their freight volume. All-weather highways account for only 67 percent of the nation's total highway mileage. Failure to consider multipurpose use of water conservancy projects has reduced the total length of navigable inland waterways by 10,000 to 15,000 kilometers since 1962. The deficient cargo-handling capacity of coastal harbors hinders the growth of for-

eign trade. There are only 137 10,000-ton class berths in coastal ports, of which only 90 are usable for foreign trade purposes. In the first half of 1979 an average of 220 foreign trade ships were in port every day, many fewer than needed. Some 27 percent of the foreign trade cargoes handled by China are shipped by chartered foreign vessels, for which 150 million U.S. dollars are paid every year. Drawbacks in the managerial system account for the lack of a rational division of labor among different kinds of transportation, so that navigable waterways remain idle, the railroads are overburdened, and trucks have to run long distances, while seagoing vessels often lie at anchor waiting for loading or unloading, resulting in waste and losses.

6. *Commerce and the service trades lag behind the growth of the national economy.* In 1978 China's population showed a 48 percent increase over 1957, the total number of industrial and office workers was three times bigger, and the volume of retail sales had also gone up more than three times. However, the number of workers engaged in commerce, the food and drink trade, and other service trades had increased only 6.6 percent. Every worker in retail business had to serve 213 people in 1978 as against 114 in 1957, every worker in the food and drink trade had to wait on 912 people as against 563, and every worker in the other service trades had to serve 1,699 people as against 1,056. In Liaoning Province the number of commercial stores and service shops and stalls had dropped by more than 80 percent in 1978 as compared with 1957, and the number of restaurants had dropped by over 90 percent. In some cities not a single shop can be found along a lengthy street, and people complain about the difficulties in buying food or finding a public bath. In 1957 there were 28,500 cooperative shops and 11,800 cooperative restaurants in China's rural areas. By the end of 1979 the number had dwindled to a mere 580, so that many communes had no shops or restaurants. Peasants going to village fairs can hardly find a place to eat, to have their pictures taken, or to turn in at night. Fuxin City had 1,020 shops for a population of 140,000 in 1958. Now the population has swelled to over 500,000, a rise of three times, but the number of shops has dwindled to 316, one-third of the original. There is a serious shortage of storehouses, granaries, edible-oil tanks, and cold storage facilities. The lack of cold storage compelled the city to suspend the purchase of pigs from the peasants on three occasions in 1979. Because of the inadequate number of shops, tens of thousands of urban residents must travel at

least one kilometer to buy grain, vegetables, or even soybean sauce. Underdeveloped commerce and service trades handicap social reproduction and inconvenience the people.

7. *Foreign trade is not keeping pace with the requirements of modernization.* China's foreign trade, too, is underdeveloped, and the volume makes up only a small proportion of the world trade volume —a mere 0.8 percent of it in 1978. China ranked fifteenth in world trade in both 1973 and 1974, twenty-fifth in 1975, and twenty-ninth in 1976. In terms of the total value at which they were purchased at home, exports averaged 4.0 percent of the gross industrial and agricultural value of output in thirty years after the founding of New China and accounted for only 3.9 percent in 1977 and 1978. The lineup of export commodities is unsatisfactory. Primary products made up 54 percent of the exports in 1978, light and textile goods 38 percent, and heavy industrial products only 8 percent. On the other hand, there has been a lack of overall balance in the import of complete equipment.

8. *Accumulation and consumption are unbalanced.* During the First Five-Year Plan period, the rate of accumulation was kept between 23.0 percent and 25.0 percent, which suited the circumstances. Subsequently the rate tended to be too high for a long time, being 33.9 percent in 1958 and 43.8 percent in 1959. It averaged 30.8 percent under the Second FYP, 26.3 percent under the Third, 33.0 percent under the Fourth, and was 31.1 percent in 1976, 32.3 percent in 1977, and 36.5 percent in 1978. The rising accumulation in the years following the First FYP period resulted from a fast rise in the accumulation fund and a slow rise in the consumption fund. After 1958, with the exception of the three years of economic readjustment, the accumulation fund grew much faster than both the consumption fund and the national income.

The high rate of accumulation was accompanied by a scale of capital construction far too large for the nation's financial and material resources. The spendings on capital construction in the First Five-Year Plan period came to 37.0 percent of the financial expenditures, which was a relatively appropriate ratio. But it jumped to 46.2 percent under the Second FYP, declined to 38.7 percent under the Third FYP, rose again to 40.2 percent under the Fourth FYP, and was 40.7 percent in 1978. The high rates overburdened the country and had a negative effect on production.

Within the sphere of accumulation, there has also been a serious imbalance between accumulation for productive purposes and accumulation for nonproductive purposes. Productive accumulation accounted for 59.8 percent in the First FYP period but rose to 87.1 percent under the Second FYP. It dropped to 65.6 percent in the three years of economic readjustment and went up again to 74.5 percent under the Third FYP, 77.4 percent under the Fourth, and 83.2 percent in 1976, 75.4 percent in 1977, and 75.9 percent in 1978. On the other hand, the proportion of nonproductive accumulation plummeted from 40.2 percent under the First FYP to 12.9 percent under the Second. It rose to 34.5 percent in the three years of economic readjustment and then dropped to 25.5 percent under the Third FYP and to 22.4 percent under the Fourth. This led to the serious imbalance between productive and nonproductive construction. Take investment in housing, for example. It made up 9.1 percent of the total investment in capital construction under the First FYP but came down to 4.0 percent under the Second FYP and 5.0 percent in the period from 1967 to 1975. In 1977 the floor space for every urban resident averaged only 3.6 square meters, or 0.9 square meters less than the 1952 figure of 4.5 square meters. The gap is even wider when compared to the housing conditions in many other countries. In addition, there are problems like insufficient water-supply facilities, crammed traffic, shortage of school buildings, and inadequate construction for cultural, educational, and public health undertakings.

The irrational economic pattern and the economic disproportions also find expression in many other fields, such as the divorcement of the defense industry from civilian industry, serious industrial pollution in some areas, science and education lagging behind the requirements of modernization, the low technical and managerial levels of the workers and staff, and the large numbers of people waiting for jobs.

THE MAIN TROUBLE WITH THE ECONOMIC PATTERN

Among the numerous problems stated above, which is the fundamental one? Three views have emerged from discussions among Chinese economists. Some pinpoint high accumulation and low consumption, that is, the imbalance between accumulation and consumption, as the main trouble and suggest its elimination as the key to the solution of all other problems concerning the economic pattern. Others consider the disproportions among agriculture, light industry, and heavy industry to be the fundamental problem to be tackled before anything else. Still others regard the serious imbalance between the two departments of social production, one turning out the means of production (capital goods) and the other the means of consumption (consumer goods), as the basic issue in a readjustment of the economic pattern. In my opinion, all three views contain some truth, but the third seems to be the most accurate.

A proper handling of the relationship between the two departments of social production is the foremost condition for smooth *reproduction*. To be more exact, two basic conditions are required for *extended reproduction:* (1) the department producing the means of production (Department I) must turn out the means of production needed for *simple* reproduction and an additional amount for *extended* reproduction; (2) the department producing the means of consumption (Department II) must turn out the means of consumption needed for *simple* reproduction and an additional amount needed for *extended* reproduction. The absence of either one of these conditions will mean tremendous difficulties in *extended* reproduction.

The basic trouble with China's economic pattern lies in the incorrespondence between Department I and Department II. Generally speaking, production of the means of consumption is lagging far behind production of the means of production. While reproduction suffers from a shortage of the means of production, it suffers even more from a shortage of the means of consumption. Thus it is very difficult to raise the living standard of the people, on the one hand, and carry on effective reproduction, on the other hand. Speaking of capitalist reproduction, Lenin said, "The point of departure in discussing social capital and revenue—or, what is the same thing, the realization of the product in capitalist society—must be the distinction between two entirely different types of social product: *means of production* and *articles of consumption.*"[2] This is also applicable to socialist reproduction. The relationship between the two departments of production should be taken as the point of departure in an effort to solve the whole series of questions concerning the economic pattern.

2. V. I. Lenin, "A Characterisation of Economic Romanticism," in *Collected Works* (Moscow: Foreign Languages Publishing House, 1960), vol. 2, p. 152.

Compared with the relationship among agriculture, light industry, and heavy industry, the relationship between the two departments of production reflects more profoundly the very nature of the process of social reproduction. In actual economic life, however, there are three tangible departments of production—agriculture, light industry, and heavy industry—and not just two. In economic planning and management the two departments of production must likewise be handled in terms of their concrete expressions, that is, agriculture, light industry, and heavy industry. In this sense, we may agree with the second view cited above. But this view contains some inaccuracies. First, although we usually regard agriculture and light industry as Department II and heavy industry as Department I, this is an inaccurate classification because agriculture and light industry also produce some means of production. Second, this dividing line between light industry and heavy industry is inapplicable in some cases. For instance, it is difficult to define the chemical industry as either a light industry or a heavy industry. Third, whether there is a proportionate relationship among agriculture, light industry, and heavy industry depends in the final analysis on whether such a relationship answers the demand of social reproduction on the two departments of production. A departure from the dividing line between the two departments of production means the absence of an objective criterion and of a scientific basis for handling the relationship among agriculture, light industry, and heavy industry.

The high rate of accumulation, which has prevailed in China over the years, has indeed been an important reason for the emergence of an irrational economic pattern. This is why a readjustment of the ratio between accumulation and consumption is essential for establishing a proper relationship between production and people's livelihood, between production and capital construction, between construction for productive purposes and construction for nonproductive purposes, and so on. But it is not correct to regard the relationship between accumulation and consumption as the basic question of the economic pattern. However important it may be, such a relationship is after all a question of distribution, which is determined in the final analysis by production. In China, as in any other country, the pattern of distribution is determined by the pattern of production. The high rate of accumulation in China is the result mainly of an overstress on heavy industry. The lopsided development of heavy industry has caused an underdevelopment of agriculture and light industry, and consequently the insufficient production of the means of consumption as compared with the production of means of production, making it difficult to establish a proper relationship between accumulation and consumption. It is generally agreed that the state of high accumulation and low consumption should be changed and the people's living standard raised as quickly as possible. But the effort is limited by the slow growth in production and by the present pattern of production, both of which make it impossible to accomplish the goal overnight. This is not to say that we should stop remedying the disproportion between accumulation and consumption as a means of readjusting the pattern of production. But it does mean that the pattern of production is decisive to the pattern of distribution and that a readjustment of the relationship between the two departments in the pattern of production provides the key to a solution of the question of the economic pattern.

SEARCHING FOR AN ECONOMIC PATTERN SUITED
TO CHINA'S CONDITIONS

What kind of economic pattern is rational for China? The question is still being explored by Chinese economists. Ma Hong, noted economist and vice-president of the Chinese Academy of Social Sciences, holds that a rational economic pattern suited to China's conditions should—

- Enable China fully to utilize her advantages and avoid the consequences of her disadvantages.
- Make for a most effective use of the nation's human, material, and financial resources and her natural riches.
- Ensure a coordinated development of the various economic sectors and geographical regions and a smooth progress of social reproduction on the present material and technical basis.
- Bring about a fast improvement in technology and a speedy rise in labor productivity.
- Create a benign cycle of high-speed development, high consumption, and high accumulation, that is, a fast growth in pro-

duction, a fast improvement in the life of the people, and a fast increase in accumulation.[3]

Other economists maintain that a rational economic pattern that meets the requirements of China's modernization must ensure a rational distribution of social labor time; the economic use of labor time; and a continual and maximum fulfillment of the ever-growing needs of the workers in their unconstrained development.

Still others say that in order to define the criteria of a rational economic pattern, it is necessary to introduce four basic concepts: economic possibilities, economic advantages, economic results, and economic needs. In other words, a rational economic pattern must be built on the basis of actual economic possibilities, give full play to a nation's advantages, produce optimum economic results, and thus meet the diverse economic needs of the whole society to the maximum extent.

According to my own studies, a rational economic pattern should be judged by four main indicators:

1. *An appropriate pattern of ownership, that is, an appropriate pattern of relations of production, which suit the condition of the productive forces.* An economic pattern consists of a pattern of productive forces and a pattern of relations of production. Marx said: ". . . the aggregate of these relations, in which the agents of this production live with regard to nature and to themselves, and in which they produce, is precisely their society, considered from the point of view of its economic structure."[4] This definition is also applicable to socialist society. Thus a rational pattern of relations of production is part of a rational economic pattern. We must deal correctly with the pattern of ownership according to the law that the relations of production must suit the condition of the productive forces.

It is important to note that the pattern of relations of production has much to do with many aspects of the pattern of productive forces. If the former is irrational, it is hardly possible to rationalize the latter. The evolution of China's economic pattern shows that a rational

3. Ma Hong, "Make a Thoroughgoing Study of the Economic Pattern and Accelerate Socialist Modernization," *Caimou Zhanxian* (Financial and Commercial Front), September 14, 1979.

4. Karl Marx, *Capital* (Chicago: Charles H. Kerr & Co., 1909), vol. 3, p. 952.

pattern of productive forces must be premised on a rational pattern of relations of production.

Because China's productive forces are marked by an extremely uneven development, it is necessary to create a multilevel pattern of relations of production. This means tolerating the existence of a multiplicity of economic sectors and forms of operation while maintaining the predominance of socialist public ownership.

A long-prevailing view asserts that it is always better to have a bigger economic organization with a higher degree of public ownership. This view has led to a blind quest for a larger scale and a higher level of socialist ownership and the enforcement of a unitary economic form. Facts have proven this view to be incorrect. It is true that the productive forces become stagnant if the relations of production lag far behind them, but it is also true that the former cease to grow when the latter go too far ahead. Yu Guangyuan, a leading economist and vice-president of the Chinese Academy of Social Sciences, pointed out: "Our basic approach to the question of socialist ownership is this: We support any system of ownership which promotes the development of productive forces to the maximum extent; we accept with reservation any system which promotes such a development to a rather limited extent; we do not support any system which does not promote such a development, and we resolutely oppose any system which hinders such a development."[5]

2. *A smooth progress of extended social reproduction.* This is the least we should demand of a rational economic pattern. No economic pattern can be regarded as rational if it does not fulfill this minimum requirement. Extended social reproduction cannot be carried out smoothly unless there is a proper handling of the relationship between Department I and Department II of social production. This means Department I should provide Department II with the necessary means of production, while Department II should provide Department I with the necessary means of livelihood. At the same time, the internal relations in each department should be handled well. This alone will ensure a smooth progress of extended social reproduction. In actual economic life, the two departments manifest themselves as the various material-producing branches of the national economy. A

5. Yu Guangyuan, "The Basic Approach to Socialist Ownership," *People's Daily,* July 7, 1980.

smooth progress of extended social reproduction also means a coordinated development of the various branches of the national economy.

A smooth progress of extended social reproduction requires not only the production of the necessary means of production and means of livelihood, but also an unblocked circulation of these products for their timely delivery or marketing. This means that a rational pattern of circulation is as indispensable as a rational pattern of production.

3. *A full utilization of the elements of production.*[6] A rational economic pattern requires not only a smooth progress of extended social reproduction but also the achievement of the optimum economic results in society as a whole. This means obtaining a maximum of economic results through a minimum expenditure of labor. It calls for a full and rational use of available manpower and material and financial resources, that is, organizing the elements of production in such a way as to bring their roles into full play. To this end it will be necessary to handle well the employment makeup and the technological makeup and their mutual relationship. Full employment must be guaranteed, for the existence of a vast number of jobless people would obviously prevent society from achieving the maximum economic results. While dealing with the technological makeup, we must take employment into account. A relative surplus of labor power means a need for more labor-concentrated industries, and a relative shortage of labor power means a need for more capital-concentrated industries.

The attainment of optimum socioeconomic results also requires a rational use of natural resources, which has much to do with labor productivity. Each region faces its own favorable and unfavorable conditions. Historically, favorable economic conditions are often connected with favorable natural conditions. Thus people in each region have to exploit their favorable natural and economic conditions. This also involves the question of ecological balance. Indiscriminate exploitation, felling (of trees), fishing, and hunting will exhaust the resources, resulting in the deterioration of soil, soil erosion, and an abnormal climate. Even if some economic results are achieved for a time, much trouble will be left to posterity. Such an economic pattern cannot be considered a rational one.

4. *A fairly speedy improvement in livelihood.* The life of the working people is an overall indicator of the rationality of an economic

6. The laborer, the instrument of labor, and the object of labor.

pattern. Although the immediate aim of production varies from one society to another, production and life, and production and consumption, are always interdependent. This is because every product acquires a practical significance only in the course of consumption. For instance, a piece of clothing becomes a real one only when someone wears it; a room without an occupant is not a real room in an economic sense. Marx says, "Without production no consumption, but without consumption no production either, since production would then be aimless."[7] This is a most profound thesis. A fast improvement in people's life means not only a fast growth in production, but also a proper relationship between production and life, between accumulation and consumption, and a fairly rational pattern of production, of distribution, of circulation, and of consumption.

If the economic pattern of a society fulfills the four requirements stated above, it is one endowed with a benign cycle. First, there is a benign cycle between the productive forces and the relations of production, that is, the relations of production suit the productive forces and promote their growth, while the growing productive forces make possible a further perfection and development of the relations of production. Second, there is a benign cycle among the various branches of the national economy, and a mutual promotion among the various departments of production, among the various departments of circulation, and between production and circulation. Third, there is a benign cycle between the human and material elements of the productive forces, plus a benign cycle between the productive forces and the natural conditions, which likewise promote each other's development. Finally, there is a benign cycle between production and life, between production and consumption. Such an economic pattern will ensure a sustained, sound development of the national economy. This is the final aim of changing the economic pattern.

HOW TO ESTABLISH A RATIONAL ECONOMIC PATTERN

The guidelines for establishing a rational economic pattern put forward by Chinese economists in recent discussions may be stated as follows:

7. Karl Marx, *Preface and Introduction to a Contribution to the Critique of Political Economy* (Beijing: Foreign Languages Press, 1976), p. 19.

- As a basic requirement of the socialist system, the economic pattern should be focused on satisfying the people's needs, including food, clothing, shelter, and other necessities.
- Priority should be given to the development of the energy industries and communications and transport, and more emphasis should be given in the next ten years to energy-saving, labor-concentrated industries to help solve the energy and employment problems.
- On the principle of self-reliance, full use should be made of the existing enterprises by tapping their potentials through technical renovation and transformation.
- Expansion of exports and elimination of the weak points in China's economy through the import of technology and the use of foreign funds.
- Integration of defense industry with civilian industry, and production of more goods for civilian use by the former.
- Much attention to science and education, demographic planning, environmental protection, the improvement of labor conditions, urban construction, public health, and so on.

In a word, suiting social production to social consumption should be the starting point as well as the objective of a change of China's economic pattern. The following is a specific program for the attainment of this objective.

1. *Developing agriculture in an all-around way to lay a solid foundation for the growth of the national economy.* At present the grain shortage is a formidable obstacle to all-around development of farming, forestry, animal husbandry, sideline production, and fishery. But historical experience in China and abroad shows that the grain problem can be solved only through simultaneous progress in all these five fields of endeavor, and grain production must rise together with increases in cash crops. It is incorrect to stress grain as the "key link" in all cases, and it is harmful to destroy forests, grasslands, or cash crop farming as a means of boosting grain production. Instead of solving the grain problem, these practices would damage the rural economy and upset ecological balance.

2. *Accelerating the growth of light industry, increasing accumulation, and improving the standard of living.* Light industry should be enabled to grow at a rate faster than that of heavy industry, and its

proportion in the country's gross value of industrial output should be increased to about 50 percent by 1985 or a little later.

3. *Readjusting the pattern of heavy industry, and giving full scope to the role of the machine-building industry in the technical transformation of the national economy.* Heavy industry has a leading role to play in the national economy. It should provide the various branches of the economy with energy, raw and semi-finished materials, and all kinds of equipment, furnish consumers with durable goods, and produce much for export. If heavy industry is to contribute to a fast development of the national economy, it must be oriented toward these purposes and must be placed at the service of agriculture and light industry to a much greater extent. Its growth rate and its proportion in the nation's gross value of industrial output must be readjusted for a change in the pattern of the national economy.

The modernization of agriculture, industry, science and technology, and national defense requires a technical transformation of all branches of the national economy. The machine-building industry must be oriented toward this transformation. Instead of producing mainly for new plants and capital construction, it should supply more equipment to the old plants to change their technologies, and do more for agriculture and light industry, for urban construction, especially housing, and for consumers, especially in the area of durable goods. Instead of being only domestically oriented, it should take the world market into full account.

4. *Establishing a rational energy structure.* Energy is decisive to the scale and rate of industrial development. The per capita energy consumption of a nation is a general indicator of its social production and living standard. China faces a serious shortage of energy. Until the energy problem is solved, it will be impossible to effect a coordinated development of the national economy or to improve the people's life steadily. In view of the condition of China's energy resources, coal should remain the chief source of energy for a fairly long time, while hydraulic resources should be developed speedily.

5. *Stepping up city planning and construction and developing the building material industry.* The housing shortage is an outstanding problem in the life of the urban population and has also become serious in the rural areas. The civilian building trade should be developed on a large scale along with an expansion of the building material industry.

6. *Lowering the accumulation rate and changing the investment makeup.* The high rate of accumulation which has prevailed in China over the years has unbalanced the economy. In light of historical experience at home and abroad and the level of China's economic development, it will be appropriate to keep the rate around 25 percent. Capital construction should be conducted on a scale which lies within the nation's capabilities. It must not be based on unguaranteed supplies, and it must not be allowed to lower the people's living standard or to create a financial deficit. Production must come before capital construction, and capital construction funds should first be used for the technical transformation of existing equipment, and so should the equipment introduced from abroad.

7. *Changing the lineups of import and export commodities.* This should be done to help rationalize the economic pattern, to coordinate the growth of agriculture, light industry, and heavy industry, and to accelerate socialist modernization. In import trade, the stress should be on key technology and equipment, goods which China lacks the resources to produce, and those it cannot produce at a favorable cost. In export trade, it is necessary to assess fully the nation's resources and the demand on the home market and, on the basis of domestic production and international demand, gradually shift the stress from farm produce and primary products to heavy and light industrial products, especially products from the machine-building industry and high-grade processed goods. Meanwhile, it will be advisable to export more labor-concentrated products, particularly China's famous handicrafts and artware.

8. *Giving full play to the advantages of various localities through a division of economic zones.* A rational economic pattern requires a scientific division of economic zones, which will create a number of local patterns for a thorough exploitation of the favorable conditions and a vigorous growth of commodity economy in all areas. Such division should be based on the distribution of natural resources, the present levels of industrial and agricultural production, communication and transport conditions, and the economic ties that have taken shape historically. The economic zones should be strictly distinguished from the administrative zones, each with an economic pattern that gives full play to favorable local conditions, including natural conditions (such as climate, soil, resources) and economic conditions (such as production capacity, the technical force, managerial expertise).

9. *Increasing transportation capacities as an important means of establishing a rational economic pattern.* The expansion of socialized production creates ever-closer ties between different branches of the national economy, between production, the procurement of the means of production, and marketing, between production and consumption, and between various localities. Consequently there will be a rising demand on transportation and postal and telecommunications, which will have to be developed even faster than the other branches of the economy.

10. *Changing the system of economic management (the economic setup) to help establish a rational economic pattern.* The serious disproportions in the national economy form a major obstacle to economic development. Until the disproportions are remedied, the managerial system cannot be changed. But without a reform of the managerial system, it will be impossible to establish and maintain a rational economic pattern that ensures a coordinated development of agriculture, light industry, and heavy industry.

In reforming the managerial system, it is necessary to act according to objective economic laws, to enlarge gradually the powers of the enterprises to make their own decisions, and to develop the supplementary role of the market and other economic mechanisms, as regulators of the economy which is regulated mainly through state planning.

3

Greater Power for the Enterprises

by Wang Haibo

THE HIGHLY CENTRALIZED SYSTEM of economic management in China is based largely on the Soviet model evolved in the Stalin era. In this system the mandatory production targets set by the central government are handed down level by level to the local authorities and the enterprises, which must fulfill them regardless of their suitability. Financially the central authorities keep a tight control on revenue and expenditure. The local governments must turn over all their revenue to the central government except for the part allocated for their use. All investments in extended reproduction and other expenses are also centrally controlled and allocated to the various localities, enterprises, and institutions through the government ministries by designated items. The recipients are allowed to spend allocations for authorized purposes only. The central government leaves a tiny portion of the tax revenue with the local authorities for use at their own discretion. Each enterprise must give the central government not only all its profit but also the greater part of its depreciation fund, which is left in the hands of the administrative authorities in charge of that enterprise. As for the distribution of products, the means of production are allocated according to state plans, while the industrial consumer goods are handled by state commercial agencies, which buy and sell everything.

The advantage of this system lies in a concentrated use of the country's funds and material resources on items vital to its economic life. It has a fundamental drawback, however: It fetters the initiative of the local authorities and particularly the initiative of the enterprises and artificially cuts the ties between trades and between enterprises, and so creates serious obstacles to the development of society's productive forces.

Such a managerial system stands in sharp contradiction to the Chinese people's historic task of socialist modernization.[1] In December 1978 a communiqué issued by the Third Plenary Session of the Eleventh Central Committee of the Chinese Communist Party stated: "One of the serious shortcomings in the structure of economic management in our country is the over-concentration of authority, and it is necessary to boldly shift it under guidance from the leadership to lower levels so that the local authorities and industrial and agricultural enterprises will have greater power of decision in management under the guidance of unified state planning."[2] Following this, the Second Session of the Fifth National People's Congress, held in June–July 1979, passed a resolution on readjusting, reforming, consolidating, and improving the national economy.

Here we will discuss the theory and practice of the experimental reform of China's economic setup since 1979.

GREATER POWER FOR THE ENTERPRISES: THE KEY TO A MANAGERIAL REFORM AT PRESENT

The Main Trouble with the Managerial System and the Key to a Reform

When treating a patient, a doctor must first diagnose the illness and then prescribe the medicine. This also applies to a study of China's economic setup. So far Chinese economists have offered three different diagnoses and prescriptions.

One school holds that the main problem with the present economic setup lies in insufficient centralization. It underscores the fact that most of the enterprises, particularly the larger ones, are in the hands of the local authorities, and too few are controlled directly by the central ministries. The local authorities are in control of too large

1. For the above analysis, see Xue Muqiao, *China's Socialist Economy* (Beijing: Foreign Languages Press, 1981), pp. 204–5.
2. *Beijing Review,* no. 52, 1978, p. 12.

a proportion of the budgetary income and material supplies, which are therefore used in a scattered way, weakening unified state planning and causing much blindness in production and construction. This school recommends the concentration of power mainly in the hands of the central ministries, the granting of a limited measure of power to the local authorities and the enterprises, and the replacement of administrative methods by economic means within a prescribed scope. Specifically, key enterprises and the bigger ones which produce for the whole country and procure their means of production on a nationwide basis are to be placed under the central ministries; major production and construction tasks are still to be assigned under mandatory plans; the major means of production and consumer goods will continue to be distributed by the state; investments in capital construction will continue to be arranged by the state; and manpower, prices, and foreign trade will remain under unified state control. On this basis companies are to be established along trade lines, greater independence may be granted to enterprises, the local authorities may be given some more financial power, and working capital and part of the capital construction funds may be granted in the form of bank loans. If this proposal is adopted the central ministries will have to take back quite a number of enterprises which were once under their administration but were later transferred to the local authorities, a still greater range of means of production will have to be distributed through state allocation, and the central ministries will become even larger and clumsier than they are at present.

A second school, diametrically opposed to the first one, holds that the main trouble with the present economic setup lies in over-centralization. It notes that, although a number of enterprises and much government revenue have been handed over to the local authorities, they actually remain in the hands of the central ministries. Enjoying little autonomy, the local authorities must refer everything, big and small, to the central ministries, which handicaps local initiative. This school recommends that under the unified leadership of the central government the powers of management be delegated to the provinces, municipalities, and autonomous regions. Specifically, all enterprises and undertakings are to be administered by the local authorities except for the railroads, civil aviation, main telecommunication lines, maritime and Changjiang (Yangtze River) shipping, interprovincial power networks, oil and gas pipelines, national defense industries, and important national institutions of scientific research and higher learning, which are to remain under the control of the central government. Economic planning should take place mainly at the provincial level. The revenue handed over to the central authorities should be limited to a certain amount or percentage. The basic supplies needed in each province should be verified, and the quantities and varieties to be brought into or out of it should be fixed for a number of years. A shortage or surplus in terms of quantity or variety may be removed through commodity exchange among provinces or between the provinces and the central authorities, or through foreign trade. The provinces may set up joint ventures and joint stock companies among themselves.

A third school maintains that the main trouble with the present economic setup lies in the incorrect relationship between the state (including the central and the local authorities) and each enterprise. In other words, the trouble lies in the fact that the economy is being run mainly through administrative organs by administrative means and not through economic entities by economic means. This reduces every enterprise to an appendage to administrative organs and prevents it from functioning as an independent economic entity, and so hampers the growth of productive forces. It is true that problems of centralization and decentralization exist in the managerial system. On the one hand, there is insufficient centralization in certain areas, such as the planning on key aspects of economic development, the balancing of proportions among important economic sectors, the geographical layout and overall program of national construction, and the formulation of economic and technical policies. Worse still, violation of objective economic laws and arbitrary, impractical decisions have resulted in serious, long-prevailing economic imbalances, an uneven distribution of productive forces, the use of funds in a scattered way, the overlapping of construction projects, and poor economic performance. On the other hand, there is too much interference from the central authorities in matters that should be handled locally, such as agricultural production, urban construction, and the planning of local undertakings and the allocation of funds for these undertakings. This fetters the initiative of the local authorities. But the main problem lies in the extremely limited powers of the enterprises. Economic management must be separated from government administration and conducted through economic entities.

Under state leadership, the enterprises should be granted greater powers to make their own decisions. Economic means should be fully utilized for economic management under the guidance of state plans. Regulation of the economy through planning should be supplemented by regulation through a market guided by state planning. Under these principles there should be a proper division of managerial powers between the central and local authorities based on the characteristics of economic undertakings. Specifically, the central government should concern itself mainly with the orientation of a planned economy, the policies for its development, and economic legislation, while the local governments should be put in charge of most economic undertakings, the service trades, and urban construction. Under the guidance of state planning, the enterprises should be empowered to handle their own human, financial, and material resources, the procurement of their means of production, and the marketing of their products within clearly defined spheres of authority, and should conduct independent business accounting by assuming full responsibility for their own profits and losses. An enterprise should make contributions to the state in proportion to the state funds it uses and be taxed by the central and local governments. In the spirit of economic readjustment and reform, a general screening should be conducted among all enterprises so that specialized companies and joint companies may be organized according to the objective requirements of large-scale social production and the intrinsic ties within the economy, breaking through the barriers between economic sectors, between administrative areas, between military and civil industries, and between state and collective enterprises. The state guides, controls, and coordinates the economic activities of the enterprises mainly through planning, economic legislation, and the use of economic means, but it should also keep certain administrative means in reserve and use them when necessary. State planning should focus on long-term and medium-term programs, while the annual plans should be based on those of the enterprises and worked out with reference to state control figures. Democratic management should be strengthened so that the workers may become true masters of the enterprises.[3]

3. See Liu Suinian, "Studies in the Orientation of a Reform of China's Economic Setup," *Jingji Yanjiu* (Economic Research), no. 1, 1980.

What Should We Learn from Previous Managerial Reforms
in the People's Republic?

In the early days after the founding of the People's Republic, it was
necessary to limit the powers of the local authorities and stress centralization in order to overcome economic anarchy, cope with foreign imperialist blockades, stop inflation, and strive for a basic turn
for the better in the country's financial and economic situation. Centralization played a vital role in winning the War of Liberation
across the country and in effecting a speedy rehabilitation of the
war-torn economy. Beginning with the First Five-Year Plan (1953–
57) and with the basic completion of the socialist transformation of
the economy in 1956, there was a further concentration of power,
and a centralized managerial system of the Soviet type gradually
took shape. Whereas industrial enterprises had generally been under
the management of the greater administrative regions, each embracing several provinces, up to 1953, large numbers of big state-owned
enterprises were placed directly under the central ministries with
the abolition of these administrative regions in 1954. The enterprises
under central management numbered over 9,300 in 1957, as against
some 2,800 in 1953. Plans for state-owned industry and communications and transport and for capital construction were in the main
dictated to the lower levels in the form of directives. Following the
completion of the socialist transformation of individual farming,
handicrafts, and capitalist industry and commerce, there was a
tightening of control over these economic sectors by means of state
planning. In capital construction, 90 percent of the investment was
allocated directly by the central ministries. Important means of production were distributed by the central authorities. In 1957 some
530 types of supplies were distributed by the central government,
against 220 in 1953. The local authorities, and particularly the enterprises, enjoyed very limited powers. The enterprises had to refer to
state administrative organs such matters as the use of human, financial, and material resources, production, the procurement of means
of production, and the marketing of products. They had to hand
over to the central authorities even such money as their depreciation
fund.

Because of China's low level of economic development and its
relatively simple economic structure at the time, such a system of
economic management was more or less in conformity with the devel-

opment of the productive forces. But the drawbacks of the system became increasingly clear with the progress in socialist construction. The main drawbacks were, first, an overcentralization of managerial powers, and second, a practice of everybody "eating out of the same big pot," meaning extreme equalitarianism. These inevitably led to poor economic results. In 1958 a reform of the setup began, centering on the extension of the managerial powers of the local authorities, including the provinces, municipalities, and autonomous regions. The following steps were taken:

1. Most of the enterprises directly under central management were transferred to the local authorities. From March 1958 to the end of the year, over 8,000 enterprises administered by the central authorities, or 87 percent of the total number of such enterprises, were placed under the local authorities. The central ministries retained a little over 1,000 enterprises because of their unusual importance or experimental and pioneer nature.

2. Financial administration was placed on two levels, central and local, through a five-year apportionment of revenue and expenditure on the principle that whoever received a larger share of the income was to pay a larger bill.

3. The number of types of centrally distributed supplies was reduced to 130 in 1958, some 75 percent less than in 1957.

4. The power of employing temporary workers was transferred to the authorities in provinces, municipalities, and autonomous regions, who could take on as many of them as needed.

5. The local authorities were also given greater power in planning. They were permitted to revise—in fact, raise—the production targets for their own areas provided they pledged to fulfill the production and construction targets set by the central government and ensured the supply of equipment, raw and processed materials, and consumer goods from their areas. The local authorities were also given some power to approve capital construction projects. A double-track system was introduced in planning, by which the central ministries worked out the plans for their respective trades and the local authorities drew up overall plans for their respective areas, while the State Planning Commission and the State Economic Commission formulated the national plans on the basis of the plans turned in by the ministries and the local governments.

Viewed from the angle of defining the central and local powers of economic management, the orientation of this reform was correct.

This accounted for some positive results. To a certain extent, the reform aroused the initiative of the local authorities, and local industries grew fast for a time.

After the transfer of managerial powers from the central to the local authorities, however, it became difficult to control national economic development. This was especially so in the field of planning, where the local authorities were permitted to set production quotas on top of the state-assigned quotas. As the quotas were passed from a higher level to a lower level, they were raised without restriction, capital construction projects were started everywhere, and the labor force and the payroll grew fast in the process. Finally, there was no planning to speak of. This naturally created serious imbalances in the economy. However, the confusion was caused mainly by "leftist" errors in the economic guidelines, characterized by unreasonably high quotas for production and construction and unreasonably high rates of accumulation in the distribution of national income. As for the relationship between the state (the central and local authorities) and the enterprises, the vital question of the economy, there was no departure from the rigid practices. The enterprises were allowed in 1958 to retain part of their profits instead of giving all of them to the state. Previously they had retained only a tiny portion of their profits as a bonus fund. Now each was able to retain a much larger portion worked out on the basis of the following figures which it had registered with the state during the First Five-Year Plan period: the bonus fund, the reward for overfulfillment of production targets, the total of four kinds of costs (the costs of taking new technical measures, developing new products, ensuring labor safety, and acquiring minor items of fixed assets), and the profit earned. Beginning in 1958 the enterprises used such a portion of their profit to cover the above-mentioned four kinds of costs, the collective welfare expenses, and the bonuses. This enhanced their initiative. Nevertheless, there was still no change in the status of the enterprises as appendages to state administrative organs, central and local. Thus economic management in 1958 and thereafter was marked not only by confusion but also by insufficient flexibility.

In view of the serious economic imbalances which had appeared during the "Great Leap Forward" years of 1958–60, the nation began to carry out a policy of economic readjustment in 1961. Amid a return to centralization, state industrial enterprises were ordered to stop keeping a portion of their profits. The central government took back all the enterprises that were considered to have been transferred inappropriately to the local authorities, along with the powers in planning and the handling of human, financial, and material resources. Things returned to what they had been before 1958, and managerial powers became even more centralized in some departments. By 1963 the number of enterprises directly under the central ministries exceeded 10,000, and more than five hundred types of supplies were placed on the allocation list of the central government. Planning and management were conducted mainly by the central ministries along the lines of the industries, supplemented by work done by the local authorities in their respective areas.

The concentration of managerial powers at the time played an important role in putting the economy back on its feet. Yet all the drawbacks of the economic setup remained. As the economic situation improved, the contradictions in the setup sharpened. Beginning in 1964 some of the managerial powers were transferred back to the local authorities. In 1970 decisions were adopted to extend the powers of the local authorities still further. Once more, most of the enterprises under the central ministries (except for the ministries in charge of the defense industries) were handed over to the local authorities, including such giant enterprises as the Anshan Iron and Steel Complex and the Taqing Oilfield. The material supplies allocated directly by the central authorities were cut by 61 percent by 1972 as compared with 1966. A system of balancing surpluses with shortages among regions[4] was tried out nationwide or in parts of the country in the case of twelve key products, including rolled steel, cement, timber, and coal. The local authorities were given greater financial power. With many enterprises transferred again to the local authorities, the basic depreciation funds of the enterprises were placed directly at the disposal of the local authorities and the enterprises themselves. Between 1971 and 1973 a system was introduced to grant some financial freedom to the local authorities. Under the conventional system, they had been required to hand over the bulk of their revenue to the central government, which in turn

4. By this system the quantities and types of material supplies to be brought into or out of each province, municipality, or autonomous region were agreed upon for one or several years between the central ministries and the local authorities concerned on the basis of those consumed in the previous year and the estimated production and needs in the current year. The local authorities undertook to provide for the needs of all enterprises in the areas under their jurisdiction, including those run by the central ministries, but excluding the defense industries, railroads, foreign trade establishments, and some special undertakings. The central government ceased to be a direct provider for most enterprises but helped to make up for shortages in types and specifications from year to year.

covered almost all their expenditure. This was called a "unified collection of revenue and coverage of expenditure." Now they were only required to hand over a fixed amount of revenue and to pay for a fixed amount of expenditure, and they were allowed to keep for their own use the rest of their revenue and all savings on their expenses. This was called a "contribution of revenue [to the central government] and coverage of expenditure by fixed amounts," a system which encouraged the local authorities to collect more and spend less in the interest of local development. The local authorities were also empowered to make overall arrangements for capital construction in their areas.

The managerial reform in these years was fruitful and did much to arouse local initiative, but it caused serious imbalances in the national economy. Such confusion, however, was mainly a result of the "Cultural Revolution" and ultra-left errors, or errors of impetuosity and adventurism in the economic guidelines.

Although the reform helped improve the relationship between the central and local authorities, it brought no fundamental change to the system of economic management along administrative lines. The only difference was the shift of some powers from the central to the local administrative organs. The basic drawbacks of the managerial system were again kept intact. Worse still, because of the disruptive activities of Lin Biao and the Gang of Four during the Cultural Revolution, industrial enterprises were even denied the right to keep a certain percentage of their profits as a bonus fund.

After the arrest of the Gang of Four in October 1976, which marked the end of the Cultural Revolution, centralized leadership in economic management was again stressed as a means of overcoming the semi-anarchic state of the economy. Enterprises that had been placed under local administration were once again taken back by the central authorities. In 1978 alone nearly one thousand enterprises, including some scientific research institutes engaged in production, were affiliated with the central government again. The central authorities also took over the distribution of most of the products which they had put in the hands of the local authorities.[5]

5. See *Theoretical Questions of a Reform of China's System of Economic Management*, ed. Liu Guoguang (Beijing: China Social Sciences Publishing House, 1980), pp. 20–27, and He Jianzhang, "Problems in the Management of a Planned Economy Under the System of Ownership by the Whole People in China and the Orientation of Reforms," *Jingji Yanjiu*, no. 5, 1979, pp. 37–38.

If we leave aside the period of national economic recovery (1949–52) and the period of the First Five-Year Plan (1953–57), during which a centralized system of economic management was only just taking shape, the managerial system has experienced two major processes of centralization and two major processes of decentralization in more than two decades. The two decentralization processes were also two reforms, consisting of readjustments of managerial powers between the central and local authorities within the nation's administrative setup.

The significance of these two reforms lay in the fact that in the course of more than two decades people gradually came to see the problems in the managerial system and attempted to improve it. Over the years, however, the reforms were limited to the question of relationship between the "vertical" and "horizontal" systems of management, that is, management by the central ministries and their lower organs and management along the lines of administrative regions, which meant centralization and decentralization. But this was a question only of division of power within the administrative setup. As long as economic activities remained under the management of administrative organs, the initiative of the enterprises could not be brought into full play, and economic life could not be enlivened, even though the highly centralized managerial powers were divided between the central and local authorities and large numbers of enterprises were placed in the hands of the latter. This was because the reforms did not touch the basic system under which the economy was run by state organs. They made the enterprises appendages only to local administrative organs and not to the central ones. And since such a process of decentralization often weakened management by the central authorities in the absence of economic means of control to replace such management, disorder appeared in the nation's economic life as the authorities at each level pushed up production targets and started a great number of capital construction projects all at once. Thus the reforms created an endless cycle of centralization and decentralization. Nevertheless, this very cycle has convinced people that, to change the highly centralized managerial system which stifles human initiative, the basic way is not to hover around a division of power between the central and local authorities but to give the enterprises power to make their own decisions. Experience proves that neither a further centralization nor a further decentralization can provide the key to a reform of the economic setup. The key lies in enlarging the powers of the enterprises under state guidance. To prove this point, some theoretical discussions may be necessary.

A Theoretical Exposition

Why do we say that, for the present, the key to a reform of China's system of economic management lies not in centralization or decentralization but in greater powers for the enterprises?

First, the enterprises owned by the socialist state are relatively independent commodity producers because they remain the basic production units in a socialist society as in a capitalist society. The history of development of social production shows that, as an organizational form of production, the basic production unit is determined by the given productive forces of society. The enterprises are the basic units of social production under capitalism. The development of the basic contradiction of capitalist society, that is, the contradiction between the social character of production and the private appropriation of the means of production by capitalists, calls for the abolition of the capitalist ownership of the means of production and the establishment of socialist public ownership. But this contradiction does not call for a change in the status of the enterprises as society's basic production units. The experience of the socialist revolutions in various countries has proved that, after its seizure of state power, the proletariat can institute a socialist system of public ownership, but it cannot alter such a status of the enterprises. Of course, with the fundamental change in the character of the ownership of the means of production, the enterprises have also undergone a fundamental change in social character, and they will become bigger in scale with the growth of social productive forces. But they continue to function as society's basic production units. These are the circumstances that determine their position as relatively independent commodity producers. Furthermore, because of the limited growth of social productive forces at the stage of socialism, and because the means of production still cannot be owned by society as a whole, associated labor cannot be conducted on a society-wide basis. The laborers continue to regard labor as a means of earning a living. Because of this situation, socialist state ownership contains some elements of ownership by each enterprise. To put it another way, it contains some elements of collective ownership by the members of each enterprise. This is the fundamental reason that an enterprise is a relatively independent commodity producer. As society's production units, the enterprises must, in the economic activities conducted among themselves, observe the law governing commodity production, that is, the law of value, if they wish to secure an income commensurate with their economic performance—to fulfill the economic requirement of a system of ownership which is to some extent ownership by each enterprise.

Second, enlarging the powers of the enterprises to make their own decisions means giving a concrete expression to the economic relations whereby state-owned enterprises operate as relatively independent commodity producers—recognizing them as such producers in a true sense. Only when the enterprises become such producers will it be possible to bring their initiative into full play, to unfetter their productive forces, and to give a powerful impetus to the development of the productive forces of the whole society. This is an automatic means of eliminating the main drawback of a highly centralized setup which runs the economy chiefly by administrative means, namely, its restriction of human initiative.

This also explains why a further centralization of managerial powers cannot provide the key to a reform of the economic setup, but runs counter to the very purpose of such a reform. The present centralized setup does not suit the objective status of the enterprises as relatively independent commodity producers, and it hampers a rise in their productivity. Further centralization means continuing along an erroneous course. Here we are speaking only of the general orientation of a managerial reform. We are not denying the need for more centralization in certain respects within a given period of time, such as in the present period of economic readjustment, which will create the conditions for an all-around reform of the managerial system. A further centralization in this sense has nothing to do with the basic orientation of the reform of the economic setup.

The above discussion also shows why decentralization of managerial powers among the local authorities cannot provide the key to reform. Although some decentralization helps to bring into play the initiative of the local authorities and accelerate the growth of productive forces to some extent, it cannot change the present position of each enterprise as an appendage to state administrative organs. Thus it is also not in keeping with the objective status of each enterprise as

a relatively independent commodity producer. It will likewise fetter
the growth of productive forces and will not help eliminate the main
drawback of the present economic setup.

RECOGNIZING EACH ENTERPRISE AS A RELATIVELY INDEPENDENT COMMODITY PRODUCER

What kind of decision-making powers should be granted to an enterprise so that it may act as a relatively independent commodity producer? In any society, no production can be carried out without the
three elements of production—the laborer, the means of labor, and the
object of labor—and no economic entity can organize production
without owning or exercising control over the means of production
and labor power, or without the right to direct the process of production. Since socialist production remains to be commodity production,
the general process of production manifests itself not just in the direct
process of production, but also in a unity of two processes, production
and circulation, while the means of production and the products take
the form of material objects as well as the form of value or money.
Thus an enterprise should exercise powers of decision not just on the
means of production, but also on its monetary expression, that is, the
capital funds, and not just on production but also on marketing, or
circulation. All these powers of decision on human, financial, and
material resources, and on production, the procurement of the means
of production, and marketing, find concentrated expression in the
power over planning. Thus an enterprise must have the power to map
out its own plans under the guidance of state plans. Specifically, an
enterprise must exercise powers of decision in four spheres:

1. *Planning.* An enterprise may draw up plans in accordance with
state requirements and market demand as well as its production conditions and financial interests, and submit them to the authorities in
charge for registration or approval.

2. *Marketing.* An enterprise may market its products by signing
contracts with customers after the required deliveries to the state, and
may export its products with government approval. On the question
of pricing, except for products governed by standard government
prices, an enterprise may set its own prices or negotiate them with
customers within prescribed limits, and report them to the price-

control authorities for approval or reference. An enterprise may sign contracts with suppliers for the procurement of means of production.

3. *Finance.* An enterprise should assume full responsibility for its profits and losses. It should pay taxes to the state as well as interest on the state funds it uses. After paying state taxes and returning its loans, including principal and interest, an enterprise may use its profit to set up a fund for the expansion of production, a collective welfare fund, a bonus fund, and a reserve fund in accordance with state regulations and use them in accordance with state laws. In case of losses caused by mismanagement, the executives and the persons involved will have to bear the financial responsibility. If an enterprise keeps losing money over a long period of time, the authorities in charge should, acting on the merit of the case, decide whether to suspend its operation, close it down, merge it with another enterprise, or change its line of production.

4. *The labor force and wages.* An enterprise may recruit workers on a selective basis and discharge superfluous ones without violating state policies and decrees, and may choose the forms of wage payment within the range of increase in the total wage bill of the state. An enterprise may raise its wage scales and improve collective welfare for its workers along with rises in production.

If an enterprise enjoys powers of decision in these four spheres or, in other words, if its powers are extended to such an extent, it will have been granted the right to conduct its production and management independently under state leadership. Since it links the results of its operation directly with its material gains, it acquires a built-in economic mechanism for making advances. Then it can truly conduct independent business accounting and assume responsibility for its profits and losses, gaining recognition for its status as a relatively independent commodity producer in actual economic life. This will inevitably emancipate the productive forces of the enterprises, which are the foundation of the productive forces of society as a whole. It will accelerate the socialist construction of the country and provide a powerful material base for the consolidation of its socialist economic and political systems.

Some people are worried that a process of "capitalist liberalization" will take place after greater powers of decision are granted to the enterprises. Well-intentioned foreign friends have similar misgivings. But this will not be the case.

In the first place, extension of the powers of the enterprises is premised on maintaining the socialist system of public ownership and is designed to perfect such a system. As mentioned above, socialist state ownership is characterized by some elements of ownership by each enterprise. For this very reason, each state-owned enterprise remains a relatively independent commodity producer. Yet the present highly centralized system of economic management deprives each enterprise of its decision-making powers and its proper interests, and so contradicts the characteristics of socialist state ownership and the real economic status of each enterprise. Thus socialist state ownership under such a managerial system is far from perfect. When each enterprise enjoys greater powers of decision, and emerges as a relatively independent commodity producer in economic life, the characteristics of socialist state ownership will find better expression in the new system of management.

Second, extension of the powers of the enterprises is premised on maintaining a planned socialist economy and is designed to perfect such an economy. This aim is to be accomplished by regulating the economy through the market under the guidance of state plans or, in other words, by regulating the economy chiefly through planning and through the market as a supplementary means. All major economic questions will be handled by the state, including the general orientation of economic developments, the rate of economic growth, changes in the nation's economic pattern, the ratio between accumulation and consumption, the scale and orientation of capital construction investment, the general wage level and price level, and key construction projects. Guided by state planning, the enterprises operate on their own. The point is that regulation of the economy through the market plays an important role in promoting a planned economic development because it helps to provide information on supply and demand as a basis for drawing up plans, to review the feasibility of plans and correct the mistakes in them, to reveal the gaps between supply and demand and the need to balance them by pricing and other economic levers, to call the attention of producers to consumer preferences, to indicate possible choices for a rational distribution of economic resources, and so on. This shows that extension of the powers of the enterprises, accompanied by regulation of the economy through planning and through the market, will put the planning system on a much sounder basis.

Third, extension of the powers of the enterprises will be coupled with a more scientific system of administration, wider socialist democracy, particularly more democratic management in the enterprises, a sounder socialist legal system, and better ideological-political work. These will ensure the socialist development of the economy.[6]

SOME EXPERIMENTS

The enlargement of the powers of the enterprises to make their own decisions was officially proposed at the Third Plenary Session of the Eleventh Central Committee of the Chinese Communist Party in December 1978. Following the session, experiments have been carried out around the country. Two steps were taken. First, the enterprises under experiment were allowed to retain a certain percentage of their profit. Then quite a few assumed full responsibility for their profits and losses.

The enterprises under experiment exceeded 4,000 in 1979 and rose to more than 6,000 in 1980. Of these enterprises, 191 are trying out a system whereby they conduct independent business accounting and make themselves responsible for all profits and losses on the basis of paying taxes to the state instead of turning over their profits to the latter. In terms of number, the more than 6,000 enterprises are only 16 percent of the 42,000 enterprises covered by the state budget, but they account for 60 percent of the output value and 70 percent of the profit earnings of all these enterprises.[7]

Profit retention by enterprises began in Sichuan Province, where the results were more impressive than in other parts of the country. One hundred enterprises were designated for the experiment in the fourth quarter of 1978. Of these, eighty-four were locally run industrial enterprises, and the rest belonged to the transport and postal and telecommunication services, which are directed by central ministries.

A fourteen-point program was announced for the tryout. The main points were:

6. These points are based on an analysis made by Ma Hong in "A Reform of the System of Economic Management and Extension of the Decision-making Powers of the Enterprises," *Hongqi* (Red Flag), no. 10, 1979, pp. 54–58.

7. See report in *People's Daily*, January 2, 1981, p. 1.

• After fulfilling state targets, an enterprise had the right to produce more to meet market demand and accept processing jobs with materials supplied by clients.

• An enterprise might sell its new products as well as products not purchased by state commercial agencies.

• After fulfilling the eight technical-economic norms set by the state regarding output, variety, quality, consumption of raw and semi-processed materials and of fuel and power, labor productivity, cost, profit, and the use of working capital, an enterprise was allowed to set up an "enterprise fund" by retaining 3 to 5 percent of its planned profit and 15 to 25 percent of its unplanned profit, that is, profit earned in excess of the plan target.

• An enterprise was allowed to retain 60 percent of its depreciation fund which had previously been placed in government hands. It might keep for the first two years the profit earned through the use of new techniques, new technological processes, and new equipment developed with its own money. The income from these two sources, plus the allocations for major overhauls, might be used to tap production potentials through technical renovation and transformation.

• By fulfilling the eight technical-economic norms, an enterprise might set aside from its retained profit a "production bonus" equivalent to 17 percent of its total wage bill.

• An enterprise had the power to appoint its cadres, except the top ones, without authorization from higher authorities.

• An enterprise might obtain loans from the banks for use as working capital on an interest-free basis for the amount set by the state, on a low-interest basis for any extra amount, and on a high-interest basis for coverage of the cost of overstocked goods.

The results of the experiment were good. During the year 1979 the enterprises under experiment did much better in output, output value, quality, variety, profit, and profit contributions to the state, compared with the previous year and with enterprises not under experiment. The total output value of 84 pilot enterprises rose by 14.9 percent in 1979 over 1978 and was 26 percent higher than that of nonpilot enterprises. Their profit rose 33 percent over 1978 and was 120 percent higher than that of the nonpilot enterprises. The profit they handed over to the state rose 24.2 percent over 1978 and was almost double the amount turned in by the latter.

In 1980 the number of pilot enterprises trying out a retention of profits rose from 100 to 440 in Sichuan Province, representing 16 percent of all industrial and transport enterprises in the province but 70 percent of the total output value and 80 percent of the total profit. During the year, Sichuan had to cope with an acute shortage of energy and a serious lack of production assignments for the heavy industries. The profit turned in by local industries decreased by 7.55 percent as compared to the previous year. This included a drop of 30.3 percent in the case of nonpilot enterprises and of 3.7 percent among pilot enterprises.[8] The latter managed to minimize the decrease by raising the quality and changing the patterns of their products to meet consumer needs.

The national situation was similar to that in Sichuan. In 1979 more than 4,000 pilot enterprises throughout China boosted their total output value by 11.6 percent over 1978, some 3.1 percent more than the growth rate of the country's total industrial output value, which was 8.5 percent.[9]

In Yunnan Province industrial output value from 100 pilot enterprises in 1979 showed a rise of 11.4 percent over 1978, or 3.2 percent higher than the provincial average of 8.2 percent. These enterprises earned 13.2 yuan in profit for every 100 yuan's worth of output value, as against the provincial average of 10.7 yuan.[10]

In Zhejiang Province, 74 pilot enterprises registered a 14.2 percent increase in industrial output value and a 21.36 percent increase in the profit handed over to the state in 1979 as compared with 1978. Both figures were much higher than those for the whole province.[11]

During 1980 many of the pilot enterprises did not get enough production assignments from the state. Their income was further affected by the rising prices of raw and processed materials and by the energy shortage, but most of them boosted production and income. A survey of 5,777 pilot enterprises throughout the country, excluding those bearing full responsibility for their profits and losses, showed an

8. *Jingji Guanli* (Economic Management), no. 6, 1981, p. 2.

9. *Xinshiji* (New Era), no. 6, 1980, p. 7.

10. *Jingji Wenti Tansuo* (Inquiries into Economic Problems), no. 3, 1980, p. 34.

11. *Zhejiang Xuekan* (Academic Journal of Zhejiang), no. 1, 1980, p. 22.

increase of 8.8 percent in output value, of 11.8 percent in profit, and of 7.4 percent in the profit turned over to the state as compared with 1979.[12] The figures were generally higher than those from nonpilot enterprises.

Why did the extension of the powers of enterprises result in better economic performance? In the first place, with some powers of decision, an enterprise has changed from being a purely productive unit devoted solely to the fulfillment of state quotas to an economic unit, endowed with an internal motive force, for both production and business operation. Before the experiments, many enterprises in Sichuan did not get enough production assignments and could not find enough customers for their products. The production plans were worked out for them by the state, and the products were all delivered to state commercial agencies. The state was responsible for all the gains and losses of an enterprise, which depended on it for everything. Now that an enterprise has acquired certain powers of decision and enjoys its own financial interests, it begins to concern itself with both production and business, to look for more work and a bigger market, and to increase its profit by making new products and improving management. The experimental reform has given business to many factories and mills. The Central-South Rubber Factory, which had operated below capacity, increased both output value and profit by 60 percent in 1979 over 1978. The Mianyang Silk Dyeing Factory, which had not found a market for its goods, sold all of them and received enough orders for full-capacity production in 1979. In the same year the Chengdu Seamless Steel Tubing Mill, which had failed to meet market demand in terms of variety and specification, solved the problem by developing more than thirty new products in a few months. The Sichuan Chemical Plant, which had also operated under capacity, did much to improve its management and reduce cost. In 1979 it increased its profit by 2.7 percent for every rise of 1 percent in output value, as against a ratio of 1.7 percent to 1 percent in the previous year. What made the difference was the initiative of the enterprises, which propelled them forward from within and not from without.

Second, with some powers of decision an enterprise has secured certain economic means for its own expansion. Whereas it was able to undertake only simple reproduction but not extended reproduction,

12. *Guangming Daily,* March 6, 1981, p. 1.

it can now rely on its own strength to conduct the latter within a prescribed scope. In other words, it is becoming an organic body capable of growing on its own. In the past the right to conduct extended reproduction was, in both theory and practice, vested in the state but not in an enterprise, which was not even empowered to handle such a matter of simple reproduction as the renewal of equipment. This accounted for the slow progress in technical renovation and transformation to tap production potentials. Now a pilot enterprise has control over 60 percent of its depreciation fund, the fund for major overhauls, and an enterprise fund deducted from its profits. Thus it may carry out extended reproduction by these internal means. An enterprise sees that technical transformation has much to do with its financial interests. Using its own money, it procures better equipment and material, reorganizes its labor force, sees to it that production and technical transformation do not affect each other, and so makes faster advances. A case in point is the Chongqing No. 2 Knitwear Factory, which had to use old-fashioned knitting machines for one-color socks for a long time because it could not get the money to renew its equipment. In 1979, when it was granted greater managerial powers, the factory decided to delay housing construction and the payment of bonuses and used an enterprise fund of 60,000 yuan, deducted from the previous year's profits, to buy twenty three-color knitting machines. It installed the new machines in April, started using them in May, and earned the equivalent of all the investment in the same month. It used its share in the snowballing profit to buy fifty-five more pieces of equipment and, by the end of the year, earned 570,000 yuan in profit. If a small enterprise like this had turned to the government for a renewal of its equipment, it would have waited throughout the year without getting any investment. According to figures from fifty-two pilot enterprises, a total spending of 38 million yuan on technical improvement brought them a profit of 9.9 million yuan within the same year.

Third, with some powers of decision, an enterprise can achieve a unity of interests between itself and the state and the worker on the basis of growing production and a better income. The workers and staff members are becoming true masters of their enterprise, and the quality of management acquires real significance. An enterprise showed a lack of democratic management because it enjoyed little power and could hardly see its own interests. A pilot enterprise is granted power in five respects: making part of its plan, marketing some of its products, retaining part of its profit, using its own fund for extended reproduction, and controlling its bonus fund. at the same time, managerial performance is directly related to the personal interests of the workers. In Sichuan, one hundred pilot enterprises planned for a profit of 490 million yuan in 1979 but actually earned 150 million yuan more, or 640 million yuan, of which 92.0 percent went to the state, 6.5 percent to the enterprises, and 1.5 percent to the workers and staff. of the 150 million yuan in extra profit, 65 percent went to the state, 28 percent to the enterprises, and 7 percent to the workers and staff. The powers and interests enjoyed by an enterprise explain why the workers and staff worry about the elimination of waste, the managerial level, the marketability of their goods, and the development of new products. Workers' congresses have been held in 80 percent of the pilot enterprises. The workers attach great importance to the election of shop and crew leaders, regarding themselves as masters of their enterprises.

Finally, with some powers of decision, an enterprise can give wider scope to the talent of its executives, managerial staff, and technicians. The ways of management have begun to show some creativeness, and shrewd socialist entrepreneurs are emerging. Under the old managerial system, even a fool could stay on as the head of an enterprise, while a most talented person might not be able to do much. How could management improve in these circumstances? Given both power and responsibility, the pilot enterprises in Sichuan have, on the basis of rigorous business accounting, made market forecasts and suited production to demand.[13]

All this shows that the extension of the powers of enterprises, characterized by their retention of some profit, corresponds more or less to their economic status as relatively independent commodity producers. This activates the management and the rank and file, resulting in better economic performance.

However, leaving some profit with an enterprise is only a minor reform, because it does not fully correspond to its economic status as a relatively independent commodity producer. To carry through the reform of the managerial system, an enterprise must be given full power to make its own decisions. Only thus can it be a truly indepen-

13. Cf. Lin Ling, "A Year's Experiment in Granting Greater Powers of Decision to Enterprises," *Jingji Guanli,* no. 6, 1980, pp. 13–14.

dent accounting unit assuming complete responsibility for its gains and losses under state supervision. But in the absence of the necessary macroeconomic conditions, such as the basic elimination of the serious economic imbalances and reforms in the financial system, the distribution of supplies, employment, wages, pricing, and taxation, only a very limited number of enterprises may assume full responsibility for its gains or losses on a trial basis. In 1980 five enterprises in Sichuan Province were selected for an experiment whereby they conducted independent business accounting, paid taxes instead of turning over their profits to the state, and assumed full responsibility for their profits and losses under the guidance of state plans. They were the Sichuan No. 1 Cotton Textile Mill, the Chengdu Electric Wire Plant, the Southwest China Electrical Appliance Plant, the Chongqing Clock and Watch Company, and the Chongqing No. 3 Printing House. The government stopped taking over their profits but collected from them a tax on fixed assets, an industrial-commercial tax, and an income tax. After paying these taxes, the five enterprises used their net income to establish a production development fund, a public welfare fund, a wage and bonus fund, and a reserve fund. Apart from paying wages, they used a larger part of their money for extended reproduction and a smaller part for public welfare and bonus. They undertook to cover any losses that might be incurred without asking for government support. These enterprises enjoyed fairly extensive powers and advantages in the following respects:

- Working out production and marketing plans and financial budgets in accordance with state requirements and market demand
- Buying equipment, materials, and fuels wherever they wanted to
- Marketing some of their fast-selling products and putting their new products in sales exhibitions
- Setting the prices of their products and readjusting them with the approval of price control authorities
- Conducting trade negotiations with foreign businessmen and keeping part of the foreign exchange earnings[14]

14. While these enterprises are entitled to receive the full value of their exports, they are required to transfer part of their foreign exchange earnings to the government, which pays them an equal amount in domestic currency.

• Receiving priority in importing advanced technology and equipment and in getting bank loans for technical improvement
• Being permitted to pay taxes after clearance of debts and being exempted from income tax for the first two years on profits earned through the use of their production development funds
• Being authorized to decide on the sizes of their labor forces, to discharge workers when necessary,[15] and to raise wage scales within a prescribed range[16]
• Having their directors elected at workers' congresses, subject to approval by the authorities

This system of responsibility for profits and losses in Sichuan yielded good results. During 1980 the five enterprises experimenting with the system reported a 42.7 percent increase in output value, an 80.7 percent increase in profit, and a 49.1 percent increase in profit handed over to the state.[17] These increases compared favorably with the average figures in the province and with those from enterprises experimenting with retention of part of their profits.

Similar experience has been gained in other parts of the country. Like the five above-mentioned enterprises in Sichuan, the Shanghai Light Industry Machinery Company shifted from a profit retention system to a system of full financial responsibility as from the beginning of 1980. Between January and July of 1980 it paid the state 42,000,000 yuan in taxes and fees, which was 4,360,000 yuan more than its profit contributions to the state in the corresponding period in 1979. The company netted an income of 6,970,000 yuan in 1980, or 1,760,000 yuan more than in 1979.[18] This meant a bigger income for both the company and the state.

Why is the system of full financial responsibility more effective than the profit retention system? In the first place, when an enterprise assumes full responsibility for its profits and losses it wins a full power

15. State enterprises in China have no right to discharge workers on economic or financial grounds, but may do so in cases of serious violation of law or discipline. The enterprises experimenting with managerial reform are permitted to discharge workers for business reasons. The discharged workers remain on the state payroll and are transferred to other jobs.

16. State enterprises in China have no right to change the wage scales, which are set by the government for the whole country and are applied according to the price level in each officially designated "price zone." The enterprises experimenting with managerial reform are permitted to adjust these scales within certain limits on the basis of their own earnings.

17. *Jingji Guanli,* no. 6, 1981, p. 20.

18. *People's Daily,* September 17, 1980, p. 1.

of decision and bases its financial interests entirely on economic performance. Good performance raises the income of the state, the enterprise, and the individual alike. Poor performance may mean inability to pay wages, let alone bonuses. In other words, profits give it an impetus, while losses compel it to make improvements. This puts an end to the practice of "everybody eating out of the same big pot," the situation where all enterprises, good or poor, depend on the state for unqualified financial support. The Sichuan No. 1 Cotton Textile Mill, for example, produced 89,280,000 meters of printed cloth between January and September 1980, a 21.6 percent increase over the same period in 1979. Its profit reached 44,020,000 yuan, a twofold increase. In the first half of 1980, it cut cost 3.28 percent by saving 50 tons of cotton and 100,000 kilowatt-hours of electricity, and shortened the period of working capital circulation to sixty-seven days, against eighty days in 1979. Seventeen more varieties and 670 more specifications of printed cloth were produced. The increase in profit during this six-month period was 14,800,000 yuan, of which 33.7 percent came from higher output, 20.3 percent from lower cost, and 40.0 percent from a change in the lineup of products.

Second, the system of full financial responsibility helps to suit production to demand and regulate the economy through both planning and market operations. On the condition of fulfilling state targets, an enterprise may work out its own plans for the procurement of supplies, production, and marketing and may adjust them from time to time. This is a departure from the situation where the government sets all production targets for an enterprise, provides it with all supplies, and buys up all its products. Now an enterprise studies the market and tries to make its goods and services more competitive. In 1980 the Southwest China Electrical Appliance Plant accepted state targets equivalent only to 40 percent of its annual capacity. Market studies pointed to a great demand for varnished wire caused by a sharp increase in the supply of television sets, electric fans, electric meters, phonographs, rectifiers for fluorescent lamps, and other electrical appliances for home use. The plant used its enterprise fund for technical innovations to produce more varnished wire below 0.45 millimeters in diameter. With a higher quality, greater variety, and lower price, its products became more competitive. Contracts were signed with 442 enterprises in twenty-five provinces, which accounted for 60 percent of the annual output value of the plant.

Third, the system of full financial responsibility puts an enterprise in a much better position to carry out technical renovation and transformation. Driven by the profit motive from within and the pressure of competition from without, it adopts every possible means to improve its technology and equipment. Using its own funds and some loans, the Chongqing Clock and Watch Company invested 15,000,000 yuan in extended reproduction, equal to the total state investment in the company in the previous eight years. The Chongqing No. 13 Printing House waited thirty years for state investment to replace its old, dilapidated equipment. Now it has decided to accomplish the job in three years by using its own money and some bank loans.

Finally, the system of full financial responsibility makes democratic management a necessity in an enterprise, because the workers' financial interests are related immediately to managerial performance. This explains why the workers' congress has become the supreme organ of power in a financially independent enterprise. All important decisions of the enterprise must be examined and approved by the workers' congress, which also has the power to supervise the leaders, elect the director, and dismiss incompetent executives.[19]

The above shows that making an enterprise responsible for its own profits and losses is an effective way to arouse its initiative and improve its economic performance. The enterprises experimenting with the system are doing so only on an initial basis, in the absence of macroeconomic conditions necessary for its strict implementation. But the system has proven its superiority over profit retention and will exhibit its full vitality when conditions are ripe. It should be pointed out, however, that a number of problems remain unsolved in the experimental reform to extend the powers of enterprises. These problems arise from the serious imbalances in the economy, a basically unchanged system of macroeconomic management, and inexperience in an undertaking like this. Because of the great variances in prices and taxes and other faulty aspects of the managerial system, the gains of the pilot enterprises do not necessarily reflect their actual achievements—a factor which limits their initiative. Because of inadequate

---

19. See Deng Youchong, "Investigation on Experiments by Five Enterprises in Sichuan," *Guangming Daily*, September 27, 1980, p. 4; and Sichuan No. 1 Cotton Textile Mill, "Assuming Responsibility for One's Profits and Losses—A Great Impetus to Production," *Jingji Guanli*, no. 12, 1980, p. 29.

planning and ineffective supervision, there have been some blindness and overlapping in production and construction, failures to implement state plans, disguised price increases, an overissue of bonuses, and attempts to cut down tax payment or profit contributions to the state and use the money for one's own enterprise.

To make the experimental reform a success, it is necessary to lay down specific policies on the ways an enterprise may use its funds, market its products, fix prices, and issue bonuses. Economic legislation must be worked out as soon as possible, so that the enterprises will have laws to follow. In short, while the powers of decision of the enterprise are to be protected, unified state leadership over them must also be strengthened.

As stated in previous chapters, the Central Committee of the Chinese Communist Party put forward, toward the end of 1980, a policy for a further readjustment of the national economy in view of the serious economic disproportions and the nation's financial deficits. Since readjustment will be the emphasis for quite some time and reform is subordinate to readjustment, the experiments are being slowed down without any change in their general orientation. They are being limited to the present pilot enterprises, which must nevertheless review their experience, consolidate their gains, and raise their standards.

4

The Market Mechanism
in a Planned Economy

by Zhou Shulian

A MAJOR ASPECT of the current economic reform in China is the integration of state planning with the market mechanism. Although planning still plays the dominant role and the market is merely an auxiliary means of regulating the economy, the new approach represents a radical departure from the old practice of trying to do everything through state planning. In particular, the major means of production, which used to be distributed exclusively by the state, are being circulated through the market.

Here we will review the experience of the People's Republic of China in handling the relationship between state planning and the market, present a theoretical analysis on the question, show the advantages of the new policy, and discuss some of the problems awaiting solution.

A HISTORICAL REVIEW

During the First Five-Year Plan period (1953–57), it was not uncommon to look at planning and market as opposed to each other. The prevalent view was that the regulatory role of the law of proportionate development and that of the law of value were mutually exclusive.[1] However, planning and the market were in fact more or less integrated at the time because socialist and nonsocialist sectors coexisted and competed with one another and because it was necessary for state economy to channel the nonsocialist sectors into the orbit of a planned economic development by means of market circulation, often by signing purchasing and marketing contracts with private businesses.

The socialist transformation of the economy was virtually completed by early 1957, when the great majority of the peasants had joined socialist farm cooperatives, individual handicrafts people had also been organized in co-ops, and capitalist firms had shifted to joint state-private operation. The production and circulation of products that had been regulated by the state through purchasing and marketing arrangement now came under direct state control through its planning. This gave some people the impression that the market had been replaced by planning and that the regulatory role of the law of value had been replaced or at least restricted by that of the law of proportionate development. The role of the market was neglected, resulting in a drop in the output, quality, and variety of certain products, mainly handicraft products, farm produce, and rural sideline products. Pinpointing this tendency, some leaders of the Chinese Communist Party warned that it would be wrong to narrow the channels of commodity circulation and reduce the range of goods. In a speech at the Party's Eighth National Congress, Chen Yun, a leading member of the Central Committee and an expert on economic affairs, recommended that some of the commodities be purchased by state commercial agencies on a selective but not a monopoly basis and that the producers be allowed to market them on their own. He suggested that the sale of minor items of local produce be permitted at rural bazaars. He said that people should not be afraid of temporary and limited rises in the prices of some goods. And he pointed out:

---

1. The law of proportionate development of the national economy means that smooth economic progress is possible only when suitable proportions are maintained among different sectors of the economy in terms of the distribution of the means of production and labor power. The law of value means that the value of a commodity is determined by the amount of socially necessary labor it contains, and that commodities must be exchanged at equal value. For details, see Glossary.

The factories manufacturing articles of daily use often concentrate only on the fulfilment of targets relating to value of production and profits, while giving insufficient attention to whether their products meet the needs of consumers. Henceforth, these targets in the state plan should be taken merely as figures for reference. Factories manufacturing articles of daily use should be allowed to make their own production plans in the light of market conditions without being tied down to the reference figures in the state plan.[2]

Chen Yun's recommendations were obviously aimed at a correct utilization of the market within the framework of a planned socialist economy after the basic completion of the socialist transformation of the ownership of the means of production. The implementation of his ideas promoted economic growth. During the First Five-Year Plan period, the annual rate of increase averaged 18.0 percent in industrial production and 4.5 percent in agricultural production, the average wages of the nonagricultural labor force in 1957 was 42.8 percent above that in 1952, and peasant income rose by 27.9 percent in the same period. Prices were stable, the market was prosperous, and living standards rose substantially.

Then a "wind of communism" blew across the country in the nationwide drive to set up people's communes in 1958. Amid a total negation of commodity production and the law of value, large numbers of peasants were ordered to leave their farms to make iron and steel without financial compensation, and their private plots were abolished. This seriously dampened their enthusiasm for production. Agricultural production, which had been governed indirectly by state planning, was virtually placed under direct planning. Thus it was subjected to blind orders from administrative agencies. Agricultural production dropped sharply from 1959 to 1961, when output was 26.3 percent below that of 1958, and a serious imbalance surfaced between industrial and agricultural production. At the same time, industrial production was guided by the slogan "Keep political, not economic, accounts." Losses mounted into the billions through a neglect of cost accounting and economic feasibilities. All these mistakes stemmed from a violation of the law of value in economic guidance.

It was by a reaffirmation of the law of value and equal exchange

2. *Eighth National Congress of the Communist Party of China* (Beijing: Foreign Languages Press, 1956), vol. 2, p. 174.

that China started to overcome the economic difficulties which arose in those years. Speaking of the equalitarian, unpaid-for appropriation of the peasants' resources, Chairman Mao Zedong pointed out that the objective law of value could be applied only when people kept accounts. He said, "This law is a great school. Only by applying it can we train our millions of cadres and hundreds of millions of people and build socialism and communism in our country. Nothing can be done otherwise."[3] It was then stipulated that the production team should be made the basic accounting unit in a people's commune. Emphasis was placed on the exchange of equal values, and expropriation of the peasants was opposed. Production teams were given full power to run their production and to distribute their income on the principle of "to each according to his work." Peasants were allowed to cultivate their private plots and undertake sideline production. In industry a number of small enterprises producing poor and even unmarketable goods at high costs were closed down, and the manpower, materials, and money thus saved were diverted into the production of badly needed consumer goods. Business accounting was stressed, and attention was paid to economic feasibility. These measures proved to be in keeping with the law of value and other economic laws. The economy gradually recovered and, from 1963 to 1965, experienced a period of steady growth.

Then came the traumatic "Cultural Revolution." The money-commodity relationship was labeled as capitalist, and the law of value was opposed as "an alien force" to socialism. The negation of commodity production and the law of value, which first occurred in the late 1950s and early 1960s, was repeated with double ferocity. In the countryside the peasants' collective ownership was undermined and the production teams' managerial autonomy was trampled underfoot. The peasants were urged to accept a higher form of public ownership despite a poor material basis.[4] Their efforts to diversify the rural economy was criticized and restricted as a crime of promoting capital-

3. Quoted in Hua Guofeng's speech at the National Conference of Financial and Commercial Organizations to Learn from the Dachai Production Brigade, *People's Daily,* July 12, 1978.

4. Since 1961 the system of ownership of the means of production in China's countryside has remained a three-level ownership by the commune, the production brigade, and the production team, with the last as the basic accounting unit. This form of ownership has proved to be in keeping with the level of the productive forces. During the Cultural Revolution, some people attempted to make the production brigade the basic accounting unit, thus raising the level of public ownership at a time when the productive forces remained at a low level and the collective economy was underdeveloped.

ism. Their tiny private plots and cottage sideline production were
attacked as manifestations of the "small producers' spontaneous tendency toward capitalism." In fact, private plots were confiscated in
many places, sideline production was forbidden, and rural bazaars
were banned. There even appeared the slogan "Run agriculture by
means of dictatorship." Again the peasants' enthusiasm for production was dampened.

In industry, production was not geared to the needs of society.
There was no business accounting or concern for economic results.
There were no management rules or regulations, no production plans,
no stipulations regarding the size of the labor force in a factory, no
norms for material consumption, and no profit requirement. Production targets could be imposed at every level. Capital construction
projects were undertaken blindly all over the country. All this went
on until the economy was brought to the verge of bankruptcy.

Nearly three decades of experience shows that observation of the
law of value results in economic growth, while violation of this law
leads to economic chaos. This is why a correct integration of state
planning with the market is vital to the healthy growth of a socialist
economy.

A THEORETICAL BREAKTHROUGH

China's practice of regulating her economy through the market under
the guidance of state planning represents a theoretical breakthrough.
For a long time Chinese economists subscribed to Joseph Stalin's
thesis that under socialism the means of production are not commodities, that the role of the law of value should be restricted, and that
socialist production can be regulated only through state planning and
not through the market. A departure from these views forms the
theoretical basis of the present policies.

Forty years of socialist construction under the leadership of
Lenin and Stalin in the Soviet Union coincided with a gradual change
in the approach to the money-commodity relationship and the role of
the law of value. While both were negated at first, the need to preserve
commodity production and exchange in a socialist society and the
objective existence of the law of value were recognized at last. Up until
his last days, however, Stalin rejected the view that the means of

production allocated by the state among its enterprises were commodities. He held that the production and circulation of means of production among enterprises under ownership by the whole people was something beyond the sphere of operation of the law of value. This was why for a long time there was no true integration of state planning with the market in the Soviet Union, and economic guidance was given largely by administrative methods according to bureaucratic will. This gave rise to a corresponding economic managerial system characterized by a lack of variety of goods, low quality, high cost, and low efficiency, all of which looked like the concomitants of a planned economy. It was this managerial system which China copied from the Soviet Union in the early postliberation years and which has been in use up to this day. For almost three decades China introduced no fundamental change into this system, not even in the First Five-Year Plan period, when some improvements were made on Chen Yun's recommendations, or in the early 1960s, when the national economy was being readjusted and the law of value was more or less observed. Thus China's economy has likewise suffered from a lack of variety of goods, low quality, high costs, and low efficiency, problems which have remained unsolved for a long time. This state of affairs has had much to do with the lack of a correct theoretical understanding of commodity economy under socialism.

According to the traditional view in political economy, commodity production and exchange do not exist within the socialist system of ownership by the whole people. It is held that commodity exchange exists only between the economic sector owned by the whole people and collective economy and among different enterprises under collective ownership. In his *Economic Problems of Socialism in the U.S.S.R.,* Stalin says that products circulated within the socialist system of ownership by the whole people retain only the "outward integument" of commodities but in essence they are no longer commodities. He insists that under socialism the means of production, which have ceased to be commodities, should not be sold to enterprises under collective ownership. Now we quote his argument in full:

Can means of production be regarded as commodities in our socialist system? In my opinion they certainly cannot.

A commodity is a product which may be sold to any purchaser, and when its owner sells it, he loses ownership of it and the purchaser becomes the owner of the commodity, which he may resell, pledge, or allow to rot. Do means of production come within this category? They obviously do not. In the first place, means of production are not "sold" to any purchaser, they are not "sold" even to collective farms; they are only allocated by the state to its enterprises. In the second place, when transferring means of production to any enterprise, their owner—the state—does not at all lose the ownership of them; on the contrary, it retains it fully. In the third place, directors of enterprises who receive means of production from the Soviet state, far from becoming their owners, are deemed to be the agents of the state in the utilization of the means of production in accordance with the plans established by the state.

It will be seen, then, that under our system means of production can certainly not be classed in the category of commodities.

Why, in that case, do we speak of the value of the means of production, their cost of production, their price, etc.?

For two reasons.

Firstly, this is needed for purposes of calculation and settlement, for determining whether enterprises are paying or running at a loss, for checking and controlling the enterprises. But that is only the formal aspect of the matter.

Secondly, it is needed in order, in the interests of our foreign trade, to conduct sales of means of production to foreign countries. Here, in the sphere of foreign trade, but *only in this sphere,* our means of production really are commodities and really are sold (in the direct meaning of the term).

It therefore follows that in the sphere of foreign trade the means of production produced by our enterprises retain the properties of commodities both essentially and formally, but that in the sphere of domestic economic circulation, means of production lose the properties of commodities, cease to be commodities, and pass out of the sphere of operation of the law of value, retaining only the outward integument of commodities (calculation, etc.).[5]

5. Joseph Stalin, *Economic Problems of Socialism in the U.S.S.R.* (Beijing: Foreign Languages Press, 1972), pp. 53–54.

Stalin's point of departure is that products can be considered commodities only when they are exchanged between different owners or, in other words, only when there is a transfer of ownership after exchange. The point is that each of the enterprises under ownership by the whole people, while sharing the common interests of socialist society, has its own particular interests as a relatively independent economic entity. Without commodity exchange, they would hurt one another's interests and encroach upon one another's independence. This amounts to a violation of the basic law governing social development, the law that the relations of production must conform to the nature of the productive forces.

In political economy, commodity denotes an economic relationship between more or less separate producers. Under the socialist system of ownership by the whole people, the entire society may be regarded as a single producer and the enterprises can no longer be separated completely from one another. But the fact remains that enterprises with their own independent economic and financial interests are after all not one and the same enterprise. When one enterprise transfers its products to another, it inevitably demands a compensation equal to the value of these products. This proves that exchange of products within the economic sector under ownership by the whole people still retains the nature of commodity exchange.

Some people quote Marxist classics to prove that commodity production will vanish after the establishment of a single system of ownership—ownership by the whole people. It is true that Marx, Engels, and Lenin did express such a view in anticipation of the disappearance of commodity production in a socialist society. But practice is the ultimate criterion of truth.

The future of commodity production under socialism will ultimately be illustrated by practice. At any rate, however, commodity production has been developing in all socialist countries up to this day, and it is not likely to disappear in the foreseeable future.

It should further be pointed out that what Marx firmly believed would disappear in a socialist society is "private exchange," not just any kind of exchange. Some people interpreted Marx's thesis on the disappearance of exchange among private individuals as replacement of commodity exchange by "allocation of products" (state distribution of products handed in by enterprises). In so doing they identified socialism with natural economy, which is not what Marx actually meant. Showing how bourgeois society differs from both the socioeconomic formations preceding it and that which follows it, Marx pointed out:

> The private exchange of all products of labour, all activities and all wealth stands in antithesis not only to a distribution based on natural or political super- and subordination of individuals to one another . . . but also to free exchange among individuals who are associated on the basis of common appropriation and control of the means of production.[6]

In principle, exchange among today's enterprises under ownership by the whole people is "free exchange among individuals who are associated on the basis of common appropriation and control of the means of production." Marx also wrote: "If we did not find concealed in society as it is the material conditions of production and the corresponding relations of exchange prerequisite for a classless society, then all attempts to explode it would be quixotic."[7] In view of the reality of present-day socialism, there is no harm in theory or practice in calling "free exchange" at the present stage "commodity exchange."

Since the end of the Cultural Revolution, Chinese economists have been making a thorough study of the theory and practice of planned socialist economy. In a paper entitled "Abide by Economic Laws and Step up the Four Modernizations," Hu Qiaomu, president of the Chinese Academy of Social Sciences, pointed out:

> Under socialism, commodity production and circulation will continue over a long period of time. In our country there is a need for their vigorous development, and the law of value is still playing an indispensable role in our economic life. . . . In drawing up and implementing our plans, we must utilize the law of value and give expression to the requirement of this law. . . . Failure to observe the objective law of value means inability to observe the law of planned, proportionate development.[8]

6. Karl Marx, *Foundations of the Critique of Political Economy* (New York: Random House, 1973), p. 159.

7. Ibid.

8. *People's Daily,* October 6, 1978.

The noted economist Xue Muqiao wrote:

> The socialist economy is based on large-scale social produc-
> tion which must have a fully developed commodity econ-
> omy as its prerequisite. . . . The state-owned economy is
> under ownership by the whole people, but it is impossible
> to carry out unified production and distribution on a society-
> wide or country-wide scale. The managerial system of
> everybody "eating out of the same pot" embodies the view
> that socialist ownership by the whole people is an absolute
> unity, which denies the fact that this unity embraces indi-
> vidual enterprises which are all living cells, relatively inde-
> pendent from and conducting commodity exchange with
> one another. . . . A socialist economy cannot do without
> planning, which is necessary for arranging production and
> livelihood for the whole nation. But to a large extent such
> planning has to be effected by regulating the economy
> through the market.[9]

The almost unanimous view of Chinese economists on the need to
promote commodity economy and act by the law of value provides a
theoretical basis for the policy of regulating the economy through the
market under the guidance of state planning.

THE MARKET AS A REGULATOR

Using the market as a regulator of the economy, especially circulating
the means of production through the market, has proved to be favorable to economic growth. Some of the advantages follow.

First, direct access to the market makes possible a closer relationship among producers and users, which in turn speeds up the distribution of the means of production. When the means of production were
allocated by the state alone, users had a difficult time getting the
machinery they needed, while producers had to cope with huge inventories of unallocated goods. Under the old system, when a factory
needed a machine, it had to apply for approval from a whole series

9. *Some Problems in Our Economy* (Beiging: People's Publishing House, 1980), pp. 240,
243, and 246–47.

of higher level administrative departments. The procedure took as long as six months, and even then the user had no idea if the machine ordered would meet its needs. Under the new system, an enterprise, which can usually judge its own needs better than the authorities in charge of allocation, has the freedom to negotiate with its suppliers so that it will obtain the kind of machinery and equipment, raw materials, and semi-processed goods most appropriate for its various production processes. Linkages between producers and users are becoming closer because it is no longer necessary to pass through the many offices, and the linkages are being improved because direct confrontation enables enterprises to better understand one another's needs and problems.

In the Beijing area, many factories that needed ball bearings could not find suppliers. When local ball-bearing plants, which had substantial inventories, began to sell their products to several leading department stores, desperate customers finally located their suppliers. Sometimes users could not buy the things they badly needed when the producers of those items were right in their vicinity. For example, a factory in Sichuan in Southwest China came all the way to Beijing to buy a silicon-controlled rectifier, which turned out to be a product of a factory in Chengdu, the capital of Sichuan province.

From the producer's point of view, direct access to the market can solve the excess inventory problem. For a long time the Harbin Electrical Meter and Instrument Factory had a stagnant inventory of several thousand meters. In 1979, after the factory received permission to sell its own products, it sent out its own salespeople to visit 340 users and in a matter of two months sold its entire inventory. The Harbin No. 1 Tools Plant held a fair at which it sold over 25,000 cutting tools in twenty days. These tools, valued at over 6 million yuan, had been lying in the warehouse for years.

Toward the end of 1979 the country's stockpile of rolled steel amounted to 18.5 million tons, and turnover took eight months. The Chongqing Iron and Steel Company's huge stockpile had begun to cause serious financial problems. In June 1979 the company could not clear its loans from the bank, and every day it had to pay a 5,000-yuan fine and another 5,000 yuan in interest for an extra loan. By the latter half of 1979 the company had begun to market a portion of its products. As a result its financial position improved dramatically. Output value rose 10.6 percent over that of the previous year, and profits rose by 31.0 percent. The company's managers naturally are all in favor of the policy that allows them to sell their own products.

Second, in speeding up the circulation of producer goods, the market also speeds up capital construction. With producer goods coming into the market, many projects no longer have to wait for supplies of material and equipment. For example, the Sichuan Hydrological Bureau badly needed but could not locate 6-millimeter and 8-millimeter steel plates for the building of auxiliary projects to some one hundred small water conservancy stations. Just as the projects were about to be halted for lack of steel, the Chongqing Iron and Steel Company put its products on the market. The Hydrological Bureau immediately bought 180 tons of rolled steel and solved its problem in time.

In the past, products of the machine-building industry were allocated first to new factories, then to factories needing expansion, and last to factories planning technical renovation. Now that any factory can buy the equipment it needs in the market, old factories, and particularly small local factories, have a better chance of obtaining the equipment they need for technical renovation.

A third big advantage of the market is that it creates competition which forces enterprises to improve the quality and variety of their products and customer service. Under state allocation of the means of production, any shoddy product could find its "market." The "Quality first" slogan could be heard everywhere, but rarely was it seen in practice. With competition, those who produce quality goods are flooded with orders and those who produce inferior goods are in trouble. Enterprise managers have a new slogan: "Variety means market; quality is lifeline."

The Lüda Textile Mill in Liaoning Province, for example, tried to strengthen its competitive position by improving the quality and increasing the variety of its products. As a result, 97.4 percent of the mill's forty-five products attained first grade in the first half of 1980, among which the bed sheets for export were all top grade and five other products were cited for national awards for excellence. The mill produced 327 new designs in 1980, 85 percent of which won orders for production at the provincial design selection conference. The mill reaped 71.4 percent more profits in the first half of 1980 than in the corresponding period of 1979. The 8.1 percent increase in the percentage of top-grade products alone brought the mill 110,000 yuan in profits. The mill's profits averaged 31,000 yuan per loom and 5,777 each person, surpassing all other cotton textile mills in the province.

Factories have begun to arrange production according to market demand. The machine-building industry in Sichuan developed 190 new products in 1979, and 150 of them have gone into regular serial production. The whole machine-building industry under the First Ministry of Machine Building topped the target for developing new products in 1979, registering a 12.5 percent increase over the previous year and a record in a decade.

The Hangzhou Oxygen Machine Plant used to refuse to accept orders for replacement parts, products not listed in its production plan or in its plant brochure, and products with the customers supplying the raw materials. Though its customers had many complaints, they dared not offend the plant because they could not get their supplies elsewhere. Today the factory accepts all these orders. In fact, many machine-building factories now offer all-around guarantees that cover repair, replacement, transportation, testing and adjustment, and technical training. Competition may prove to be a cure for bureaucratism in industry and commerce.

Fourth, utilization of the market has improved management. Competition forces enterprises to make full and efficient use of their human and material resources. Spurred by competition, the management of the Tongchuan City Rectifier and Transformer Plant in Shaanxi Province promoted sixteen college graduates to be leaders of technical sections or workshops. Since 1979 the plant has appointed two engineers, an accountant, seventeen assistant engineers, and eighteen technicians. Two college graduates assumed leading positions in the plant. After he became a deputy leader of the equipment and power section, college graduate Chen Shuangchuan introduced strict scientific management into his section. As a result, the percentage of operable equipment rose from 44 percent to 89 percent. After the designing section was reinforced by five college graduates, the plant began to produce seven types of transformers, compared with four in the past. Previously the plant could not obtain enough orders to keep all its equipment running; now the plant is operating to capacity.

An example of dramatic changes in overall management which resulted from its product entering the market is the Zigong Steel Plant in Sichuan Province. The plant has set up an economic management committee to serve as an advisory organization for the plant leadership. It introduced a system for all the workshops to conduct independent business accounting and for each production team to calculate its costs. A complete set of management regulations was implemented. As a result, its 10-ton electric furnace turned out 10,115 tons of steel in 1979, more than doubling its designed capacity. It has become one of the best steel plants in the country for both quality and quantity of output. In February 1980 the plant's scrap rate of cast steel was as low as 0.9 percent, close to advanced levels in the world.

Finally, regulation through the market also encourages enterprises to set up different types of joint economic ventures. In the past, when such organizations were set up through administrative measures, resistance was strong. With competition, enterprises have come to see the advantages of association as a better way to develop technique and strengthen their competitiveness. To survive in competition, enterprises must increase productivity, which means they must improve their division of labor through specialization, coordination, and integration.

The distribution of the country's machine-building industry is irrational. Some places have too many machine-building factories making similar products. Take the automobile industry, for example. Although the country produces only about 100,000 cars each year, there are over one hundred automobile plants. Some of the plants are so small that they each assemble no more than one or two hundred cars a year. There are even a few each assembling only a few dozen cars a year. The products of these factories were shoddy and expensive, but it did not matter to them because they could easily sell their products. Many of the plants were ordered to shut down, but when old ones were closed new ones would crop up elsewhere. At the end of 1979 the First Ministry of Machine Building called a national conference of the automobile industry to organize coordination in producing cars with raw materials and semi-processed materials supplied by customers. Any enterprise could order cars or parts if they could provide the material. At the conference, orders were accepted for 15,000 cars and more than 6,000 diesel engines.

After the conference, many factories reconsidered their positions in the automobile industry. A small car plant in Guizhou Province used to assemble only 200 to 300 cars a year. Its cars were poor in quality and very expensive. This plant has now shifted from making cars to producing pistons and other motor parts to be sold nationwide. It now earns much bigger profits than before.

More than ninety machine-building factories in Sichuan have pooled their resources to set up a joint company to produce equipment for hydroelectric power stations. Without investing additional capital, equipment, or manpower, the new company is able to produce twice as much equipment as these factories could individually before the merger.

Shanghai's Watson Electric Fan Factory had more than sixty years' experience in making electric fans. It also had a strong technical force. Limited by its small factory building and insufficient labor power, however, it fell far short of market demand in both the output and the quality of its products. In 1979 Watson's merged with an electroplating factory, two hardware factories, an electrical appliance and instruments factory, and a blower factory. The new Watson Electric Fan General Plant has doubled its floor space and nearly tripled its staff. By the end of the year, the plant had turned out more than 400,000 electric fans, some of which were for export.

PROBLEMS AND PROSPECTS

Regulation through the market has pumped new blood into the country's industry. It has given new momentum to production and circulation and forced enterprises out of their inertia. Many long-standing problems have begun to be solved. On the other hand, regulation through the market has also given rise to a new set of problems.

First, there is sometimes a conflict between the tasks assigned by the state plan and tasks that enterprises seek themselves. Because of deficiencies in planning, state plans are sometimes slow to get to the enterprises, so enterprises must often seek orders on their own instead of waiting for the state plan. After they have accepted their own orders, they may later discover that the state plan has increased their tasks, in which case they have a hard time fulfilling both obligations.

Shanghai's First Bureau for Mechanical and Electrical Engineering Goods has formulated a set of principles for handling the relationship between state assignments and orders the enterprises have sought themselves. Priority must go to assignments given by the state plan. Enterprises under this bureau must put the needs of the state before those of the locality, completing key projects before ordinary ones. In drawing up contracts with customers, enterprises should give priority to products that are in great shortage in the market. For products in regular surplus, they may accept orders amounting to 50 percent of their annual capacity. As for overstocked goods, they may accept orders amounting to 75 percent of their annual capacity. Contracts must contain this proviso: "The date of delivery is subject to change through consultation in case this contract runs counter to major assignments given by the state plan." These policies have ensured fulfillment of state plan targets. The year 1980 was the best on record for the enterprises under this bureau in terms of fulfilling state plan assignments. The bureau itself fulfilled its eleven key state assignments ahead of schedule.

The second problem is the lack of good market analysis. Few enterprises are in a position to conduct thorough market analysis. When certain products become hot on the market, all kinds of factories scramble to produce these items. For example, many enterprises under the First Machine-Building Ministry simultaneously started producing electric fans, which they thought would sell fast. The ministry's Yunnan Bureau conducted a market survey and warned the enterprises that the province's demand for electric fans was in fact very limited. The bureau urged enterprises to take local conditions into account and pay attention to both the immediate and the long-range needs of the market. It suggested that enterprises concentrate their efforts on developing high-precision machinery that would suit the geographical features of the Yunnan highlands. Under the guidance of the bureau, the Kunming General Machinery Plant began to produce brick-making machines, cement mixers, derrick-type cranes, and other light equipment for the construction industry, which found a ready market among building companies and rural communes in that mountainous province.

Some factories have already developed fairly sophisticated market analysis. The Dongxin Electrocarbon Plant in Sichuan predicted that the country annually needs roughly 20 tons of carbon plates for making synthetic diamonds. They based this figure on a survey of the capacity of all the synthetic diamond presses in all the grinding wheel factories in China. The plant has built files on each of its customers. Their research has provided the plant with a clear picture of market demand for the coming two or three years.

Third, many enterprises still have too little decision-making authority to allow regulation through the market really to play its role. As long as an enterprise has pledged to fulfill its duty to the state plan, it should be allowed to arrange production or take up coordination or association according to market needs. Aside from the materials allocated to it by the state plan, an enterprise should be able to purchase the materials it needs from other enterprises within the scope permitted by state laws. No locality or department should be permitted to obstruct this. Even materials under unified state allocation should be gradually distributed in a way that allows enterprises to have freedom to choose its own suppliers. No locality or department should be allowed to interfere with the power of enterprises in production, procurement, marketing, or matters concerning labor power, capital, and materials. Contracts and agreements signed between enterprises should be honored by both parties and protected by state laws. Any party that violates the contracts or agreements it has signed should bear full economic and legal responsibility. The enterprise has the right to resist and sue for any violation of its autonomy in management.

Fourth, more channels are needed for the circulation of commodities. Between different localities and between rural and urban districts, sales departments may be set up, commodity fairs organized, and sales agents appointed. It is necessary to break down barriers between regions and departments because a unified national market is the prerequisite to competition on a national scale. Therefore no districts or departments should be allowed to place blockades on the market or prevent goods from entering local markets. Local raw materials and semi-processed goods should be shipped out to other places according to state plans. It is unlawful to take administrative measures to protect the backward and suppress the advanced and block the proper circulation of commodities.

The fifth problem is the blockade on new techniques. Some enterprises try to conceal key techniques, and others try their best to get hold of the blueprints on technology for fast-selling items, paying little or nothing at all to the factories that developed them. In a sense this is a reaction to the old equalitarian practice. In the past, whenever a new technique was developed through tremendous efforts on the part of an enterprise, it was shared with other enterprises free of charge. This practice might seem beneficial to the dissemination of new technology, but in reality it encourages enterprises to feed on the fruits of others' labor and dampens enthusiasm for innovation and invention. Now that there is competition, the introduction of new techniques is closely linked with the economic interests of the enterprise, and no enterprise is willing to make free transfer of its new techniques. Technical blockade hampers the popularization of new techniques and leads to duplication of labor, which is a waste of society's labor, material, and funds. We can neither let this problem drift nor revive the old equalitarian practice. We must find a form of technology transfer which protects the rights and interests of inventors and at the same time helps disseminate new techniques.

Finally, regulation through the market has spotlighted the problem of prices. The current pricing structure presents a major stumbling block to the thorough implementation of economic reforms. Though competition manifests itself in the quality and variety of products and services, it is ultimately reflected in prices. But because the irrational pricing of industrial goods has produced great disparities in the profit earnings of different industrial sectors, many enterprises show a lack of interest in the reforms.

The existing pricing system is too centralized. Advanced enterprises whose costs are low cannot lower their prices, whereas backward enterprises whose costs are high can still thrive, thanks to the price system. These backward enterprises vie with the more advanced enterprises for fuel, raw materials, and markets, preventing the latter from making the best use of their productive capacity and sometimes even forcing them to cut back production.

A number of measures for solving this problem have been suggested. For example, the state should list the commodities for which prices can float within specified limits. Enterprises should have the power to lower the prices of producer goods in accordance with state policy in light of market fluctuations, as long as such price cuts do not affect their contributions to the state. Any upward adjustment of prices must be made strictly in accordance with price control regulations and submitted to the state for approval. Meanwhile, prices of all major commodities vital to the people's livelihood should be kept stable.

Many of these problems can be traced to the fact that the work of restructuring the economy has just begun. Until the economy is more balanced, the functions of the market cannot be brought into full play. But the underlying cause of most of these problems is poor planning. Planning work was much better during the First Five-Year Plan period. After the ups and downs of the following decades, and especially after the chaos of the Cultural Revolution, planning deteriorated. We have not yet completely resumed a whole set of good systems and methods. And with the introduction of regulation through the market, some people have concluded that planning is no longer that important and have become slack in their planning work.

We must strengthen planning. The mere mention of unified planning and centralized guidance leads some people to take back from enterprises decision-making authority in matters of finance, procurement, and manpower. They would quickly revert to the old practice of regulation solely through planning. It must be made clear that strong unified planning does not require a concentration of authority on matters of finance, procurement, and manpower in the hands of the state. Unified planning is characterized not by how concentrated power is but by how well society is able consciously to take effective measures in advance to ensure a balanced development of the economy and an efficient use of social labor.

How are we to strengthen planning? We should first focus on drawing up long-range plans, especially five-year plans, so as to work out the right strategy for overall development of the national economy. This means setting the major targets for economic development and defining the proportions among the major economic sectors, including the ratios between accumulation and consumption, the scope of capital construction, the correct orientation for allocation of investments, targets for industrial and agricultural growth, and improvements in living standards. A five-year plan should set targets for each year, and the annual plans should lay down concrete policies and measures for the attainment of those targets. A state plan embodies a forecast of rational economic development and so provides guidance for the economic activities of enterprises and localities. The state directs the activities of enterprises into the orbit of its planning mainly by economic means and also by administrative means.

The market in a socialist economy cannot operate spontaneously independent of the guidance and regulation of state planning. Rapid industrialization and modernization require substantial changes in the industrial structure and in the distribution of the productive forces. And this requirement cannot be met if individuals in the market are allowed to make decisions and act freely. In the economic development of socialism, macroeconomic questions cannot be resolved merely through the market mechanism. The choices made by individuals in the market according to their own needs and the choices made by individual producer units according to their own interests may not conform to the overall interests of society. Individual decision-makers may ignore the impact of their decisions on the economic activities of other enterprises. External diseconomies may be disregarded, so that enterprises or groups are harmed by one industry's expansion. This is the case, for example, with the various types of pollution.

In a socialist economy there exist differences in the incomes of producing units which arise from objective conditions, such as the natural environment, location, and so on. If these varying incomes were regulated only by the market and there were no regulation through state planning, the originally rational differences in the material interests among different sectors and regions would grow into irrational differences.

State guidance is essential, because enterprises do not have an overall picture of the national economy. The market situation on which they base their plans is closely bound up with the orientation and overall situation of national economic development. Enterprises cannot grow without information provided by the state. The more scientific and realistic the state plan, the more reliable its guiding role will be to enterprises in their decision-making, and the more earnestly these enterprises will make their activities conform to the requirements of the state plan.

Some people, both in China and abroad, have misgivings about the ability of a socialist society to control the millions upon millions of commodity producers and consumers who act and make choices on their own in the market. But if guidance and coordination by planning are handled well, regulation through the market will vitalize the economy and speed up China's modernization. We are confident that misgivings will disappear as the restructuring of the economy proceeds and planning is strengthened.

5

Competition Under Socialism

by Wang Haibo

FETTERED BY CONVENTIONAL IDEAS, economic researchers and administrators in the People's Republic of China believed for a long time that socialism precludes competition. In the past few years, however, they have taken another look at the question amid a series of new developments. Soon after the end of the "Cultural Revolution," a nationwide political-theoretical debate resulted in most people endorsing the principle "Practice is the sole criterion of truth."[1] In economic life, as discussed in detail in Chapter 3, experiments in granting greater decision-making powers to enterprises were carried out across the country. And as Chapter 4 shows, management of the nation's economy by state planning alone has gradually been replaced by a new system whereby the market is used to regulate the economy under state guidance. In the course of this ideological and socioeconomic evolution, more and more people have come to see that competition does exist under the socialist system.

As a matter of fact, commodity production goes on for a long time in the historical period of socialism. It is carried out in the various economic sectors—in the state economy, the collective economy, the individual economy, and the economy under state capitalism.[2] For this reason, competition takes place both among enterprises

1. See the Introduction, p. 2.
2. For the various economic sectors existing in China today, see Chapter 10.

114

belonging to these different sectors and among the enterprises within each sector. In this chapter we shall discuss mainly the competition among enterprises under socialist state ownership, because theoretically that is the most controversial type of competition.

THE NATURE AND INEVITABILITY OF SOCIALIST COMPETITION

Marxism holds that every economic inevitability arises from specific economic conditions. The conditions that give rise to socialist competition are those of socialist commodity production, and competition among socialist state enterprises arises from the fact that each of these enterprises is a relatively independent commodity producer.

As stated in Chapter 3, workers associated in a socialist enterprise look at its business operation as a means of earning their livelihood. Thus the enterprise demands an income commensurate with its economic performance. Fulfillment of this demand requires two conditions: first, the commodity produced by the enterprise possesses a use value that satisfies a particular kind of social want, and second, there must be a balance between the supply and demand on this commodity so that its price corresponds to its value. Without either of these two conditions, the enterprise cannot sell its commodity or realize its value and cannot fulfill its economic demand. Even under socialism, however, these two conditions do not exist from the very beginning. In other words, one cannot expect a balance between commodity production and social want, or between supply and demand, from the very beginning. True, the socialist economy is a planned economy, which makes it possible to regulate commodity production by state planning, gear it to social want in a basic sense, and achieve a balance between supply and demand. But state planning alone cannot ensure a complete, accurate, and immediate balance between supply and demand, first because state planning can cover only a few major commodities and not the tens of thousands of others; second, various limitations prevent state planners from achieving full conformity with the real conditions; and third, supply and demand change so fast that it is impossible to consider the fluctuations promptly in the course of planning. Thus state planning may be correct at one time but wrong at another because it is limited in scope, accuracy, and timeliness. This limitation must be overcome through competition among state enterprises, which can help readjust the supply and demand on commodities the state plan does not cover as well as some of those it does.

On the other hand, because of their status as relatively independent commodity producers, state enterprises must be granted a managerial autonomy under state leadership. Such autonomy covers production plans, the marketing of products, the procurement of supplies, financial accounting, and the handling of the labor force and wages. Given such autonomy, state enterprises find themselves in a position to undertake competition and help readjust market supply and demand.

Thus competition among state enterprises is not an accidental phenomenon but an objective necessity.

Some theoreticians, however, deny the existence of competition under socialism. They argue that Marx and Engels looked at competition as the product of a commodity economy based on the private ownership of the means of production and that they believed competition would vanish with the elimination of capitalist private ownership and the establishment of socialist public ownership. These theoreticians also quote the words of Joseph Stalin, who once stated: "The law of balanced development of the national economy arose in opposition to the law of competition and anarchy of production under capitalism. It arose from the socialization of the means of production, after the law of competition and anarchy of production had lost its validity."[3]

Can these references be used to deny the existence of socialist competition? No. The commodity economy that Marx and Engels examined was one based on the private ownership of the means of production, including simple commodity production and capitalist commodity production, mainly the latter. So it is fully understandable that they linked competition with the private ownership of the means of production. They imagined that the proletarian socialist revolution would triumph in countries where capitalism had achieved a high level of socialized production. In that case, the elimination of capitalist private ownership would be followed by the establishment of a system of socialist public ownership embracing the

3. Joseph Stalin, *Economic Problems of Socialism in the U.S.S.R.* (Beijing: Foreign Languages Press, 1972), p. 7.

whole society, and commodity production would no longer exist. Neither would competition.

The point is that socialist revolutions have not taken place in the countries where Marx and Engels thought they would. They have triumphed not in highly developed capitalist countries but in countries where capitalism achieved only a medium level of development, such as Russia, or even a low level of development, such as China. In countries like these, a multiplicity of economic sectors inevitably exist for a long time after victory in the socialist revolution, and commodity production continues in all these different sectors, which makes competition inevitable. If we are to act in the scientific spirit of Marxism, we must not try to tailor actual economic life and cut it to the size of one particular Marxist thesis or another. Instead, we should reexamine, reformulate, and develop the theories of Marxism by drawing on the wealth of data provided by actual economic life. Here it may be noted that the Marxist thesis on the disappearance of commodity production after the establishment of a socialist system of ownership embracing the whole of the society remains a hypothesis, which has to be proved through future experience. The socialist experience we have gained so far shows that the status of enterprises as relatively independent commodity producers can hardly change during the stage of socialism.

As for Stalin's theses on commodity production, it must first be noted that he made an important contribution to the development of Marxist political economy by pointing out, on the basis of Lenin's theory and the socialist experience in the Soviet Union, that commodity production did not vanish but continued to exist even after the virtual completion of the socialist transformation of the system of ownership. Nevertheless, Stalin's theory on this question not only lacks thoroughness but also is self-contradictory in certain respects. It is not thoroughgoing, because he confines commodity production to the sphere of relations between socialist state enterprises and collective enterprises, refusing to admit that commodity relations also exist among state enterprises. It is self-contradictory because, while recognizing the existence of commodity production in a socialist economy, he refuses to admit the existence of the law of competition, which is an intrinsic law of commodity production, just as the law of value is. These defects in Stalin's theory are not accidental. While they may be attributed to his mechanical approach to the hypothesis of Marx and Engels on this question, they have a deeper root in the system of economic management practiced in the Soviet Union in Stalin's time, a highly centralized system under which the enterprises were deprived of their status as relatively independent commodity producers. Since the enterprises were mere appendages to state administrative organs and did not enjoy any freedom, how could they compete with one another? Stalin mistook this state of affairs for a reflection of the essence of the socialist relations of production and so denied the existence of the law of competition. The managerial system in the Soviet Union, which denied the economic status of the enterprises as relatively independent commodity producers, was a wrong one, and so is the theory that reflects such a system.

SOCIALIST AND CAPITALIST COMPETITION

What are the essential features of competition in a socialist economy? What are the differences between socialist competition and capitalist competition?

First, the participants are different. In a capitalist society, capitalist enterprises are the main participants in competition. As a class, the capitalists owning these enterprises are united in their exploitation and oppression of the working class. But in the competition for market they are divided by a conflict of vital interests. Thus capitalist competition is a life-or-death struggle between capitalists. In contradistinction to this, the participants in socialist competition are socialist state enterprises that are relatively independent commodity producers. They share the same vital interests but differ in their particular interests. Thus socialist competition among state enterprises is a means by which they promote one another's growth on the basis of a community of vital interests and differences in their respective interests.

Second, the aims are different. In capitalist competition, the capitalists try to maximize their profits. Socialist production has a dual purpose, and so does socialist competition, that is, mainly to serve the interests of the working people in the entire society and partially to further the interests of the working people in an enterprise. Competition among socialist state enterprises is reflected, for instance, in their efforts to earn more profits. In this respect it looks much like capitalist competition, but there is an essential difference. The profits of the socialist state enterprises are not used by capitalists to enhance their capital and personal enjoyment; they are used mainly to develop socialist production and raise the living standard of all the working people, and only partially for the well-being of the workers in an enterprise.

Third, there are differences in the means of competition. In addition to improving the quality of the products and lowering the costs, capitalist competition may involve deception and other unethical means. Socialist competition must be guided by state plans, policies, and laws, and the enterprises compete with one another by improving management and business accounting, increasing the variety and improving the quality of the products, reducing the consumption of fuel and materials, lowering production costs, raising labor productivity, and improving service. One enterprise or another may resort to methods that violate socialist principles because of the contradictions between the particular interests of the enterprises and society's general interests, the influence of the exploiting classes, and the imperfection of the present system of economic management and legal system. But such practices are regarded as illegal under socialism and can be curbed by economic, administrative, and legal means.

Finally, the results of competition are also different. Capitalist competition brings success and wealth to some capitalists and failure or bankruptcy or even death to others. It aggravates the anarchy in production and the basic contradiction that threatens the very existence of capitalism, namely, the contradiction between the social nature of production and the private capitalist appropriation of the means as well as the fruits of production. Socialist competition does bring more economic benefits to the better-run enterprises, but these benefits do not come from exploitation and will not turn workers of the successful enterprises into capitalists. Some poorly run enterprises will drop out in the course of socialist competition, but the workers of such enterprises will work elsewhere instead of becoming jobless. Guided by state planning, socialist competition may nevertheless cause some blindness in production and business operation, but it will not lead to anarchy in production in society as a whole. It pushes socialist production forward and strengthens the material basis of the economic and political system of socialism.

These differences between socialist and capitalist competition are also a reflection of the superiority of the socialist relations of production.

PROS AND CONS ON SOCIALIST COMPETITION

Chapter 4, on the functions of the market mechanism in a planned economy, has already shown how competition can be used to promote socialist economic growth: Competition forces enterprises to suit their production to market demand, improve the quality of goods, increase variety, raise technical and managerial levels, make better use of human resources (particularly the engineering staff denigrated during the Cultural Revolution), and form associations on the basis of economic feasibility.

But competition cannot develop on a full scale in China at present because no fundamental change has been effected in the economic setup, which runs the economy chiefly by administrative means, or in the status of the enterprises as appendages to state agencies. While competition is protected and encouraged by Party and government policy, it is still a subject for controversy.

One objection to competition is that, with many enterprises rushing to produce the best-selling goods, it will worsen the present economic imbalances and may even result in economic anarchy.

Leaving aside the basic principle that competition in a socialist country is guided and conditioned by state planning, we would like to point out that, while competition may cause blindness on the part of the producers, it may also serve as a means of overcoming such blindness. Blindness in production and business means failure to make a realistic appraisal of supply and demand. If the market situation compels producers to turn out goods in short supply and cut back the production of oversupplied goods, there will be a balancing of supply and demand and, in effect, a remedy for the present economic imbalances. As analyzed in Chapter 4, a balance between supply and demand cannot be achieved merely by state planning, which cannot possibly be adapted to a fast-changing market. In this sense, socialist competition will not only be necessary for economic reform in the long run, but will also benefit the present economic readjustment. Any blindness may be curbed by such economic means as pricing and taxation and by administrative means when necessary.

A second objection is that competition will put many enterprises out of business.

From the standpoint of society as a whole, it will be a good thing if the many poorly managed enterprises, which have been running at a loss for years, drop out in the course of competition because they are a liability rather than an asset to the country. The manpower, money, equipment, and material spared from these establishments can be used for other productive pursuits. In actual practice, however, socialist competition will not cause the closing down of a great number of enterprises, because the state can usually find a suitable job for each enterprise—a sophisticated job for an advanced one and a relatively simple job for a backward one—and financial aid may be provided for the revival of a collapsing enterprise. This is particularly true for China at present, when there are still too few producers for too many consumers. Generally speaking, each enterprise has its strong points and weaknesses, and each can make its contribution to society in its own way by adapting itself to society's needs.

A closing down of large numbers of enterprises did happen in China before, but that was a consequence of ill-considered economic guidelines and not a result of market competition. During the "Great Leap Forward" beginning in 1958, it may be recalled, a myriad of enterprises were set up through much blindness all over the country, disrupting the balance of the national economy and making it necessary to close down many of them during the economic readjustment in the early 1960s. Similarly, a shakeup of enterprises involving the closing down of some of them and the merger of a greater number of others must be carried out in the current economic readjustment as a means of remedying the economic disproportions. Since competition helps to suit production to demand, it will serve as a necessary complement to state planning or an economic barometer showing where state plans should be readjusted from time to time. Far from throwing the economy off balance, it may be used to maintain or restore balance, and as far as the enterprises are concerned, it may revitalize many of them instead of ending their lives.

A third concern is that competition may create a serious problem of unemployment.

As stated above, socialist competition in China's circumstances will not result in the closing down of a great number of enterprises. Even though it will be necessary to close down some enterprises, suspend their operation, merge them with others, or shift them to other lines of production, the workers who become superfluous to these enterprises will all be taken care of by the state and assigned to other jobs. A socialist government cannot deprive citizens of their constitutional right to earn a living by work. The point is whether competition will do good or harm to the national economy. Will it help eliminate economic disproportions? Will it expand production? Will it increase national income? Will it reinforce the material basis of socialism? If these questions are to be answered in the affirmative, we may conclude that it will not take away people's jobs but lay the basis for wider employment.

The above apprehensions seem to have arisen from two sources: (1) habitual adherence to the conventional economic concepts and practices in China and other socialist countries; and (2) familiarity with capitalist competition and lack of experience with socialist competition. The misgivings are not surprising and can be dispelled only when competition has unmistakably promoted socialist economic growth.

But competition cannot fulfill such a purpose without correct state guidance. Its healthy development must be guaranteed by legislation and effective policies and economic leverages. First, competitors must adhere to the socialist code of ethics in the economic field. Cheating, bribery, embezzlement, manipulation, and profiteering are punishable by law. Priority should be given to better competitors, which produce more at a lower cost, in the supply of energy and raw and semi-processed materials. Less competitive enterprises should be helped to catch up with the more competitive ones by streamlining their organization and management. The authorities and enterprises in developed areas should help those in underdeveloped areas. Pricing, taxation, and bank credit and interest rates should be designed in a way that ensures fair competition. Finally, market analyses and forecasts should be provided, so that enterprises may avoid inappropriate undertakings in production and construction.[4]

4. See "Provisional Regulations of the State Council on Developing and Protecting Socialist Competition," *People's Daily,* October 30, 1980.

6

Readjustment and Reform in Agriculture

by Zhang Yulin

SINCE 1979, CHINA'S RURAL AREAS have undergone socioeconomic changes comparable in scope to the land reform and cooperative movement in the 1950s. In place of a lopsided stress on grain production, official policy today encourages the development of a diversified economy, which is basic to modernization. Better prices have been set for state purchase of farm produce. The basic farm collectives (i.e., the production teams) now enjoy much more freedom to make decisions about their affairs. The peasants' private plots and the country bazaars at which they may sell their surplus produce, both denounced as "tails of capitalism" during the "Cultural Revolution," have been revived and expanded.

Most important is the adoption of a flexible system that allows different ways of organizing and remunerating the farming population, based on the principle that whoever brings in a better output should truly earn more. This system, known as "the system of responsibility in production," seems to give the peasants more incentive than anything else since the shift to cooperative farming in the mid-1950s. It accounted for the record harvest of 1979 and explains the second best harvest expected in 1981, a year of unusual natural disasters.

This chapter will review the achievements and setbacks in China's agricultural development since the founding of the People's Republic in 1949, analyze the latest socioeconomic changes in the countryside, discuss the pattern of China's agriculture, and touch on some basic questions of restructuring the rural economy.

ACHIEVEMENTS AND SETBACKS

China's agriculture, like her national economy as a whole, has developed along a tortuous course.

The rural areas in old China became destitute under the ravages of imperialism, the feudal forces, and the Kuomintang government. Productivity in agriculture was extremely low. New China rebuilt her agriculture under difficult conditions. On the strength of a collective economy, which took shape during the cooperative movement after land reform, a myriad of rural construction projects were completed and farm production grew. Despite mistakes and setbacks, total agricultural output value rose 3.63 times during 1949–78. This includes an increase of 2.98 times in crop farming, of 18.5 times in forestry, of 3.8 times in animal husbandry, of 12.4 times in sideline production, and of 40.6 times in fishery. In terms of the amount of output, there was a rise of 2.7 times in grain, of 4.9 times in cotton, and of 2.0 times in oil-bearing crops.

Farm conditions also improved. During 1952–78 the government earmarked a total of 170 billion yuan for agricultural development. Of this sum, upward of 60 billion yuan were spent on capital construction in rural areas. It is important to note, however, that in terms of human and material resources, the farm collectives contributed far more to rural projects than did the government—the peasants provided for themselves while working at these projects, bringing their own bedrolls and food supplies plus a subsidy from their collectives. As a result of this endeavor, 80,000 reservoirs were built, with an aggregate storage capacity of 400 billion cubic meters, and 460 million mu (30.6 million hectares or 76.6 million acres) of farmland were brought under irrigation. The number of big and medium-size tractors used in the countryside went up 954 times. Power-driven irrigation and drainage equipment increased 513 times in terms of horsepower, totaling 160 million horsepower in 1978. The number of combine-harvesters rose 68 times and that of farm trucks 261 times. The amount of chemical fertilizer applied in 1978 came to 43.68 million tons, an increase of more than 141 times over 1952. Electricity used in the rural areas in the same year was 25.3 billion kilowatt-hours, an increase of 506 times over the 1952 figure of 50 million kilowatt-hours.

Still, China's agricultural development remains backward when compared with the advanced world levels. Besides, much of the increased farm produce has been used to cover consumption by added mouths, the population of China having doubled since Liberation. This affects a rise in labor productivity and in the per capita consumption of farm produce. In terms of overall production capacity, every peasant or farm worker in China produced, in 1976, 972 kilograms of grain, 26.5 kilograms of meat, 7 kilograms of eggs, 3.5 kilograms of milk, and 7 kilograms of cotton. The per capita consumption of major farm produce in 1978 included 318 kilograms of grain, 2.25 kilograms of cotton, 1.75 kilograms of edible oils, 8.5 kilograms of meat, and 2.5 kilograms of sugar. In 1978 the amount of fixed assets on Chinese farms averaged some 250 yuan for each peasant or farm worker, or 50 yuan on each mu of cultivated land, which means about 140 U.S. dollars for each person and 170 U.S. dollars per acre. Agricultural productivity in most of China's rural areas equals that in developed capitalist countries at the beginning of this century, and only the level in a few advanced areas can match theirs in the 1940s.

Considering China's natural resources and the tremendous amounts of manpower, material supplies, and money the People's Republic has put into its agricultural development, the country should have achieved a faster growth under the socialist system. However, a number of mistakes and twists in the collectivization effort and in production guidelines have retarded progress.

Land reform, carried out across the country by stages during 1951–52, eliminated land ownership by the feudal landlord class and realized the slogan "Land to the tiller." Each given a share of land, the poor peasants and farmhands from the old society rose to become "middle peasants" (small-holders). The whole Chinese countryside became an ocean of small peasant producers each working on his own. In these circumstances, the Party Central Committee and Chairman Mao Zedong pointed out that "there must be a transition from individual ownership to collective ownership, to socialism."[1] This transition to socialism was to be effected without being preceded by a spontaneous growth of capitalism and a polarization between rich and poor. The changeover to collective or cooperative farming had to be based on the principle of voluntary participation and mutual benefit, and active leadership from the Party and the government was to be combined with a gradual, steady advance. The Party Central Commit-

1. *Selected Works of Mao Zedong* (Beijing: Foreign Languages Press, 1977), vol. 5, p. 134.

tee pointed out that the peasants should first be encouraged to form seasonal mutual-aid teams in which they would conduct some kind of collective labor in one farm season or another. These teams could develop into year-round teams characterized by a more or less permanent division of labor and ownership of certain common property. If the results turned out to be satisfactory to most participants, the year-round mutual-aid teams could be changed to *elementary* agricultural producers' cooperatives of a semi-socialist nature, in which the members would pool their land and work collectively and receive payment on the basis of their shares of the land and their contributions in labor. If things went well, these elementary co-ops would be upgraded as *advanced* agricultural producers' cooperatives of a fully socialist nature, in which land would be owned in common and everyone would get his income by work alone.[2] The Party envisaged a fifteen-year period for the completion of this whole process, beginning in 1953, the year when China launched its First Five-Year Plan for national economic development. According to this schedule, agricultural cooperation or collectivization would not be accomplished in China until 1968.

The cooperative movement thrived in the first three years, that is, from 1953 to 1955. By mid-1955, some 650,000 cooperatives had been established in the country, mostly elementary cooperatives characterized by the members pooling their lands and drawing dividends on these land shares. They were comprised of 16.9 million peasant households, or 15 percent of the nation's total of 110 million peasant households. Over 80 percent of the cooperatives achieved increases of 10 to 30 percent in production. at this point a few more years should have been allowed for these elementary co-ops to consolidate and build up their strength until their production and income multiplied and the peasants' dividends on their land shares became meager compared to their earnings from collective labor, and the majority of the membership saw that retaining the private character of landownership would hinder a further growth in production. Only then would it have been the right moment to upgrade the elementary co-ops as advanced ones, in which the land shares would be abolished. But the initial

2. See "Decisions on the Development of Agricultural Producers' Cooperatives," by the Central Committee of the Communist Party of China, in *Cooperative Farming in China* (Beijing: Foreign Languages Press, 1954), pp. 2–3.

success turned people's heads. In violation of the principle of voluntary participation and mutual benefit, administrative means were adopted in many localities to compel the peasants to switch over to advanced co-ops, which appeared almost everywhere in 1956 to embrace 87.8 percent of the total number of peasant households. This placed the relations of production on a higher level than the productive forces and so disrupted the correspondence between the two.

This rash step developed into a "Left" deviation in 1958, when a "Great Leap Forward" was started and people's communes were established in most parts of the country in no time. Each commune, embracing one thousand or more peasant households, practiced unified planning and accounting irrespective of the differences in productivity and income among its subdivisions. Yet the new organization was lauded to the skies for its "large size and high degree of public ownership." The countryside was swept by "three winds": a "communist wind" characterized by extreme equalitarianism and the indiscriminate, unpaid-for transfer of resources from one collective to another or from one level of ownership to another; a "wind of boasting," or a tendency among cadres to exaggerate production achievements, especially the figures; and a "wind of blind direction," or a tendency among the authorities to issue arbitrary, uninformed, and unsuitable orders on the spur of the moment. The tremendous waste and losses caused by these "three winds" contributed to the nation's serious economic difficulties during 1959–61.

Under these circumstances the Party Central Committee, with Mao Zedong and Liu Shaoqi at its head, decided to readjust the people's commune system and the relevant policies. Resources indiscriminately appropriated during the high tide of the movement to set up people's communes were returned to their rightful owners as far as possible. The production team, with an average of twenty to thirty peasant households (or roughly equivalent to the size of an elementary co-op), was made the basic unit of collective ownership and accounting in a people's commune. This stabilized the relations of production in the countryside and brought about a fairly speedy recovery and growth of farm production. But there was no thorough analysis of the mistakes committed during the "Great Leap Forward" and the movement to set up people's communes, and no serious attempt to take warning from them. As soon as the economy showed a turn for the better, "Left" thinking gained ground again.

The "Left" mistakes were pushed to their extreme by Lin Biao and the Gang of Four during the "Cultural Revolution." Disregarding the low productivity in the countryside, they tried to make the production brigade (and not the production team) the basic accounting unit. They exaggerated class struggle and conducted it on an excessive scale in the countryside. Rural economic undertakings other than the main line of production, the peasants' private plots, the country bazaars, and all mercantile activities were dubbed "tails of capitalism" that had to be cut off. Equalitarianism reigned supreme in matters of income distribution, violating the socialist principle of "to each according to his work." The normal ways of organizing the labor force were largely abolished. The standards for working out remuneration were no longer seriously observed, and people just had to "share the food cooked in the same big pot." Unable to speak their minds, the rural cadres and the peasant masses nevertheless offered passive resistance to these attempts and practices. This was why they were able to keep farm production at roughly the same level as before or, in some cases, achieve a slight increase.

The above provides the background to the policies for readjustment and reform in the rural economy, particularly those adopted at the Third Plenary Session of the Party's Eleventh Central Committee in December 1978.

AROUSING PEASANT ENTHUSIASM BY READJUSTING THE RELATIONS OF PRODUCTION

The experience of agricultural collectivization in China proves the inviolability of the law that the relations of production must suit the level of the productive forces. It shows that the growth of productive forces would be held up by relations of production which are either too backward for them or too advanced. If the relations of production are too advanced for the present level of productive forces, they cannot be established in practice and, even if they are established, they cannot be stabilized. The key to a readjustment of China's rural economy lies precisely in changing the relations of production that have been placed on a higher level than the productive forces and in gearing the former to the latter, and whether the former are truly geared to the latter must be judged by peasant enthusiasm and rural productivity.

After all, what is the state of the relations of production in China's countryside today? The farm collectives there may be divided into three categories:

1. About 25 percent of the farm collectives enjoy a stabilized collective economy and have achieved big rises in production, either because production conditions have been historically good or because these conditions have been improved radically through the large-scale construction of farmland projects and the determined efforts made by the peasants since Liberation. of course, the production relations in these collectives still have to be readjusted in some ways in order to give fuller scope to the growth of productive forces.

2. About 50 to 60 percent of the farm collectives are in an intermediate state, that is, they present a greater number of problems in the relations of production. But the collective economy can be stabilized and developed through readjustment and reform.

3. About 20 percent of the farm collectives, located in economically poor and backward areas, have for years failed to achieve a rise in production. The collective economy is far from stabilized and in some cases exists in name only. It will take a long time to stabilize the collective economy there through a major shakeup.

No one in China doubts the principle that readjustment of the rural economy should, generally speaking, be carried out on the basis of the collective ownership of the means of production, although it may be necessary to preserve a smattering of private individual ownership among widely scattered households in mountainous areas. Neither is there any disagreement over the point that the production team, with an average of twenty to thirty households, should remain the basic unit of production, income distribution, and accounting because this alone suits the level of productivity in most areas. There are a few places where some early steps have been taken to upgrade collective ownership by making the production brigade the basic accounting unit, but such cases are not many and do not affect the overall situation, and it will not be difficult to effect a reversion to the production team as the basic accounting unit. The main problem with the relations of production in China's countryside today lies within the production team, involving the forms of operation, the organization of the labor force, the standards of remuneration, the methods of income distribution, and so on, all of which embody the economic ties between the collective and the individual and among the individuals themselves. If these questions are not handled well, peasant enthusiasm will be affected, and so will production and the well-being of the masses.

Before the Cultural Revolution there could hardly have been any satisfactory solution to these questions under the lasting influence of the 1958 drive toward "a larger size and a higher degree of public ownership." Things got worse during the Cultural Revolution, when a specimen of ultra-leftism, the Dazhai Production Brigade in Xiyang County, Shanxi Province, was publicized as never before. What was called the "Dazhai experience," held up as a national model, consisted of an exaggeration of rural class struggle and a glaring departure from the socialist principle of "to each according to his work."[3] This resulted in the denunciation of many flexible forms of operation and methods of remuneration as "capitalist practices" and much confusion in management in the production teams, in which the normal organization of the work force based on a division of labor and economic feasibility began to fall apart and income distribution was governed increasingly by absolute equalitarianism. The situation was particularly serious in the poor, backward areas, where the peasants said, "We are being roped together to live a poor life."

Examining this state of affairs, the Third Plenary Session of the Eleventh Central Committee of the Communist Party of China, held in December 1978, decided to solve managerial problems within the production team as the key to a readjustment of the relations of production in the countryside.[4] The purpose was to heighten peasant enthusiasm by decentralizing management in the production team, encouraging a variety of forms of labor organization and methods of remuneration, and minimizing equalitarianism in income distribution. This was considered necessary in view of the vastly different conditions in China's countryside and the extremely uneven development of the collective economy, as one could see from the situation with the three types of farm collectives enumerated above. Everything would have to depend on production requirements and the preferences of the

3. For a fuller explanation, see the entry " 'Left' (ultra-left) experience of Dazai" in the Glossary.

4. The session adopted the "Decisions of the Central Committee of the Communist Party of China on Some Questions Concerning the Acceleration of Agricultural Development (Draft)." After the decisions in the document were carried out on an experimental basis, the draft was promulgated nine months later by the Fourth Plenary Session of the CPC Central Committee in September 1979. For the text of the decisions, see *People's Daily*, October 6, 1979.

masses in each locality, and there should be no hard-and-fast rule on how people in each production team should go about their collective undertakings and divide their earnings on a fair and mutually satisfactory basis.

Experiments carried out along these lines gave rise to a system of responsibility in production that assumed two different forms: remuneration according to the fulfillment of work quotas and remuneration according to farm output. Both differed from the previous system of payment according to work points, under which a peasant earned a certain number of work points every day and drew his pay from his production team at the end of the year on the basis of his accumulated work points. Under the system of remuneration on the basis of work quotas, a crew of peasant workers receives quotas from the management of the production team, takes responsibility for their fulfillment, gets a reward for overfulfillment, and suffers a reduction of pay in case of nonfulfillment. But farm work is different from industrial work and many other types of work in that there is no precise measure of good or poor performance until people see the final crop, which alone speaks for the quality of work and the quantity of labor put into the job, leaving aside, of course, the weather factor. In this sense remuneration according to the fulfillment of work quotas leaves a certain amount of room for equalitarian practices, making it possible for people to equate a better job with a worse one, even if unconsciously. This is why remuneration according to farm output is considered a much better practice in that it encourages a crew responsible for a certain crop to work for the best possible yield in a creative way. This practice, which has become the principal form of the production responsibility system in China's countryside, has been tried out in various ways, the three main ones being:

1. *Remuneration on the basis of output by contracts on different lines of work.* This is usually done in production teams with a relatively high productivity, a well-diversified economy, and a competent management. While the production team management directs all production matters and conducts business accounting on a unified basis, it signs a contract with a group of team members, a family, or an individual for the accomplishment of a certain job, depending on the special skills of the group, the family, or the individual, in such fields as crop cultivation, afforestation, livestock breeding, sideline production, fishery, or industrial and commercial undertakings. The pro-

ducer or producers signing the contract pledge to bring in a certain amount of output or earnings in return for a certain number of work points. The output or earnings go to the production team for unified distribution among the team membership. The producer or producers are rewarded with an increase in work points if they bring in more than the contracted amount, and they are penalized through a decrease if they bring in less.

The First Production Team of the Yuzhai Brigade, Xiaoqiao Commune in Xinzheng County, Henan Province, has 125 acres of farmland, 38.5 acres of orchards, 83 head of draft animals, a tractor, a truck, and some diesel engines, electric motors, pumps, sprayers, and other farm machinery. It has a good foundation for developing a diversified economy. Starting in 1979, it assigned farm work and sideline undertakings to its members on a contract basis. Each producer received an average of 243.3 yuan from the team in 1980, some 104 yuan more than in 1979.

The above method is being used by only a smaller number of the production teams in the country, but it is expected to be adopted on an increasing scale because it conforms to the orientation of large-scale socialized production and factorylike management.

2. *Contracting output quotas to producers under unified management.* This method is roughly the same as the first method as far as income distribution and remuneration are concerned. The difference lies in the lack of specialization in the areas where it is applied—areas where productivity is relatively low, the economy is far from diversified, and the managerial level is poor. Until the economy becomes diversified and people acquire special skills in the process, production teams there can only contract basically similar jobs, practically all in crop cultivation, to the producers, who receive extra work points for output above the contract figure and face a deduction of work points for achieving less. But as production teams in these areas gradually build up a diversified economy, it is highly probable that they too will begin to contract jobs to producers along the lines of specialization or, in other words, they will change to the first method. On the other hand, producers are based in individual families, and this is still true in China's countryside today. Thus contracting jobs to producers often means, in effect, contracting them to individual families or households. This creates the possibility of changing to a third method: contracting output quotas to individual households.

3. *Contracting output quotas to individual households,* [5] *either with or without unified accounting and income distribution by the production team.* It may be recalled that "contracting output quotas to individual households" was listed during the Cultural Revolution as one of the crimes of Liu Shaoqi, the late Chairman of the People's Republic, and denounced as a return to individual farming. The practice was initiated in 1957, that is, almost immediately after the universal formation of advanced farm cooperatives in 1956, and reintroduced in 1961 and 1964. Each time it was criticized as a wrong tendency to let the peasants farm on their own and a sign of capitalist restoration, but at no time was it discredited in the eyes of rural cadres and masses. After the Cultural Revolution it was introduced, for a fourth time, in 1979–80, and this time it has proved to be a welcome solution to the problems in many of China's rural areas. We will not here go into the theoretical rights and wrongs of this practice.[6] We will only show what the system is like and let readers form their own judgments.

The system is being carried out by two different methods. In both cases the production team retains its collective ownership of the land and the other basic means of production, but in one case it conducts unified business accounting and distributes collective income among the team membership. In the case where the production team conducts business accounting and distributes collective income among the team membership, it contracts all farm jobs and output quotas to individual households. The output target is based on the potential of the land, and the remuneration in work points is computed according to the targeted output. The household signing the contract turns over the targeted output to the team management for unified distribution among the team membership, gets remuneration according to the number of work points provided in the contract, and keeps all extra output for itself. The number of work points is reduced if the contractor fails to meet the output target.

In the other case, where the production team no longer conducts

5. Otherwise translated in publications from the People's Republic as "fixing farm output quotas for each household."

6. For an analysis of the various forms of the production responsibility system in China's countryside, including the form discussed here, see Wu Xiang, "The System of Responsibility for Output in Agriculture—The Three Main Forms," *Zhongguo Shehui Kexue* (Social Sciences in China), Chinese ed., no. 4, 1981, pp. 63–76.

unified accounting and income distribution, it contracts its farmland to peasant households for cultivation on a more individual basis. While the production team retains ownership of land and large and medium-size machinery, it divides up ordinary farm tools among the households, which may buy them if they want to. Each household invests in the land worked by it in its own way, using seeds, fertilizers, insecticides, and so on, as it sees fit. While it has to turn in an agreed amount of output for payment of the state agricultural tax and as a contribution to the production team's public accumulation fund and public welfare fund, it keeps the rest for itself. In the language of the rural cadres and peasants, this is a practice whereby each farm household "ensures payment to the state, sets aside enough for the collective, and leaves everything else to itself." The system of remuneration in terms of work points no longer exists in such a case.

The contracting of output quotas to individual households, carried out in either of the above two ways, began in the last few years in areas where the collective economy had been bungled by ultra-left policies and where productivity was quite low. Far from being mechanized, farm work was done almost completely by hand, a form of labor suited to individual, not collective, operation. Having been "roped together to live a poor life" for years, the peasant masses were apathetic about collective operation and demanded to work on a household basis. Considering the state of affairs in these areas, the Party and the government went along with the demand in order to give full scope to the enthusiasm for individual household operation, on the condition that collective ownership of the basic means of production be kept intact.

The results justified the decision. Chuxian Prefecture, Anhui Province, lies to the south of the Huai River. A frequent victim of flood, waterlogging, and drought, it has always been one of the poorest areas in the province. Toward the end of 1978, a small number of production teams there began to try out the system of contracting output quotas to individual households. A year later these teams brought in yields several times higher than those of the other teams. Quanjiao County in the prefecture reported in 1979 a 12.4 percent increase in grain output, while production teams in that county experimenting with individual operation won increases averaging 35.7 percent. Similarly, the ratio of increases in grain output was 0.7 percent, as against 37.1 percent in Jiashan County, presenting a contrast between hardly any increase and a substantial increase. In 1980 the number of production teams using the system swelled to 48.4 percent of the total in the prefecture. The area suffered from much waterlogging that year, with a rainfall second only to that of 1954, a year of serious floods. But peasant households that had contracted the output quotas tried every means to minimize the damage and managed to wrestle a good harvest. Grain output for the whole prefecture rose by 10.0 percent over 1979, oil-bearing crops by 41.0 percent, and cotton by 12.9 percent, all surpassing previous growth rates.

Because of the incentive it gave the peasants, the system was soon adopted by production teams of a medium economic level and by some better-off ones. It is practiced by 80 percent of the production teams in Wuyi County, Hebei Province, and in Qixian and Shenqiu counties, Henan Province, and by half the production teams in many areas throughout the country.

But while the system encouraged the peasants to produce more, it limited the inherent advantages of collective farming. The peasants were aware of this because they had experience with both individual and collective farming, so they began to put under unified management by the production team things like pump wells and water conservancy works, large and medium-size farm machines, the breeding of draft animals, crop planning and seed selection for large tracts of land, and certain types of plowing, harrowing, and sowing. For this purpose the individual households contracting output quotas must also contribute to the production team's public accumulation fund and day-to-day production budget in the interest of unified management and long-term development. This gave rise to another form of contracting output quotas to individual households, characterized by unified management of several important items of work but without unified accounting and income distribution by the production team.

Thus we have three forms under which output quotas are contracted to individual households: (1) contracting through unified income distribution by the production team; (2) contracting without unified income distribution by the production team; and (3) contracting without unified income distribution by the production team, but with its unified management of certain types of work.

In any case, however, contracting output quotas to individual households frees the production team from direct management of farm work and the village labor force, which is now scattered in the households. Each household now uses its surplus labor power for various sidelines. Does this mean a growth of individual economy? Not necessarily. There are cases like several families pooling their efforts to make bricks and tiles or process farm produce. Some families put money together to buy a tractor for common use. A survey of three communes in Kaifeng Prefecture, Henan Province, shows that there are 332 joint economic undertakings involving 1,770 households, 6.7 percent of the total in these communes. They may be seen as the buddings of new collectives based on specialization.

The emergence of the various forms of the production responsibility system in the countryside, particularly the contracting of output quotas to households, has a political significance. The peasants, who can now decide what is to be planted (as well as when and how) on the plots they are using, feel more like "masters of the house." The cadres too have to work hard to earn their living. With many fewer resources at their disposal, they find it much more difficult to seek special privileges or take more than their due. The overstaffed, costly administrative setups in the countryside have to be and are being revamped and simplified. On the educational side, many peasants, particularly the younger ones, are eager to acquire general knowledge and learn agrotechnique in order to work better and earn more.

While the production responsibility system improves, the peasants are encouraged to work their private plots, raise animals, and develop household sidelines to increase their income, provided they do not conduct these undertakings in a way detrimental to the collective economy. In places where the system of contracting output quotas to households is not followed, the total area of the peasants' private plots and fodder plots may cover a maximum of 15 percent of the cultivated land of a production team. Country bazaars have been opened (after they were stopped during the Cultural Revolution) to allow peasants to sell their household sideline produce, and production teams to sell their surplus produce after meeting state purchase quotas. This will help develop China's commodity economy, reinvigorate its rural economy, and increase the supply of farm and sideline produce to the urban-industrial population.

Introducing the production responsibility system was a matter of readjusting the relations of production within each production team. At the same time, it was found necessary to readjust the relations between Party and government agencies, on the one hand, and the communes, production brigades, and production teams, on the other hand. Party Central Committee directives stressed the need to protect the proprietary rights and decision-making powers of these farm collectives and forbid any encroachment on their interests. In particular, it was made clear that the production teams, the basic units of the collective economy in the countryside, must enjoy the right of independent operation so that they would become economic cells full of vigor.

Starting from the time when summer grain came on the market in 1979, the state raised its prices for the purchase of grain by 20 percent. Prices for grain purchased in excess of state quotas were raised by 50 percent over the new prices. Corresponding rises were announced for the prices of cotton, oil-bearing crops, sugar crops, animal by-products, aquatic products, and forestry goods purchased by the state. The Party and government took these steps to increase the peasants' income at a time when the country faced much financial difficulty, considering them necessary for improving the relations between the state on the one hand and the rural collective economy and the peasant masses on the other hand.

According to the State Statistical Bureau, Chinese peasants earned 13 billion more yuan in 1979 and 1980 from the substantial increases in state purchase prices for farm and sideline produce. The amount does not include their earnings from the sales at the country bazaars. In the meantime, the state reduced the total grain purchase quota by 2.5 million tons from 1979. The reduction, coupled with a rise in production, enabled each peasant to receive an average of 60 extra kilograms of grain during 1979–80.

IMPROVING THE PATTERN OF FARM PRODUCTION

Another important task of readjustment in China's agriculture is to improve the pattern of production, since ultra-leftist policies created imbalances affecting ecological balance and modernization. Based on a self-sufficient, small-peasant economy, agriculture in old China showed a unitary pattern. The pattern was improved after the birth of the People's Republic, with forestry, animal husbandry, sideline production, and fishery growing at a faster rate than crop cultivation, and with cash crops developing faster than grain crops. But before there was time for a radical improvement, the Cultural Revolution came. Grain production was pitted against a diversified economy, and the development of the latter was repudiated as a "capitalist" tendency. Consequently, grain production was stressed to the neglect of cash crops in many areas, and people concentrated their efforts on the existing cultivated fields while devoting little attention to the vast expanses of hilly areas, forest land, pastoral areas, grasslands, and water resources. This meant a reversal of the attempt to improve the agricultural pattern. In 1978 only 12.7 percent of the land in China was covered by forests, much less than the world level of 22.0 percent. The output value from animal husbandry made up only 13.2 percent of the gross agricultural output value, only one-third of the 50.0 percent in countries with a highly developed agriculture. (See Tables 6.1 and 6.2.)

The prolonged emphasis on grain crops hindered the growth rate of China's agriculture and, what is more serious, damaged ecological balance to the point of a decline of natural resources. The low percentage of forest acreage and the devastation of part of the grasslands left as many as 1.5 million square kilometers of land suffering from soil erosion. Almost 5 billion tons of silt flow into the seas every year, containing 40 million tons of nitrogen, phosphorus, and potassium, equivalent to the annual amount of chemical fertilizer applied in the country. The low percentage of animal husbandry, along with irrational farming methods and overuse of cultivated land in some areas, has caused a loss of soil fertility. Surveys made in Foshan and Chan-

TABLE 6.1
PERCENTAGE BREAKDOWNS OF GROSS AGRICULTURAL OUTPUT VALUE,
1949 VS. 1978

	Crop Cultivation	Forestry	Animal Husbandry	Sideline Production	Fishery
1949	82.5	0.6	12.4	4.3	0.2
1978	67.8	3.0	13.2	14.6*	1.4

*Brigade- and team-run industries included.

TABLE 6.2
PERCENTAGE BREAKDOWNS OF FARM CROPS (IN TERMS OF SOWN ACREAGE),
1949 VS. 1978

	Grain	Cotton	Oil-bearing Crops	Jute & Ambari Hemp	Sugar	Tobacco	Others
1949	88	2.20	3.40	0.02	0.10	0.05	6.23
1978	80	3.20	4.10	0.30	0.60	0.40	11.40

jiang prefectures and the suburbs of Guangzhou in Guangdong Province show that the organic substances contained in the soils generally went down 0.7 percent to 0.8 percent in 1978, compared with 1960. The organic content of Chinese soil is estimated at 1 percent, against 3 percent in the soils of agriculturally developed countries. About 116.7 million acres of grassland have become sand or have degenerated. The per-acre output of grass has decreased from more than 1,200 kilograms to between 300 and 600 kilograms. There are also signs that fishery resources have deteriorated because of inappropriate reclamation of land from lakes or haphazard fishing operations.

China is known for her area of 3,491,502 square miles, which is slightly larger than that of the United States, lying between 3° and 55° north. Most parts of China are in the north temperate zone, with a smaller portion in the tropical and subtropical zones. Almost all living beings on earth can find a suitable habitat in the country. The ratio between cultivated land and uncultivated land is 1 to 8. The per capita average of cultivated land is 0.33 acres, less than half as much as the world's per capita level of 0.80 acres. But China has rich resources. There are more than 260 million acres of unused land, of which over 83 million acres can be turned into cropland. There are also 720 million acres of grasslands, more than double the size of the country's cultivated land, providing favorable conditions for animal husbandry. The country's territorial seas cover a total area of 1.03 million square nautical miles, including 0.81 million square nautical miles of fishing grounds, and China's fresh waters extend over 41.67 million acres. These conditions for fishery are rarely seen in other countries. Among the 800 million people living in the countryside, there are 300 million ablebodied workers, constituting a rich source of labor power. Anyone free from the standpoint of the small farmer can see that a great future lies ahead for China's agriculture.

Since the Third Plenary Session of the Eleventh Central Committee of the Communist Party of China in December 1978, economic researchers and administrators have analyzed the imbalances in agriculture and taken the following measures to improve the pattern of farm production:

1. *Redefining the guidelines of agricultural production.* Drawing on the farming experience in the early post-Liberation years, the Party worked out a guideline for agricultural development in the late 1950s and early 1960s: "Take grain as the key link and ensure an all-around development." This meant both concentration on grain production and building a diversified economy, a policy that conformed with China's realities. The guideline was carried out with good results in the period of economic readjustment in the early 1960s. Between 1962 and 1965, grain output rose by an annual rate of 6.7 percent, the output from cash crops grew even faster, and the proportions of forestry and animal husbandry in the rural economy also increased. The trouble was that, during the ten years of the Cultural Revolution, the "key link" (grain production) was played up to such an extent that the "all-around development" (a diversified economy) was written off. Even people in forestry and pastoral regions and cash crop areas were ordered to "take grain as the key link" and achieve self-sufficiency in food grain. This seriously undermined forestry, animal husbandry, and the production of cash crops and did not help grain production either. Seeing the harm of this one-sided approach, the Third Plenary Session of the Party Central Committee reformulated the guideline, pointing out that there should be a "simultaneous development of crop cultivation, forestry, animal husbandry, sideline production, and fishery" under the policy of "taking grain as the key link, ensuring an all-around development, and putting appropriate emphasis on certain lines of production according to local conditions." Attention should be given to ecological balance. An important task in building a modern agriculture is to change the pattern of agriculture and the composition of people's diet.[7] Later it was made clear that, since China has

7. See the "Decisions of the Central Committee of the Communist Party of China on Some

more hilly regions than flat, arable land, it is actually more difficult for the country to increase grain output than to increase the output from other lines of agricultural production. While there should be no letup in the effort to produce more grain, China should take the multiple use of resources as a strategic measure to build up a prosperous rural economy. Thus people in different areas may choose their main line of production on the basis of local conditions. Collective or individual operation may be carried out wherever feasible, provided everybody works in the direction of strengthening the collective economy.

2. *Reforming the planning system.* This should be done in such a way as to allow the communes, production brigades, production teams, and the peasants to use local natural and human resources to their best advantage. Under the overcentralized planning system in the past, farming plans were passed down from above, restricting peasant initiative and impeding the all-around development of agriculture according to local conditions. Now the Party and the government have announced that the basic accounting units (production teams) of the people's communes have the right to grow crops according to local conditions and farm seasons and to decide on the measures for increasing production, provided they adhere to the socialist orientation, observe state policies, laws, and decrees, and accept the guidance of state plans. Production teams have the right to reject arbitrary, uninformed orders from leading organs or leaders. In this spirit, some local authorities assign to grass-roots units only the purchase quotas for grain, cotton, and other major farm and sideline products, as well as the minimum acreages to be sown with a few crops. The grass-roots units are thus free to arrange everything else. They may process and sell some products after fulfilling the state purchase quotas. Limited amountsof farm and sideline produce and native and specialty produce may be sold at prices negotiated between buyer and seller instead of state prices.

3. *Drawing up regional programs for agricultural development.* On instructions from the State Council, special agencies are being set up to organize multisubject surveys of the agro-climate, soils, landforms, forests, water conservancy facilities, aquatic resources, and other conditions in each locality. This will provide scientific data for

Questions Concerning the Acceleration of Agricultural Development," op. cit.

establishing a wholesome agro-ecological system and a rational pattern of agriculture. Regional and national programs are being mapped out for the utilization of natural resources. Some projects have already been put into effect, such as those for the building of shelter belts (afforested zones holding off sandstorms) in northeastern, northwestern, and northern China.

4. *Building up bases specializing in cash crops, forestry, animal husbandry, fishery, and so on.* This is a departure from the conventional preoccupation with the building of water conservancy works and other farmland improvement projects, a practice determined by the almost exclusive attention paid to grain production. In the interest of ecological balance and an all-around development of agriculture, more financial and technical assistance is being extended to areas specializing in the above lines of production. However, the effort is restricted by the country's insufficient grain production. To meet the needs in these areas, China is importing more grain for a few years while trying to raise the country's own output. By so doing China will not have to spend too much effort on food grain production and may devote more attention to animal husbandry and cash crop farming, changing the pattern of the rural economy and tapping agricultural resources to a fuller extent. Importing more food grain does not go against the country's policy of self-reliance. Once a diversified economy takes shape, the Chinese will enjoy a different diet and consume less grain. This means a better living standard and perhaps an automatic solution to the food-grain question.

It has been only two years—much too brief a space of time for changing nature—since China decided to improve her agricultural pattern, but the country has clearly made advances:

A clear direction has been set for the all-around development of agriculture instead of an almost exclusive devotion to a few grain crops.

Bases offering much agricultural produce for sale are being revived, established, or expanded, such as the stockbreeding areas in Inner Mongolia, Qinghai, and Xinjiang, the traditional cotton areas in Nantong and Yancheng in Jiangsu Province and on the Jianghan plain (the plain drained by the Yangtze and Han rivers) in Hubei Province, the linseed areas in Inner Mongolia, Qinghai, and northwestern Shanxi, and the sugar crop areas in Guangdong, Fujian, Jilin, and Heilongjiang provinces.

The irrational distribution of crops is being changed and ecological balance gradually restored. Some of the fields used to raise grain crops, which were actually unfit for such crops, are being changed back to woods, pastures, fish ponds, and so on. For this reason the arable land available for grain cultivation was reduced by 3.33 million acres and the total area sown to grain crops was reduced by 11.66 million acres during 1979–80. In spite of this, good harvests were gathered because the crops were planted rationally according to local conditions and efforts were made to raise per-acre yields. In 1979, grain output rose by 27.35 million tons over 1978. In 1980, a year of abnormal weather, grain output dropped by 15 million tons from the 1979 figure. But it was still 10 million tons above the 1978 level and the second best in the thirty-one years since the birth of the People's Republic. The 1981 output was estimated to be close to the 1979 peak. On the other hand, the acreage sown with cotton, oil-bearing, and sugar crops was extended, and output rose year after year. The 1980 cotton output was the highest since 1949, and a further rise was expected in 1981.

The output value from animal husbandry rose from 19.3 billion yuan in 1978 to 22.119 billion yuan in 1979. Its proportion in total agricultural output value grew from 13.2 percent to 14.0 percent. In 1980 the combined output of pork, beef, and mutton came to 11.29 million tons, an increase of 0.66 million tons over 1979. The per capita amount of these three kinds of meat increased to 11.0 kilograms in 1980 from 8.5 kilograms in 1978.

How does all this affect the income of the peasants? In 1979 and 1980 they earned 25.8 billion more yuan by selling their farm and sideline products because of the increases in state purchasing prices and other factors. The average income of each peasant rose from 117 yuan in 1977 to 170 yuan in 1980. Peasants' savings deposits in banks increased to 12.66 billion yuan in 1980 from 4.65 billion yuan in 1977.

PROBLEMS OF RESTRUCTURING THE AGRICULTURAL ECONOMY

Modernizing China's agriculture according to her conditions requires the solution of many more problems. Two of them are under serious study by Chinese economists:

1. *The formation of associations embracing agriculture, industry, and commerce.* In a number of places in China with better economic conditions—those near big cities or in cash crop areas, and those where economic work has been more successful—commune- or brigade-run industrial enterprises, including those processing farm and sideline produce, are thriving because labor productivity is relatively high and the peasants produce much for the market. In Wuxian County, southern Jiangsu Province, which is near Shanghai, the output value from industries run by communes, brigades, or teams makes up 30 percent of the total agricultural output value and is as high as 50 percent in some communes. Across China, these industries employ about 30 million people, and their annual output value amounts to some 50 billion yuan. Also, a number of state farms have been set up in the border regions, coastal areas, and other parts of the country. They cultivate a total of 10 million acres of land, employ 5 million workers, and have a great deal of farm machinery. These farms also run many industrial enterprises of a fairly high level. With the Party carrying out flexible economic policies in the rural areas, enlivening the commodity economy there, people in these regions have found it beneficial to form associations embracing agriculture, industry, and commerce. The Party and government encourage such integration. As a first step, a number of associations have been set up on a trial basis on state farms and in a few dozen countries. The results seem to be good.

In Sichuan Province, more than twenty associations have been set up since 1978 in places with better processing equipment and transport facilities. They do crop farming, forestry, and livestock breeding or grow tea, fruit, medicinal herbs, and tung trees. There is no change in the ownership system, affiliation, or financial status of any of the economic entities participating in these associations. They process farm produce and go in for commerce. By signing contracts or forming joint stock companies, they have each formed an integral system for the procurement of supplies, production, and marketing and have achieved good results by bridging the gaps between the cultivation of crops, the processing of farm produce, and the marketing of the final products. This eliminates some intermediate links in commodity circulation and changes the auxiliary status of agriculture as a mere producer of raw materials. The Changjiang (Yangtze River) Agricultural-Industrial-Commercial Association in Chongq-

ing was formed by twenty-six state farms specializing in crop cultivation, forestry, and fishery on the outskirts of the city, which
signed contracts with more than fifty nearby production teams. Producing milk, fruit, tea, and processed fish and running commerce, it
has established business ties with more than forty enterprises in
eighteen provinces and municipalities. In one year it increased industrial and agricultural output by 17 percent, industrial output
value by 23 percent, and labor productivity by 16 percent, while
reducing the cost of production by 4.5 percent.

Most Chinese economic researchers and administrators agree
that the establishment of associations embracing agricultural, industrial, and commercial enterprises is an inevitable trend toward modernization in better developed rural areas. But since this development
involves both the reform of the entire system of the agricultural economy and the relations between state farms and farm collectives, on the
one hand, and state industry and commerce, on the other hand, no
hasty steps should be taken to extend it to the whole country.

2. *The future of the people's commune system.* Rural people's
communes in China have always been organizations under socialist
collective ownership and grass-roots organs of socialist state power
in rural areas. Experience over a long period of time shows that this
system prevents farm collectives from becoming independent economic entities and keeps them in the position of appendages of government agencies. This is why the rural economy is often run by
purely administrative methods and not according to economic and
natural laws. In the past, this system has fostered the indiscriminate,
unpaid-for transfer of property between collectives, encroachments
on their interests, and a blind, uninformed direction of production.
In varying degrees, the decision-making powers of the production
teams are still being restricted by this system. An important aim of
China's economic reform is to enable the producers to manage their
economic organizations directly and make the collectives independent productive enterprises jointly owned by its members, who handle production and business on their own with full economic vigor.
"Combining commune management with government administration" contradicts this requirement, and many economic administrators and researchers call for a change in this system. But how should
it be changed? Is government administration to be separated from
the commune? Are the communes to become economic associations

of production teams? Are they to become associations embracing agriculture, industry, and commerce? More studies are needed, and experiments must be carried out before a universally acceptable program can be put forward.

7

Changing the Leadership System in State Enterprises

by Xiao Liang

WITH THE PROGRESS in the reform of China's system of leadership and economic management, the system of leadership in industry must also change. The question is how to change it and in what direction.

Currently in China the leadership system in industry is comparable to that in a company or factory in the West, where an administrator runs things under a board of directors. Under China's socialist system, both in state-owned enterprises and in enterprises owned by urban collectives, the factory director manages under the leadership of the Communist Party committee. Despite its historical justification and some positive aspects, this system has major drawbacks, particularly in the confusion between the Party's political responsibilities and the factory director's managerial responsibilities. As stated in previous chapters, large numbers of Chinese enterprises have been granted greater decision-making powers, but how these powers should be exercised, and by whom, are questions that have major implications for China's economy.

THE FORMATION OF THE PRESENT SYSTEM AND ITS PROBLEMS

The current leadership system in industry developed historically when a number of publicly owned industrial, financial, trading, and communications enterprises were set up in the revolutionary base areas

147

during the years of struggle before Liberation. In those days the director ran the factory under a collective leadership, usually a triumvirate consisting of the Communist Party branch secretary, the factory director, and the trade union chairman. The form of collective leadership could also be that of a factory management committee or joint meeting. In some cases the factory director ran things under a higher authority. In the later stages of the War Against Japanese Aggression, unified leadership was exercised by the Party committee.

After nationwide liberation in 1949, this system was enforced in all state enterprises, but soon it was changed into a factory management committee system in accordance with the "Draft Regulations Concerning the Establishment of Factory Management Committees and Workers' Representative Conferences in State and Public-Owned Enterprises" announced by the North China People's Government in August 1949. By this system the director was put in charge of day-to-day operations under a management committee elected by the workers' representative conference which automatically included the director, deputy director(s), chief engineer, and trade union chairman. Lacking experience in running large, modern enterprises, China copied the Soviet system in which the director assumed overall management responsibility. But this proved to be a problem, because most factory directors had no experience or training in management. In some instances, Party leadership was not respected; in others, workers' reasonable proposals were ignored. Many inept decisions were made by these factory director-managers, and this was naturally especially discouraging to workers as "masters of the house" under socialism. This situation led to a change in 1956 to a system in which the factory director or manager took responsibility for production under the leadership of the Party committee. This was firmly established as the basic managerial system in China's socialist enterprises in March 1960, when the late Chairman Mao Zedong, after examining a report submitted by the Anshan City Party Committee, approved it and described it as the antithesis of the system of the factory director assuming overall responsibility.

The last two decades of experience under this system, in which the factory director manages under the leadership of the Party committee, shows that it has played a positive role in carrying forward the Party's fine tradition of relying on the masses and in helping to overcome the defects caused by copying the Soviet system. The departure from the Soviet model was in itself an experimental reform in the leadership system. Nevertheless, we cannot ignore the problems that have developed.

In the first place, what has happened under the current system is that, in place of the director taking overall responsibility, the Party committee secretary has become the number-one boss. This has come about because the system has confused the Party's political leadership responsibilities with the factory director's managerial responsibilities, so that the director cannot run things in a coherent way, the Party committee having become an integral and leading part of the administrative management of the enterprise, with the Party committee secretary edging the director into a lesser light. Ideally there should be collective leadership by the Party committee, but in fact the Party secretary has the final say in everything, including managerial affairs. This is what we usually refer to as the Party committee taking everything upon itself, or the substitution of the Party for the administration, or the confusion of the Party with the administration, or the lack of clearly defined duties among responsible officers. The system prevents the factory director from establishing his own chain of command from which to direct production and management independently and efficiently. Consequently, many urgent matters are delayed. Things became worse during the Cultural Revolution, when inner-Party life was disrupted and "revolutionary committees" took power.

Second, although it may seem that the present system strengthens Party leadership, in fact it does not. Under the present system, the Party organization often directly runs the enterprise, and the Party committee is so immersed in administration that it has no time to consider the enterprise's vital problems or to do political work. As the vanguard of the proletariet, the Party ought to lead the enterprise by ensuring the implementation of the Party's line, principles, and policies as well as the plans of the state. The onerous burden of routine work only takes away from the Party organization's real purpose. Also, the Party organization differs from administration in that it cannot issue orders to workers directly but must rely on ideological and political work and on the exemplary behavior of its members, especially its cadres. However, in the present system, the Party organization does become involved in giving orders. All this weakens the Party's real function of exercising political leadership.

Third, this system discourages the workers and staff by hampering democratic management, which is fundamental to a socialist enterprise. Democratic management is possible only when the means of production are placed under public ownership and class exploitation is abolished in a socialist society. But under the existing system, the Party committee is the actual decision-maker and the workers' congress merely an advisory board. How can the workers be real "masters of the house" if the workers' congress has no authority?

Fourth, the existing system may be suited for conducting political movements, but it is not suited for giving proper expression to the roles of the Party, the administration, the trade union, and the Communist Youth League organization, or for establishing a normal order in production. In particular, this system lacks accountability, so that a leader may act without a sense of responsibility and a person in a responsible position cannot exercise leadership. More often than not, the Party committee arrives at a decision without being held responsible for its consequences. The system also facilitates the making of uninformed decisions by Party committee secretaries who know little about production, technology, or management, while at the same time nothing is done to encourage the training of competent socialist entrepreneurs.

Finally, the current leadership system cannot be applied to joint ventures with foreign investment, or to the associations formed by domestic enterprises. To promote China's modernization, it is necessary to absorb capital from abroad and establish joint ventures with foreign interests. On the domestic scene, China had formed by 1980 some 3,400 associations of every description based on voluntary participation, mutual benefit, and economic feasibility, breaking the barriers between industries, regions, enterprises, and systems of ownership. These associations have developed fast with impressive economic results in the past two years. Clearly each of these associations can be governed only by a board of directors or management committee formed by the participants, and not by an agency based on the present leadership system.

THE ORIENTATION AND STEPS OF REFORM

The system of leadership in Chinese enterprises should be changed by making the workers' congress or general assembly the basic form of democratic management. At the same time, the Party's leadership must be improved and given correct scope so that the factory director or manager can take charge of directing the production and administrative affairs of the whole enterprise. In this way, we can properly handle three questions: Party leadership, democratic management, and administrative command. This will enable us to distinguish Party leadership from administration, to make the workers true "masters of the house," and to strive for excellence in running socialist enterprises. This is an important way to give expression to the superiority of the socialist system.

The leadership of the Party committee comes first in looking deeper into these three questions. The Chinese Communist Party, as the core of leadership for the Chinese people, is of course the force directing a socialist enterprise. When we talk about changing the leadership system in socialist enterprises, we do not mean denying or weakening the leading role of the Party committee. Instead, we mean to strengthen and improve it. How should this be done? The Party committee must first stop meddling in production matters and taking upon itself all administrative work. Instead, it must put its energies into ideological and political work while supporting the factory director or manager in directing production. The Party committee must ensure the implementation of the Party's line, principles, and policies and guide the workers in exercising their right to govern. It must do a good job of building up the Party, both ideologically and organizationally; develop criticism and self-criticism; carry forward the Party's fine tradition and style of work; and oppose and rectify all harmful trends and practices. It must demand that its members serve as models in production and other fields of work. It should give better leadership to the workers' congress, the trade union, the youth league, and other mass organizations. But it cannot concentrate its efforts on these tasks unless it separates itself from the administrative setup.

Democratic management is the basic content of any reform of the leadership system. With the expansion of the enterprise's decision-making powers, a question arises: Who will enjoy these powers, the workers or a few leaders? Because the workers should have the final say in a socialist enterprise, powers should be given to them. There are many ways for workers to exercise these powers: raising proposals for improvement of work, organizing inspection tours, the three-in-one combination, the system of eight representatives, and so on.[1]

1. The three-in-one combination refers to cases where leading cadres, technicians, and workers in an enterprise pool their heads to solve questions of production and technology. The eight representatives are elected by workers in a workshop, each supervising one of the following items of work: (1) safety and environmental hygiene, (2) planning and statistics, (3) collective

But the basic way is to vest power in the workers' congress or general assembly under the leadership of the Party committee.

As a matter of fact, the workers' congress was first instituted in the late 1950s simply as a form to attract worker participation in enterprise management. It could make proposals and supervise, but it made no decisions. In other words, the congress was not an agency of power. Even at that it was severely damaged in the days when Lin Biao and the Gang of Four were rampant. But in October 1978 a major step to enlarge the right of democratic management was taken when, addressing the Ninth National Trade Union Congress on behalf of the Party Central Committee and the State Council, Deng Xiaoping announced:

> To bring about the four modernizations, all our enterprises must, without exception, practice democratic management and combine centralized leadership with democratic management. From now on, the workshop directors, section chiefs, and group heads in every enterprise must be elected by the workers in the unit concerned. All major issues of the enterprise must be discussed by the workers' congress or general assembly.[2]

A further step was taken on June 15, 1981, when the Party Central Committee and the State Council released the "Provisional Regulations for the Workers' Congresses in the State-Owned Industrial Enterprises," a document with the impact of law on democratic management in China's industrial enterprises. This document clearly demonstrates that the present workers' congress is not a merely advisory organization but an agency with real power through which the workers can directly manage an enterprise and supervise the cadres. The regulations stipulate that the workers' congress of an enterprise —in accordance with state policies, decrees, and plans—has the power to—

> 1. Examine and adopt resolutions on the work report submitted by the factory director, the production and con-

welfare, (4) business accounting, (5) the care of work tools, (6) political education, (7) examination of quality, and (8) sports and recreation.

2. *People's Daily,* October 12, 1978.

struction plans, the budgets and final accounts, and major plans concerning technical innovations and management.

2. Discuss and decide on the use of the funds for labor protection, the welfare funds for the workers and staff, and the funds for bonuses, as well as other issues of vital interest to the workers and staff, such as the regulations for awarding and punishing workers and staff members and the allocation of housing for the workers and staff.

3. Discuss and adopt resolutions on matters related to the reform of the enterprise's setup, plans for wage adjustment, vocational training for the workers and staff, and major rules and regulations to be applied throughout the enterprise.

4. Supervise the leading cadres at all levels in the enterprise. The workers' congress recommends those cadres who work hard and have a record of success to the higher authority for commendation or, in the case of outstanding achievements, promotion. It has the right to propose to the higher authority the criticism, punishment, or removal of cadres who cause losses as a result of negligence of duty. It may propose to the Party discipline inspection commission and judicial agencies action against cadres who are guilty of dereliction or serious violation of law or discipline.

5. Elect enterprise administrators in accordance with guidelines set by the higher authority, subject to approval and appointment by the appropriate authorities.

The regulations also stipulate:

The factory director submits work reports to the workers' congress regularly, is responsible for carrying out the resolutions adopted by the congress concerning the production and administrative matters of the enterprise, and places himself under supervision by the congress. The workers' congress should support the director in the discharge of his functions and powers and defend the authority of the chain of command in production. It should educate the workers and staff members so that they act with a high sense of responsibility as masters of the house, consciously observe labor discipline, and carry out the system of responsibility concerning production and technical matters. . . .

The workers' congress may raise its voice if it disagrees with any decision or directive of the higher authority. If the higher authority upholds its original decision or directive after deliberation, the workers' congress must implement it.[3]

People may ask, Since the workers' congress is an agency of power, why must the cadres elected by the congress be approved and appointed by a higher authority, and why must the congress act under the higher authority's decisions and directives? The reason is that China's state enterprises are owned by the whole people under the centralized leadership of the government, and all these enterprises enjoy only a *relative* independence, an independence confined to the use and control of the means of production and to questions of management. The workers in any enterprise must exercise their powers not only according to their own interests but also according to the interests of the whole people. That is to say, democratic management must combine both national and local interests. On the one hand, the power of the workers' congress is limited in that it comes under the guidance of state plans and must be subordinate to the need to uphold the ownership of the whole people. On the other hand, national interests and unified planning must be based on worker enthusiasm and the democratic power of independent management in the enterprise. As for each collectively owned enterprise, the workers' congress or general assembly should be the highest agency of power.

Experience over the years shows that the workers' congress is of immense importance to good management in a socialist enterprise. First, it enhances the workers' awareness of their position as masters of the house, fires their enthusiasm, helps them observe labor discipline and various systems of job responsibility, and improves their knowledge and ability to run the enterprise. Second, it can pool the wisdom of the workers by tapping the strength of the collective to help solve all production, technical, and managerial problems. Third, it helps to coordinate the interests of the three (the state, the enterprise, and the individual), to handle correctly the contradictions within the enterprise, and to forge closer ties between the Party and the masses. Fourth, it upholds the authority of the administrative command by

3. *People's Daily,* July 20, 1981.

linking centralized leadership with democratic management. Fifth, it is conducive to strengthening and improving the Party's leadership over the enterprise.

The administrative command of the factory director is an important aspect in any change in the enterprise leadership system in that it is essential for the establishment of an authoritative chain of command and the combination of democracy and centralism.

The provisional regulations on workers' congresses stipulate that in the future the workers' congress will elect administrators of an enterprise in accordance with the guidelines set by the higher authority. These administrators will naturally include the factory director or manager. A factory director or manager elected by the workers' congress and approved and appointed by the higher authority is the commander of the enterprise in production and administrative matters and is the legal person representing the enterprise. Responsible for all the enterprise's production and construction work, the factory director must be obeyed by the workers through various responsibility systems and a unified chain of command. Under the director, the deputy director, chief engineer, chief accountant, and so on, must each perform his clearly defined duties independently. This system rules out once and for all the past practices of overlapping leadership without reward for good performance or punishment for negligence.

The combination of the three aspects—leadership of the Party committee, democratic management by the workers, and administrative command by the factory director—is a system of leadership in a state enterprise which we have worked out over the years within the framework of China's socialist system and national conditions. Because this is a reform that involves the overall economic situation, it must be carried out through experimentation in a systematic and planned way. At the same time, rather than following a uniform pattern, the system should be adaptable to specific conditions.

Economic researchers and executives in China disagree over the question of reform in the enterprise leadership system. Some support the system in which the factory director takes responsibility for production under the leadership of the workers' congress, some support the system with the factory director assuming responsibility under the leadership of an enterprise management committee, and others support the existing system of the factory director acting under the Party committee. Proponents of the last view argue that the prevailing problems in the enterprise leadership are caused by many factors, not necessarily by the leadership system itself. Some people are concerned that any change in the current system might weaken Party leadership. In view of this the Party Central Committee has decided that, except for a few cases where experiments are under way, the present system shall remain in force for the time being.

In any case, reform of China's enterprise leadership system can only be brought about one step at a time. The current changes are minor, paving the way for drastic reforms in the future. Conditions will ripen as the powers of the workers' congress expand with the progress in readjusting and restructuring the economy.

SOME PROBLEMS AWAITING SOLUTION

Having defined the general direction the reform of the enterprise leadership system should take, we need to look at some details.

First, should the workers' congress have a standing agency with the power to exercise the will of the workers' congress when it is not in session, one similar to the standing committee of the people's congress? Most people favor flexibility on this point. Generally, a standing agency would work better in a large enterprise, while in a small or medium-size enterprise it might prevent the factory director or the workers' congress from performing their duties. But the presidium of the workers' congress can be made a permanent setup, with a few executive presidents, who are not divorced from labor, taking turns chairing it. Its task would be to organize congress sessions, call meetings of delegation heads and representatives, and, as entrusted by the congress, deal with any important problem that crops up unexpectedly.

Second, what should be the relationship between the workers' congress and the factory director? The factory director or manager must be answerable to both the workers' congress, an agency of power, and the state, which appointed him. If the director thinks that a certain resolution adopted by the workers' congress goes against a Party or government policy or decree, he may ask the workers' congress to reconsider the case. If after deliberation the congress upholds its resolution while the factory director continues to disagree, the latter may postpone the implementation of the resolution, at the same time reporting the case to the higher authorities for adjudication. Both the workers' congress and the factory director must obey the ruling of the higher authorities.

In day-to-day operations, the factory director should run the enterprise efficiently by respecting the powers of the workers' congress, carrying out its resolutions, and accepting its supervision. For its part the workers' congress should support the factory director in discharging his duties, uphold the authority of the chain of command in production, educate the workers and staff to enhance their sense of being "masters of the house," and urge them to observe labor discipline and strictly carry out the various responsibility systems in production and technical matters. The establishment of the system of workers' congress and the institution of democratic management of the enterprise should be in full accord with strengthening the factory director's power to administer. Only when the two sides support each other in earnest can they bring about a unity of centralized leadership and democratic management.

Third, what about the relationship between the workers' congress and the trade union? The trade union, a mass organization embracing almost all the workers and staff of an enterprise, should make as a focus of its own general work any matters related to the workers' congress, which is an agency of power. As the representative of the masses, the trade union shares the same tasks as the workers' congress. The trade union council at the grass roots should act as an agent to help implement the decisions made by the workers' congress. Lenin described the trade union as a school in communism, a bond linking the Party with the masses. For the workers, the trade union should also serve as a school in management, teaching them to do well in production and to safeguard the interests of the state and the collective. It also has the duty to supervise the enterprise leaders in carrying out state decrees concerning the workers' interests and welfare, to protect the workers' democratic rights and material interests, and to organize them in running the enterprise as "masters of the house." There are also concrete matters the trade union needs to tackle while the workers' congress is not in session (such as preparing for the convocation of the congress, electing delegates, sorting out proposals, and seeing to the implementation of congress resolutions, dealing with workers' appeals, canvassing reactions, and so on).

Fourth, there is the question of the role of the specialists. Industrial management is a matter of science. Experience at home and abroad shows that industry needs a group of special personnel well versed in technology, production, economics, and enterprise management to serve as consulting assistants to the factory director so that he can make prompt and authoritative decisions. Undoubtedly, the elevation of the workers' congress to an agency of power can improve industry in its democratic management. Elected by the masses and coming from the masses, delegates to the workers' congress are widely representative and are able to reflect the opinions and demands of the masses. But as individuals they are not necessarily capable of running the enterprise, especially when it comes to planning, the procurement of supplies, production, sales, designing, scientific research, and training. There is no conflict here—detailed work by specialists can ensure the implementation of the decisions of the workers' congress. Furthermore, important issues may crop up in the day-to-day operations of an enterprise which require prompt solution. And the workers' congress or general assembly cannot be in session at all times. So these matters must be handled by the factory director or manager, who may well need advice. This is all the more so in the bigger enterprises where operations are closely related to market conditions and decisions must be coordinated among different departments at different levels.

This problem of the role of the specialists must be properly solved in the course of changing the enterprise leadership system. The crux of the matter lies in the form to be adopted—the enterprise management committee, the factory-level meeting, or some other form. This is still open for discussion. The factory-level meeting is relatively simple. The factory director calls together the department heads and the specialists for a meeting, which is limited in its power and responsibility. The use of the management committee raises certain questions: What is the nature of the committee? What are its functions and powers? How are its members to be chosen? How can an appropriate proportion of specialists on the committee be guaranteed? What is the relationship between the management committee and the workers' congress, between the committee and the factory director? And so on. Even if these questions are answered, the problem of enterprise leadership and management will still require more in-depth study.

8

The Rehabilitation of Collective Enterprises in Urban Areas

by Xiao Liang

URBAN COLLECTIVES, including those that have mushroomed in the last few years and those that appeared long before, are vital to China's economic health. This has been widely recognized and supported since the national forum on such enterprises in January 1980.

Previously downplayed as a transitional form for changing individual economy, the collective enterprises, owned and managed by the laboring people with state support, are now seen as an ideal method to respond to some of China's real economic and social problems, both at present and for a long time to come.

It is now agreed that in theory the collective ownership sector and the sector owned by the whole people form the mainstay of China's national economy as the "twins" of socialism, each complementing the other in its role to further the modernization program.

However, in reality, urban collectives in China today face many problems, the legacy of over two decades of repeated unfavorable policy decisions which emphasized state ownership and which culminated in the "Cultural Revolution" attacks against the collective sector as being a "tail of capitalism." These problems must be solved before the collective sector can fulfill its mission.

SUITABILITY TO PRESENT PRODUCTIVITY

The root of the vitality of collectively owned enterprises is that—in line with Marxist-Leninist theory—they are suited to the character and level of the social forces of production in the country. Because the level of the productive forces in China is low and unevenly developed and the degree of socialization of production is also low, the economy in which the means of production are owned by the whole people cannot embrace all trades and departments. Collectively owned enterprises, on the other hand, can take in vast numbers of workers in a variety of departments and trades. Organized on a voluntary basis, they can explore both new job possibilities for the large numbers of people in China waiting for work, and new ways of tackling the many tasks waiting to be done in the cities and towns in industry, handicrafts, building, repairing, transportation, the restaurant trade, tourism, poultry-raising and fish-breeding, utilities, gardening and afforestation, cultural services, health, and other work.

The enthusiasm shown for collective enterprises in China can be demonstrated by the example of Ningbo City, Zhejiang Province, where between 1965 and 1978 the output value of industrial enterprises owned by the whole people rose two and a half times, while that of industrial enterprises under collective ownership increased more than five times. This was true in other places as well during that period, which covered the Cultural Revolution years of 1966–76, and it is interesting to note that while many state-run enterprises stopped operations to "make revolution," it was generally business as usual for collectively owned enterprises.

That the collective sector could thrive under such adverse conditions testifies to some inherent strengths in the basic principles of collective ownership:

• The workers are both producers and owners, and as such are real "masters of the house" under democratic management. In principle, all activities of the enterprise—whether production, exchange, distribution, or management—are decided by the workers collectively or by leaders elected by them in accordance with the collective will.

• Collectives pay state taxes, keep their own business accounts, and assume sole responsibility for their profits or losses. This independence and flexibility in matters concerning manpower, money, material, supply, production, and sales puts them in a position to do things that are beyond the means of some state enterprises, at least for the present.

• Workers in collectives have a real stake in the successful operation of the enterprise, eliminating the defects of the "iron rice bowl" and "sharing the food from the same big pot" prevalent in state-owned enterprises. Wages, welfare, and bonuses for workers and staff—even their very jobs—are directly linked to the growth of production.

• Collectives require small investments and gain quick returns. Scattered all over, they are easy to set up and can be flexible in responding to the needs of the people. Under the unified guidance of state plans, they can organize and control production according to market demand.

• Collectives are free from overlapping administrative levels and tedious work procedures. In other words, they tend to be less bureaucratic. Most administrators are former laborers familiar with production, which makes it easier for the collectives to operate in an industrious and thrifty way under democratic management.

Because of these strong points, collective enterprises suit the requirements of the present development of China's productive forces. They may exist side-by-side with enterprises under ownership by the whole people for a long time. The two may learn from and compete with each other to make joint progress. The growth of collective enterprises is vital to the development of China's socialist economy.

THE NEED FOR REHABILITATION AND READJUSTMENT

Few existing collective enterprises are operating under the ideal conditions outlined above. Immature attempts to change collective ownership to state ownership has stripped most urban collectives of their proprietary rights and left them under the control of local governments. They remain collectives only in the sense that the state levies taxes on them instead of taking over all their profits. In fact, they are far closer to enterprises under state ownership or ownership by the whole people than to enterprises under collective ownership, because the workers no longer control the means of production. Actually they are, in the words of the late Chairman Mao Zedong, "owned by the collective in name but in reality by the whole people."[1] The point is that present-day collective enterprises in China have not yet reached that stage of development where they can be converted into enterprises owned by the whole people, and will not necessarily in the future.

To show the confused relationship between the state and collective sectors, it is necessary to review the history of the urban collectives. From the outset, urban collectives in China inspired the socialist enthusiasm of workers and staff and boosted production. Handicraft cooperatives and groups were first set up before 1955 by organizing individual handicrafts people, small merchants, and peddlers into collectives of a socialist nature with democratic management and independent business accounting in which each collective assumed sole responsibility for profits and losses. In 1952 some 228,000 handicrafts people, or 3.1 percent of the nation's total work force in handicrafts, joined cooperatives with an output value of 255 million yuan, or 3.5 percent of the total handicraft output value. By 1956, when the socialist transformation of the means of production in the handicraft industries had mainly been completed, this number had grown to 6.03 million people, or 91.7 percent of the total handicraft work force, organized into some 100,000 cooperatives with an output value of 10.876 billion yuan, or 92.9 percent of the total output value from the handicrafts. The gross handicraft output value grew by an annual rate of 12.4 percent in the first four years of the First Five-Year Plan period, which meant an increase of 47.9 percent in the output value for every member of the handicraft cooperatives. In those first five years, cooperative organizations paid over 700 million yuan in taxes to the state. Most of the cooperative members—about 90 percent— earned more than they had before they joined the co-ops.

However, the collective movement began to be stifled in late 1957 as ultra-left thinking gained ground and a number of handicraft cooperatives were made into local state-owned enterprises or cooperative factories. A further consolidation drive in 1958 virtually wiped out

1. *Selected Works of Mao Zedong* (Beijing: Foreign Languages Press, 1976), vol. 5, p. 283.

collectives, and the agencies in charge of administering them as the handicraft collectives were converted into "big collectives" affiliated with industrial departments at the city or district level or "small collectives" affiliated with neighborhood offices or residents' committees. These were "collectives" in name only, because profits were turned over to the state and workers earned fixed wages instead of drawing pay according to their collective earnings. By the end of 1958, only 15 percent of the handicraft cooperatives still existed, while the rest had been converted into state-owned factories (41 percent), cooperative factories (19 percent), and commune-run factories (25 percent). As an example of what was going on, in 1957 Tianjin had 853 handicraft cooperatives with 107,195 people, or 29.66 percent of the city's total industrial work force. After 1958 this force was cut by more than half as 416 cooperatives with 62,675 people were "upgraded" into state-owned factories. Further, 43,052 handicrafts people in other cooperatives were switched to work in various branches of industry. In Shenyang, 629 handicraft cooperatives with 65,000 people were merged to form 198 cooperative factories in the second half of 1958, which accounted for 86.5 percent of the city's original cooperative handicraft work force. Only 110 cooperatives and groups with 10,100 people were retained. And by 1960 all the cooperatives had been converted to cooperative factories or state enterprises except 38 cooperatives in the arts and crafts and repairing trades, employing a mere 2,880 people.

It was soon clear that this intense drive to move quickly through the collective economy of a cooperative nature as an interim form of ownership and go directly to ownership by the whole people was both unproductive and demoralizing. There appeared the phenomena of the "iron rice bowl" (the complacent attitude that the state will take care of everything) and "sharing food from the same big pot" (the disregarding of economic accountability). Handicraft laborers—who in the forced "transfers" had in fact been expropriated by the state— were late to report to work, lax during working hours, and quick to leave the work site at the sound of the whistle. The quality and quantity of manufactured goods declined day by day.

In response to this situation, the Central Committee of the Chinese Communist Party set forth in June 1961 "Some Policy Regulations on the Handicrafts in the Urban and Rural Areas (Preliminary Draft)," otherwise known as the thirty-five-article document on handicrafts, which clearly stipulated that handicrafts should be enterprises operated in a democratic way under collective ownership. In 1962–64 this document, along with the policy of "readjustment, consolidation, filling up, and raising standards," was implemented, and part of the state-owned and cooperative factories were turned back into cooperatives. A national organization of handicraft cooperatives was restored.[2] For a time, industrial enterprises under collective ownership revived and expanded, with the production and supply of goods for daily use greatly improved. According to statistics supplied by the enterprises directly under the Second Light Industrial Bureau of Beijing, output value in 1965 rose by 46.9 percent over 1957, labor productivity increased 2.8 times, exports 13.5 times, and profits 4.1 times.

But the remedies were not thorough, nor did they last long, because of the Cultural Revolution begun in 1966 and its push along an ultra-left line toward "a larger size and a higher degree of public ownership." Collectively owned businesses in the urban areas were once again devastated, this time amid the troubles caused by Lin Biao and later the Gang of Four. They repudiated collective economy both as a "tail of capitalism" and as a "soil that engenders the bourgeoisie," criticized the laboring people in cooperatives as "spontaneous forces of capitalism," and condemned the drawing of dividends among cooperative members as "taking the capitalist road." They closed down cooperatives and merged those that survived, continued the "transition" from collective ownership to state ownership, and ordered enterprises to hand over their profits and to switch to the manufacture of other products. Between 1966 and 1970 more than 50,000 handicrafts people in the arts and crafts trade in Beijing were forced to suspend operations or switch to making other products, with a sharp decline in exports.

Over the years, the development of collectively owned enterprises has also been restricted by the erroneous view that they are suited only for manual labor, when in fact these enterprises can accommodate both production by hand tools and mechanized production. At the time of cooperative transformation of handicrafts in 1956, mechanized operations involved only 3.75 percent of the total work force in the handicraft cooperatives in the country. By 1978 mechanized opera-

2. It was actually dissolved during the chaos of the Cultural Revolution and no longer exists.

tions had grown to cover 40 percent of the enterprises under the second light industrial bureaus throughout China and 60 percent in Beijing, Tianjin, Shanghai, Guangzhou, and other big and medium-size cities as back-breaking manual labor was replaced by machinery in a number of trades.

The cooperatives founded at the time of socialist transformation survive in limited numbers, the majority having become cooperative factories or state-owned enterprises. But in the past two decades or so, urban enterprises under collective ownership—despite the repeated devastation suffered under erroneous policies—have managed to grow in number, work force, and output value. A case in point is what happened in 1958. While many handicraft cooperatives were being merged or converted into state-owned factories, dependents of workers and staff, housewives, and retired workers organized themselves into a variety of collective economic organizations. These are called the "58" type. Then in 1968 many enterprises, government offices, schools, army units, and neighborhoods set up "May 7th" factories, workshops, and productive and service groups after the publication of a directive issued by Chairman Mao Zedong on May 7, 1966, in which he emphasized the need for Party and government cadres, students, and army men to run enterprises and take part in productive labor. The enterprises that came into being at this time came to be known as the "May 7th" type. More of these turned up in 1970. By the end of 1978, collectively owned enterprises in the urban areas totaled more than 100,000, employing 12 million people with a total output value of some 60 billion yuan. And since 1979, an even greater number of collectively owned enterprises have been established to provide jobs to urban youths with some education. These are referred to as the "79" type. Today collectively owned businesses in the urban areas are made up largely of these three types, forming the collective sector of China's urban economy which must be rehabilitated and readjusted if it is to realize its superiority.

To restore true collective ownership and untangle the confused relationship between the collective sector and the state sector, the government must first extricate itself from management of collective enterprises and also provide the collective sector with flexible regulations that will foster its growth. Of course, socialism advocates a planned economy, and collectives should operate under the guidance of state planning in matters of general direction, variety and specifications of products, prices of goods, and safety and health codes. Without state regulation the collective sector tends to develop blindly, leading to waste and anarchy in the economy. Such problems exist now. For example, because plastic goods sell fast at a profit, plastics factories have been established in many places and in many industries far beyond the available supply of raw materials and market demand. Likewise, because cigarette-making is profitable, the opening of many cigarette factories under collective ownership has consumed raw materials intended for large, modern factories, which in turn operate under capacity. Since it is more advisable to establish specialized factories than to install the same production technology in every factory, consolidation may be necessary for some collective enterprises. If some collectives must be shut down or merged, this readjustment and consolidation should proceed in a way that respects collective ownership.

To respond to these problems, it is necessary that a set of unified regulations—like the regulations on people's communes—be formulated to be observed by all for the collectively owned enterprises in cities and towns. The thirty-five-article document on handicrafts, now out of date, is being revised by departments in charge of light industry.

Since 1979, various provinces, municipalities, and autonomous regions have repudiated the leftist ideological line and have worked out methods and rules to expand collective enterprises under more flexible policies. In the past, collective enterprises were not allowed to engage in the restaurant trade in some cities; this ban has been lifted. In the past, state commercial enterprises refused to supply raw materials to collective enterprises in the restaurant trade; they now provide supplies. Many local governments have given tax relief and favorable loans to collective enterprises.

But on the whole, most local governmental policies continue to discriminate against collectives both politically and economically. For example, certain localities impose all kinds of restrictions on the growth of collective enterprises. Plans made by labor departments took the uncalled-for step of setting a limit on the number of workers and staff members that can be added to the collective enterprises in the next few years. Also, workers and staff of collective enterprises receive lower wages, fewer welfare benefits and food rations, fewer nonstaple foodstuffs, and less labor protection than their counterparts at state-owned enterprises. This further discourages the rehabilitation and development of the collective businesses in that job-awaiting youths prefer to land a place in a state enterprise for its better benefits. Even if they do go to work in a collective enterprise, they plan to stay only until they can move over to a state enterprise.

Until a set of regulations for collectively owned enterprises is formulated and, further, an administrative agency is established at the national and provincial levels to represent collective enterprises and study their problems, the collective sector will be vulnerable. Collective enterprises need an organization of their own to promote cooperation among the enterprises, strengthen the ideological education of workers and staff, assist in technical training, and actively report their conditions and suggestions to the government.

A common complaint is that nobody speaks for collectives. State administrative agencies manage collectives largely in the same way they do state-owned enterprises. For instance, the eight technical-economic norms[3] of a mandatory nature are issued to all enterprises, large or small, whatever their products. All raw materials—which are in serious short supply—are distributed in a unified way. Since many regions refuse even to transfer materials to other areas, collective enterprises are severely restricted in obtaining them. On the other hand, all products are purchased and sold by government commercial agencies so that the manufacturers have no direct contact with the market. Channels of sales are often blocked, so collectives are never assured of a ready market for their products. This is one of the biggest problems facing the collectives—the lack of flow in the channels of procurement of supplies and sales and the dislocations between procurement, production, and marketing. Contracts to safeguard the rights and interests both of collectives and of the state would help. The state is unable to control everything, and collective enterprises should be allowed to purchase goods and sell their products outside state plans. But these are matters concerning the reform of the economic management system and enterprise management system which must be handled with care. In addition, the state labor departments control far too tightly matters of labor management, including wages and rewards, leaving little room for the collective enterprises to maneuver. And in financial management, officially the state levies only industrial and commercial business taxes and income taxes according to specific

3. See Glossary.

rules and regulations. In fact, collective enterprises are plagued by all kinds of appropriations from local governments, such as those for defense-preparation engineering expenses, afforestation fees, voluntary labor service, dam repairs, aid-to-agriculture fees, city construction fees, education fees, and so on. Some local authorities even impose on collective enterprises to pay for their film tickets, the night-shift allowance for police, and pensions for families of traffic victims. This leaves very little profit to the collective enterprises.

All these problems essentially boil down to this: The proprietary rights of the collective enterprises in the urban areas have been so encroached upon over the years that to a large extent they have been destroyed. Collective enterprises should have the right to decide on matters involved in daily operations, keep their own accounts, and assume responsibility for their profits or losses. The power of the enterprise should rest with a congress of the cooperative members or congress of the workers and staff (general assembly). Often these groups do not even exist. And under the influence of ultra-left thinking, the agencies directing the collective enterprises have all become local representatives of state power. These agencies, for the sake of their own convenience and interest, generally favor transferring financial and material resources away from the collectives. In this way, collective enterprises have generally lost their special features.[4] A recent study reveals that at present all the earnings and expenses, profits, and losses of the "big collective" enterprises are controlled by the departments in charge in all large and medium-size cities. The profits netted by the collective enterprises after paying taxes are handed over totally or largely to the company or municipal bureau in charge. The collective enterprises retain only a very limited portion to cover the depreciation of their equipment. With no funds at hand, the enterprises must apply to the immediate higher organization for even minor expenses. The proceeds of the "small collective" enterprises in industrial and service trades are in most cases handed over to residents' committees or neighborhood offices to cover administrative and other expenses.

---

4. Some executives in government departments do not agree that the government's collection of the profits of collective enterprises means a transfer of financial and material resources from them, but most theoreticians share the view that the very practice of the government being responsible for the profits or losses of the collective enterprises is tantamount to such a transfer.

GUIDELINES FOR REHABILITATION

The aim of rehabilitation and readjustment is to enable the collective enterprises to regain their original nature as a system of socialist ownership. This is a kind of socialist public ownership under which the means of production are collectively owned by a group of laborers. The collective enterprises are set up by these laborers with their own funds or with earnings from their collective labor. The means of production and products are neither private property nor state property, but the property of the collective. The laborers have the right to handle their means of production and products and to manage their enterprise and its production. This form of ownership precludes any possession, control, or management of the collective means of production by any group or individual outside the collective. This form of socialist public ownership must therefore bear the following features:

- The collective, formed by a group of immediate producers, has the exclusive right to own, control, and handle its means of production and products.
- The collective keeps its own accounts and is responsible for its own profits or losses.
- The collective of producers conducts, in a democratic way, all its economic activities, including production, exchange, and distribution, and its leaders are elected by the masses and run the enterprise in accordance with the collective will.
- All matters concerning amalgamation, association, joint operation, or cooperation based on specialization between one collective and another, or transition to a higher form of collective ownership or to state ownership, must be handled according to the needs in production in the enterprise and on the principle of voluntary participation and mutual benefit.

These should also serve as the basic principles for a shakeup of the urban collectives, because the ownership of the means of production is the basis of the relations of production.

In accordance with these principles, government administrative agencies must be separated from collective enterprises so that these enterprises may really become independent units of production and operation. State administrative agencies may, according to law, apply economic levers and use economic means to influence, guide, regulate, manage, and supervise the operational activities of the collective enterprises, but they must not poke their noses into the production, exchange, or distribution of these enterprises or interfere with their internal affairs. Purely economic affairs and the organization of production should be handled by economic organizations of an entrepreneur nature, which have yet to be established in China. This is a fundamental question of orientation. Only when the government is separated from the enterprises, including the cooperatives, will it be possible to restore the nature of collective ownership and run collective economy well. When the government is really separated from the collectively owned enterprises, and when the latter become truly independent enterprises, there will be no need for the concepts of "big collectives" and "small collectives" to remain. It is important to restore the two basic features that characterized the handicraft cooperatives and groups first set up prior to 1957: independent business accounting and democratic management. Experiments have been made to do this in Liaoning, Anhui, Jiangxi, and Tianjin since the second half of 1979 with the gratifying results of more tax returns for the state, bigger accumulation for the enterprises, and increased income for individuals. But this is only a first step.

The blurred line between ownership by the whole people and collective ownership has created situations where many enterprises owned by the whole people employ workers and staff originally belonging to collective enterprises, and vice versa. Some state enterprises even set up workshops or groups under collective ownership. In Beijing, for instance, approximately 75,000 workers and staff members belonging to collective enterprises are scattered in state enterprises. This mixing of the two kinds of ownership causes problems of a transfer of resources and confusion in financial management so that it is of advantage to neither state nor collective enterprises. Even if production entails joint operations between the two kinds of ownership, a clear line still should be drawn between them—they should keep separate accounts and assume separate responsibility for profits and losses—for the good of everyone. Efforts have begun in many places to sort out the one from the other, but it has not been easy. In Beijing, work started in 1980 to try to separate the workers and staff belonging to collective enterprises from state enterprises step-by-step.

However, people who once belonged to collectives are reluctant to leave state enterprises, and leaders in the latter would not let them go. Thus it will take time for the job to be completed.

One problem—after so many years of severe criticism of collective ownership and promotion of a "larger size and higher degree of public ownership"—is to make it clear to people that urban collective economy is not a "tail of capitalism" but an indispensable component of the socialist ownership structure. The national forum on urban collective enterprises in 1980 recognized this need to rehabilitate the reputation of the urban collective economy. Neither collective ownership nor ownership by the whole people should be put one above the other. At a time when the level of productive forces in China is low and commodity production is underdeveloped, a big expansion of collective economy will promote the production and circulation of commodities, revitalize socialist production and circulation, and thus help raise the standard of living. It will never lead to capitalism. Friedrich Engels said: "At the time of transition to totally communist economy, we must adopt cooperative production as the intermediate link on a large scale. This Marx and I have never doubted."[5] With the growth of productive forces, in the future collective ownership will most likely fuse with the ownership by the whole people to form a kind of socialist public ownership that is more perfect, more advanced, and more advantageous to the development of the productive forces. The current expansion of collective enterprises is of great importance for the development of China's socialist economy.

5. Frederich Engels, letter to A. Bebel, January 20–23, 1886, in Marx/Engels, *Werke* (Berlin: Dietz Verlag, 1973), 36:426.

9

The Revival of Individual Economy in Urban Areas

by Fang Sheng

FU CHANGYOU is a young man, twenty-four years old, who knows how to repair shoes. He learned the trade from his father, who had his own shoe repair shop before Liberation. A few years ago, having graduated from school, Fu had nothing to do. He was waiting for the government to assign him a job. But in big cities like Shenyang, where he lived, there were more young people than jobs and the wait could be a long one. So Fu decided to carry on the family tradition and opened up his own business—the Youth Shoe Repair Shop.

In the past it had been quite a hassle for big-city residents to get their shoes repaired. Shops were scarce and lines were long. When Fu opened up his shop, business thrived. He has been making about four or five yuan a day, which means a monthly income of over 100 yuan, higher than the average worker's. Needless to say, Fu is pleased. He has added two rooms to his courtyard home and bought furniture and new clothes. Asked about his future plans, Fu replied, "Shoe mending is not a bad job. It earns me a lot of money. I'd like to do it all my life, but I'm afraid no girl would marry me."

Now why would any girl be reluctant to marry such an enterprising fellow? The answer has a lot to do with the history of individually owned and operated businesses in China—a highly controversial sector of the economy. In this chapter, I will try to explain young Fu's dilemma by analyzing some of the theoretical problems involved and their policy implications.

THE VICISSITUDES OF INDIVIDUAL ECONOMY

In China, "individual economy" is the sector in which the means of production are owned and operated by independent laborers. Businesses in this category are usually operated by urban residents in handicrafts, commerce, repair, and other services on a family or individual basis. Individual handicraft workers and merchants have been through many ups and downs since Liberation. The period from the birth of New China in 1949 through 1976, when the Gang of Four was toppled, can be roughly divided into three stages:

First stage: 1949–55. Individual economy in urban and rural areas made up a fairly large percentage of the national economy: its earnings accounted for 71 percent of the national income in 1952 and an average of over 50 percent in the following two years. In 1955 businesses operated by small merchants and peddlers totaled 2.8 million, or 96 percent of all privately owned commercial enterprises, they employed 3.3 million people, or 91 percent of the total work force in the private sector. Their sales came to 65 percent of the total volume of commodities in circulation.[1]

Second stage: 1956–65. Socialist transformation of the ownership of the means of production was by and large completed in 1956. The number of individual handicraft and commercial enterprises declined sharply. By the end of 1956, there were only 544,000 individual handicraft workers, or 8.3 percent of the total work force in the handicrafts industry—91 percent less than in 1955. The number climbed a bit to 640,000 by the end of 1957, but fell to 300,000 by 1961. In 1962, as a result of overall economic readjustment, the number of individual handicraft workers rose to one million. The story is generally the same for private small traders and peddlers. They totaled 490,000 in 1956, some 85 percent less than in the previous year. The figure rose to 700,000 by the end of 1957, but plummeted to 130,000 in 1961. There were some increases in 1962, and by 1964 small traders and peddlers numbered 568,000.

Third stage: the "Cultural Revolution" of 1966–76. Individual handicraft and commercial enterprises were devastated. By 1976 the number of people operating such businesses had dwindled to a mere

---

1. The figures used in this chapter have been collected by the author and verified with the General Administration of Industry and Commerce of the People's Republic of China.

190,000. Statistics for individual cities dramatize this decline: in Xi'an there were 19,900 individual handicraft workers and merchants in 1965, but by 1975 there were only 300 left; in Chengdu they numbered 3,300 in 1965, but their ranks had shrunk to only 1,200 by 1973.

Despite all these twists and turns, private businesses have survived. This once again bears out the Marxist truth that a social order never perishes before all the productive forces for which it is broadly sufficient have been developed. One reason behind the vicissitudes in the fate of private business in China is the profusion of theoretical misconceptions about the nature of individual economy. Many myths must be expelled from people's minds before individual economy will be able fully to play its positive role in the economy.

MISCONCEPTIONS AND PREJUDICES

Many people in China believe that individual ownership is not compatible with socialism. They tend to think that bigger is always better: the bigger the scale of production, the better; the higher the degree of public ownership, the more advanced. But is the publicly owned sector necessarily more advanced than individual economy? Is it inherently superior to the latter? This question cannot be discussed in the abstract; it can only be analyzed in relation to the productive forces: "In the social production of their existence, men inevitably enter into definite relations, which are independent of their will, namely, relations of production appropriate to a given stage in the development of their material forces of production."[2]

The productive forces determine the relations of production, and the latter must be suited to the nature of the former—this is the fundamental law governing the development of human society. What then is the nature of the productive forces in China today? Certain industries are modernized: they use advanced technologies in large-scale socialized production. But the economy as a whole remains backward, and agricultural production is still basically conducted by manual labor—in some places it is still at the slash-and-burn stage. Even in the industrial, commercial, and service sectors, a considerable portion of the work is done manually on a small scale.

2. Karl Marx, Preface and Introduction to a Contribution to the Critique of Political Economy (Beijing: Foreign Languages Press, 1976), p. 3.

This unevenness in the development of the productive forces should be matched by a simultaneous existence of different systems of ownership. Individual economy remains an indispensable form in the national economy, because businesses in this category generally engage in small-scale, flexible, diversified production and operate in a dispersed and mobile fashion. These features are suited to the use of simple tools.

What kinds of relations of production are advanced? Any relations of production are advanced and superior as long as they correspond to the level of the productive forces, even if they are not characterized by large-scale production or public ownership. Conversely, all relations of production that do not correspond to the level of the productive forces can only fetter the growth of the latter, even if they are characterized by large-scale production and public ownership. In this sense, it is rational and necessary for individual economy to exist within certain limits, because it will facilitate the development of the productive forces.

Another widespread notion is that individual economy means capitalism. Proponents of this view use as their basis an oft-quoted statement of Lenin's: "Small production engenders capitalism and the bourgeoisie continuously, daily, hourly, spontaneously, and on a mass scale."[3] Note that Lenin said "engenders" rather than "is." Besides, the living soul of Marxism is the concrete analysis of concrete conditions. Clearly it is not a Marxist approach to make a universally applicable truth out of a statement Lenin made in 1920 in the context of the specific conditions in Russia. He was referring to a situation in which private economy was still predominant and the question of which would win out—socialism or capitalism—was still at issue.

Individual economy is not necessarily related to capitalism. It came about long before the birth of capitalism. Historically, there has been individual economy related to the slave system, to the feudal system, and to the capitalist system. It was at the latter period of feudalism that capitalism emerged through the polarization of individual businessmen. In China today, where socialist public ownership predominates, the objective conditions for engendering capitalism no longer exist. Of course, certain people will take advantage of running individual businesses to engage in such capitalist activities as specula-

3. V. I. Lenin, *Left-Wing Communism: An Infantile Disorder* (Beijing: Foreign Languages Press, 1965), p. 6.

tion and profiteering, but these are illegal and are to be forbidden. Besides, that is a question essentially different from the nature of the individual economy we are dealing with. Even if a few bourgeois elements are born, we cannot say that individual economy is capitalist in nature.

Another feeling shared by many is that big incomes mean capitalism. Because some individual businessmen have impressive incomes, sometimes more than the average earnings of a worker in a big enterprise, people say, "What else could this be but capitalism?" This is a superficial prejudice. Big incomes and fat wallets mean getting rich and nothing more. We are against getting rich through exploitation; we are for getting rich through labor. A capitalist is a capitalist not because he is rich but because he accumulates capital by exploiting the workers he hires. Individual handicraft workers and merchants make a living by their labor. Some of them earn more because they work more. Different people earn money for different purposes. A capitalist lives to earn money; an individual laborer earns money to live. This reflects the essential difference between individual economy which bears the imprint of a commodity economy and capitalist commodity economy.

Individual businesses rely mainly on manual labor. The income of an individual laborer is in great measure determined by the duration and intensity of his labor, both of which have definite limits. Certain individual laborers might earn more for a time by offering products in short supply or by providing badly needed services, but their earnings will eventually be reduced by the functioning of the law of value. In the long run, income disparities among individual laborers will not be too great, and their incomes will not be much higher than those of workers in large enterprises.

Perhaps this particular objection to individual economy stems from misconceptions regarding "exploitation." The Chinese government's present policy allows individual laborers with special skills to take on one or two apprentices. Some people are opposed to this, saying that it is a form of exploitation. We hold that the practice of taking on apprentices should be judged case by case. An apprentice recognizes someone as his master mainly to learn skills. The master commits no exploitation as long as he earns money mainly through his own labor and not by relying on his apprentice. If a master takes on more than two apprentices and earns money mainly through their labor instead of his own, then it probably involves exploitation. But this may still be permissible if it does not go beyond the limits prescribed by state policy.

THE NATURE OF INDIVIDUAL ECONOMY
UNDER SOCIALISM

What is the relationship of individual economy to the other economic sectors? Individual economy does not exist cut off from the socioeconomic conditions around it. It is not and can never become the dominant mode of production; it is always conditioned by the dominant mode of production. Before the revolution, individual economy in China consisted mainly of the self-sufficient economy of the small peasants operating under the feudal system of landownership. Today the state and collective sectors form the mainstay of the socialist economy, while individual economy is subordinate to them. Individual businessmen cannot possibly get raw and semi-finished materials, market their products, or obtain loans without the assistance of the state and collective sectors. Being small, individual businesses are engaged mainly in operations which are not undertaken by big enterprises, or work directly for the latter. Thus, the scope of operations for individual businesses cannot but be conditioned by the nature of the economy in which the means of production are owned by the public. In a word, individual economy must depend on the mainstay of the socialist economy both in production and in circulation. Otherwise it will be deprived of support and can hardly develop.

Since individual economy under the socialist system should not be described as capitalist in nature, is it right to regard it as socialist? One prevailing view is that, when analyzing the nature of individual economy under the socialist system, it is not enough to look only at the businessmen's private ownership of the means of production; it is also necessary to take into account the role such an economy plays and the position it occupies in the entire structure of ownership. According to this view, individual economy within the socialist system is socialist in nature. I agree that it is not enough to look only at the private ownership; to avoid turning ownership into something abstract, we must also look at the economic realization of this ownership. But I cannot agree with the view that the nature of individual economy should be judged by its position and role in a given structure of ownership. The nature of a thing is determined by the contradiction within the thing itself, not by the relationship between itself and other things. External relationships can only exert an influence and cannot determine the nature of a thing. This tenet of Marxist philosophy must be applied to our analysis of the nature of individual economy within the socialist system.

Individual economy has existed in several different social formations, but as a form of ownership, it possesses a common, qualitative determinant: the individual laborer owns his means of production and through labor makes his own living. This characteristic distinguishes individual economy from both capitalist and socialist economy. Conditioned by the environment in which it exists, individual economy functions differently in different societies, but this does not and cannot alter the inherent nature of individual economy.

Under the socialist system, individual economy has been absorbed into the sphere of socialist economic development and thus will not spontaneously engender capitalism as it does in capitalist society. It enjoys the support and assistance of the socialist publicly owned economy and will not be squeezed out or attacked, as it is in capitalist society, where the means of production are private property. In socialist society, individual laborers working on their own are on an equal footing with others and will not become objects of exploitation by the bourgeoisie, as they do in capitalist society. These are all special features of individual economy under the socialist system, but they do not constitute a fundamental change in the nature of individual economy. In the individual economy under the socialist system, the means of production are owned by individuals who work on their own. The income of an individual laborer is on the one hand related to the quality of his labor, which makes it possible for the principle "more pay for more work" to be applied in varying degrees; on the other hand, his income is also related to his ownership of the means of production, which in principle precludes compensation according to work. Thus it is theoretically untenable to equate individual economy under the socialist system with socialist economy or to regard it as an economy of a socialist nature.

When we say that businesses owned by individual laborers under socialism are an appendage and supplement to the socialist economy, we are referring to the position they occupy and the role they play in the entire socialist economic system. This does not mean that individual economy is socialist in nature. It is wrong to confuse the position and role of individual economy with its nature. However, in disagreeing with the view that individual economy under socialism is socialist in nature, I do not have the slightest intention of overlooking its role.

THE ROLE OF INDIVIDUAL ECONOMY IN SOCIALIST DEVELOPMENT

Individual economy in China is showing its vitality in national economic development. It facilitates the development of production and of commercial and service trades. For some trades, operations by individuals can save more labor and pay off better economically than operations by the state or the collective. For example, individual handicraft workers can make use of industrial scrap to produce marketable commodities. It is more convenient for large factories to ask individually owned shops to process or repair certain parts and accessories than for them to take on the job themselves. Flexible and diversified in operation, individual traders and peddlers can fill in the gaps in the channels of circulation operated by state-owned and collective commercial enterprises.

Individual economy can also fill in the gaps at the retail level. Statistics show that in 1978 the number of shops in the retail, restaurant, and service trades was 51 percent less than in 1957. In some provinces the figure had dropped by as much as 86 percent. In 1957, for every 10,000 residents in cities at the county level or above, there were 100 retail and service shops, and now there are only 10. The shortage is even more serious in rural areas.

Individual economy can suit the convenience of the people in their consumption needs. The consumer needs of the people vary greatly and cannot be met by the state and collective enterprises alone. Big enterprises are often reluctant to produce or sell some of the goods the people want. Residents in many large and medium-size cities find it difficult to get clothing made, have their hair cut or styled, eat out in restaurants, buy nonstaple foodstuffs, buy furniture, or get repairs done. But the state and collective enterprises are unable to solve these problems for the time being. This makes it all the more desirable for individual businesses to fill in the gaps.

Individual dealers can offer many services by setting up booths or stalls in the streets, making the rounds of the lanes and alleys, and delivering goods from door to door. Individual groceries are usually run by husband-and-wife teams. These stores can be seen on almost every corner in residential districts. They keep long hours, from dawn till midnight, even serving customers after hours because the owners usually live right in the shops. They sell a wide variety of merchandise, stressing quick turnover and catering to the daily needs of the people in the neighborhood. No wonder the people call these stores "convenience shops."

Shortly after Liberation in 1949, there were upward of 10,000 restaurants operated by individual businessmen (including a large percentage of sidewalk stalls) in Beijing employing 16,000 people. By 1956, there were only 3,900 left, employing 4,600 people. It fell further to a mere 96 by 1965. At present, because of the inadequate number of state and collectively owned restaurants, eating out in Beijing is often an unpleasant experience. After standing in line for what seems like forever, you finally sit down, only to find the next wave of customers crowding in to grab your seat the minute you put down your chopsticks. During the past year or so, several Beijing families have opened new restaurants, and residents of the capital will be truly relieved when more people do so.

In addition to filling the gaps in the circulation and supply channels, individual economy can contribute to solving the employment problem. An outstanding contradiction in China is that large numbers of people are waiting for the state to assign them jobs, while a considerable amount of productive, commercial, and service work is left undone. At present, an additional 7 million people are joining the waiting lists for jobs every year. It is estimated that every million yuan worth of fixed assets in heavy industry can provide only 94 jobs, but the same sum in light industries or textiles can provide 257 jobs. If heavy industry were to absorb all the young people joining the labor force each year, the state would have to invest 77.78 billion yuan annually. Even if these young people all went into light industries and textiles, the investment would still run to 28 billion yuan a year. Under China's current economic conditions, the state is not in a position to provide jobs for all these new workers. However, individual businesses can be set up, making do with what is available without asking the state for investment or managerial personnel. Combining state assignment of jobs with job-seeking through individual economy is one way to relieve the employment problem. Moreover, once individual businesses are operating, they will add to state revenue and even earn foreign exchange by exporting arts and crafts and other products.

A number of traditional arts and crafts and services best suited for individual operations have virtually disappeared, and some traditional techniques and skills full of national flavor are in danger of being lost. Revival and expansion of individual economy may preserve and promote these traditional products, techniques, and service items. The famous glass grapes blown by the Chang family in Beijing, once on the verge of extinction, have been revived since the return of individual businesses. In Shenyang, Liaoning Province, hometown of our young shoe repairman, flexible policies were introduced a few years ago, and individual economy has quickly expanded. A look at some of these new businesses shows how the individual economy has livened up local economic life.

Hei Yueting is sixty-three years old. In early post-Liberation days he ran a small restaurant until it became a joint state-private business in 1958. After a stint in the service, he opened up a snack shop in 1962, but in 1969 it was forced to close down as a "remnant of capitalism." Hei then worked in a local factory until 1979, when he decided to go back into the restaurant business. In 1980 he cut the ribbon for his Muslim Dumpling Restaurant. His delicious steamed dumplings, known for their traditional flavor, attract over one hundred customers a day. The restaurant serves from 10 A.M. to 8 P.M. His business volume averages 3,000 yuan a month, with net profits running to 750 yuan.

Fifty-five-year-old Han Xiuwen, a retired knitwear maker, has opened up a Stage Shoes Repair Shop. She designs, embroiders, makes, repairs, and mends all sorts of shoes and boots used on the stage. Understaffed at first, her shop could not meet the demand. With a 300-yuan loan from a local bank, she bought a sewing machine and a shoemaking machine. Her earnings amount to 200 yuan a month.

Thirty-year-old Qu Yiying and her husband, Zhao Binghui, have three children. Two years ago they were both jobless, living with their parents, and having a hard time. Last June, Qu Yiying began dealing in small articles for daily use, such as fans, buttons, dusters, watch chains, needles, and thread. Qu's Novelty Shop was born. Her business earns her about 100 yuan a month, and the life of her family is now secure.

Ma Jinghe is a fifty-eight-year-old retired worker. In May 1980 he opened up a grocery selling over fifty kinds of articles, such as cigarettes and tobacco, wine, sugar, tea, food, edible oils, salt, soy sauce, vinegar, and stationery. The shop provided about 10,000 residents with daily necessities and operates until midnight. His business thrived, the retail volume averaging 45 yuan a day. His monthly retail sales came to some 1,300 yuan, bringing him a 10 percent profit or a monthly income of more than 130 yuan. He and his family are living better than ever.

WHERE DO WE GO FROM HERE?

During the economic readjustment and reform of the last few years, the government has adopted a number of policies that more realistically suit the development of the productive forces. In December 1978 the Third Plenary Session of the Eleventh Central Committee of the Chinese Communist Party adopted a series of guidelines for economic reform which have injected the economy with a new vitality, including the policy to encourage the growth of individual businesses. In 1979 about 100,000 individual businesses were licensed, an increase of 70 percent over 1978, bringing the total number of individual handicraft and commercial enterprises to 250,000. The figure rose to nearly 400,000 in 1980 and to 600,000 in the first quarter of 1981. But on the whole, development of the individual economy is not fast enough: it still lags far behind the needs of society. So while energetically developing the state and collective sectors, we must create the conditions for effecting a big expansion of individual economy.

First, we must straighten out people's thinking. The policy of the central government[4] is as clear as it can be: on the condition of the predominance of the state and collective sectors, nonagricultural individual businesses in urban areas should be revived and expanded. Local governments and the departments dealing with finance, commerce, light industry, supplies, banking, and industrial and commer-

4. See "Some Policy Regulations on Nonagricultural Individual Businesses in Urban Areas," *People's Daily,* July 16, 1981.

cial administration are required to support urban individual businesses with regard to funds, the supply of goods, taxation, sites and premises, and market control. But there are many obstacles to implementing this policy, particularly the mental leftovers from bygone days. Even among the ranks of cadres, there are still many who look down upon or despise individual businesses. The authorities should protect the lawful operations of individual businesses, their legitimate income, and their property. As to individual laborers, we must help dispel their misgivings. In view of past suffering, a good number of individual operators have lingering fears and are overcautious. Many people who could easily operate individual businesses do not do so because they fear that some day they will be forced to regret it. Therefore, to develop individual economy in a sound way, it is necessary to eliminate the influence of ultra-left thinking and acquire a correct understanding of individual economy. When it comes to selecting a job, people as a rule first choose to work in a state-owned enterprise, thinking it to be somehow more official. Work in a collective enterprise is considered unofficial, and work in private individual businesses is simply indecent. We must make it clear that individual laborers are just as important as people in other economic sectors and, as people living on their own labor, must be treated with equal respect.

Second, we must work out rational policies. It is necessary to work out a comprehensive set of rules and regulations to suit the concrete conditions in different localities. Existing policies that retard the growth of individual businesses should be changed. In taxation, for instance, the fourteen-grade progressive rates imposed in the past were much too heavy. Recently they have been replaced by the eight-grade progressive rates levied on income in excess of specific amounts. The old practice of additional rates on huge incomes has been abolished. The average tax rate has been lowered by 70 percent. To encourage the establishment of individual repair, processing, restaurant, and service businesses, which are badly needed by the public, those who choose these lines of business may apply for tax reduction or exemption. Individual businesses should also be supported in the supply of goods, bank credits, and so on.

Those who run their own businesses well should be allowed to earn more than the average worker in a state-owned enterprise. Here a distinction must be made. The policy stipulates that individual economy should "continue to exist within a limited scope." This means that individual enterprises can choose their lines of business only within the limits permitted by law; they cannot do whatever they please. They may choose such lines of business as small handicrafts, retail sales, restaurants, service trades, repairs, transportation with nonmechanized vehicles, repair of houses, and trades needed by the public but not sufficiently developed by state-owned and collective enterprises. But within the legally defined limits, they should be encouraged to develop, and no restrictions should be imposed upon them. To restrict the growth of individual economy is to restrict the development of social production, limit consumption, narrow employment opportunities, and reduce state revenue, all to the detriment of the modernization program. In addition, state policy also stipulates that individual laborers enjoy the same political rights and social status as workers in state and collective enterprises. Young people engaged in individual businesses must not be discriminated against when they want to join the army or enroll in schools. And their lengths of service as workers should be counted from the time when these businesses are licensed by the authorities. In a word, there must be a shift from a policy of restriction and exclusion to one of guidance and assistance.

Third, perfect and strengthen management. For the present and some time to come, individual businesses are expected to develop at a fairly rapid rate to suit the needs of the modernization program. Management must keep pace with this growth. In management, attention should be given to the special features of individual economy, such as its capacity for decentralized, dispersed, and mobile operations. To avoid binding individual operators hand and foot, management must be flexible. Needless to say, all illegal operations must be banned with a firm hand. But this does not mean that we will once again try forcibly to transform individual businesses or push blindly and rashly for a transition to higher forms of ownership.

Many past problems stemmed from ignorance about a transition to higher forms of ownership. Such a transition aims at effecting a fundamental change in the relations of production by converting the individual economy in which the means of production are privately owned into an economy in which they are owned by the public. The timing of this transition depends on the level of development of the productive forces. Individual economy, which embodies a kind of relations of production, will remain as long as productive forces characterized by the use of simple tools exist as an objective reality and as long as it is needed by society. The lawful existence and appropriate development of individual businesses is not an expedient, but a fairly long-term policy. We should never repeat the mistake of rushing into a transition to collective or even state ownership in disregard of the low level of productive forces. In the future, when the productive forces are highly developed, when production is highly socialized and the publicly owned sector is able fully to satisfy the needs of the people, then individual economy will finally be converted into public economy. But this transition will take a long time.

10

The System of Ownership: A Tendency Toward Multiplicity

by He Jianzhang and Zhang Wenmin

THE CURRENT ECONOMIC REFORM in China is characterized by the rise of new, and controversial, forms of ownership, including a smattering of state capitalism. Basically China's economy remains as it has been since the late 1950s, dominated by two forms of socialist ownership—ownership by the whole people as in all state enterprises, and collective ownership by the working people as in the rural people's communes. But especially since 1979, new forms of ownership have emerged to include joint ventures between state enterprises and economic collectives; enterprises, both state and collective, operating with private investment from their staff and workers; and individuals being allowed to operate their own businesses. Also, besides joint ventures financed by the Chinese government and foreign companies, some capitalist firms in China are now being run by businessmen from Hong Kong and Macao, overseas Chinese, or foreigners.

The present chapter will discuss the background of this development toward multiplicity, the present condition of these new economic forms, and the controversy that surrounds their development.

THE SOCIALIST TRANSFORMATION IN RETROSPECT

By the late 1970s China's urban economy consisted of state enterprises with a sprinkling of collective undertakings, while its rural economy

186

consisted of people's communes which were not purely economic collectives but also served as basic units of state administration in the countryside. This system of ownership evolved from an economy divided into five sectors immediately after the founding of the People's Republic in 1949:

1. State enterprises, already socialist in nature, converted from firms owned by the Kuomintang government or its officials and known as *bureaucrat-capital.*
2. Cooperatives—mainly supply and marketing co-ops organized by the people's government to supply industrial goods to the peasants and to purchase their farm produce. (Few producers' co-ops among the peasants or handicrafts people had yet evolved.)
3. Enterprises operated jointly by the state and by capitalists.
4. Capitalist enterprises continuing from the old society.
5. Individual economy—the economy of small producers, including peasants, handicrafts people, and small businessmen. Individual peasants and handicrafts people had also been left over from the old society. Land reform carried out in the early post-Liberation years, which abolished exploitation by landlords, also created large numbers of independent peasants from among the former tenants and farmhands who farmed on their own after receiving land during the reform.

After a period of economic rehabilitation from 1949 to 1952, China started a drive to socialize the means of production in 1953— a task known as the socialist transformation of individually owned agriculture and handicrafts and of capitalist industry and commerce, which was scheduled to be completed in fifteen years, or by 1968. In fact, the job was basically accomplished in less than five years, by early 1957. By that time capitalist factories and stores had shifted over to joint state-private operation by whole trades, and both the peasants and the handicrafts people were organized in producers' cooperatives.

In other words, acting in great haste, the country had by 1957 reduced the original five sectors of the economy to three: state ownership, collective ownership, and individual ownership. The last, however, existed in very few instances anywhere.

Further steps were taken in 1958, the year of the "Great Leap

Forward," when large numbers of co-ops in cities and towns were changed to state enterprises, in fact if not in name, and a persistent effort was made to wipe out all traces of an individual economy. This was then followed by the ten years of the "Cultural Revolution" (1966–76), during which anything suspected of being a "tail of capitalism" was done away with, leading to the domination of the economy by state enterprises by the late 1970s.

Although a success in a general sense, the socialist transformation of ownership of means of production in China was flawed by going too far and too fast in imposing a high level of public ownership out of line with the country's low level of productive forces. The haste with which it was carried out caused many problems and difficulties in all areas of the economy.

In September 1956, at the height of socialist transformation, the dangers of the speed at which the process was going were pointed out by Chen Yun, a leader of the Chinese Communist Party known for his expertise on economic affairs. Speaking at the Eighth National Congress of the Party, he pointed out:

> Mistakes of a temporary and local nature have occurred which we must now rectify as soon as possible. These mistakes are as follows: (1) While cooperation was extending into the field of handicraft industry, too much emphasis was laid on amalgamation and unified management with profit and loss shared in common by all the different units drawn into a cooperative. This has not benefited the management of handicraft production. This is why some handicraft products have deteriorated in quality or become less varied since the handicraftsmen ceased working on their own. Furthermore, both customers and handicraftsmen themselves have experienced many inconveniences since some handicraft service establishments were brought together and placed under unified management. (2) Cases in which amalgamations were blindly carried through also occurred when the transformation of capitalist industry and commerce was at its height, and this gave rise to the same problems as ill-considered mergers of handicraft establishments. (3) When bringing cooperation to agriculture, we did not pay sufficient attention to those subsidiary occupations which were suitable only for cooperative members to run as household

industries. Coupled with negative influences from other directions, this has caused a certain drop in the output of some agricultural subsidiary occupations. . . .

It is essential that a considerable proportion of industrial and handicraft establishments, agricultural subsidiary occupations, and commercial enterprises should be separate units of production under separate management. The tendency blindly to amalgamate and unify managements, which results from a one-sided view of things, must be checked.

Chen Yun also stressed that "the different cooperative teams and individual households should themselves shoulder responsibility for their own profit and loss" and that "the method with which small traders and peddlers ply their separate trades within a cooperative team should be preserved for a long time to come."[1]

Unfortunately Chen Yun's arguments and recommendations were hardly listened to. What happened in agriculture, industry, and trades was the following:

1. The socialist transformation of agriculture was characterized by a blind effort to seek a larger scale of collectivization and a higher level of public ownership despite a poor material basis. In some cases, farm co-ops were established through compulsion, in violation of the principle of voluntary participation. In the methods of management, all farms were required to model themselves on a so-called pacesetting collective, disregarding the tremendous variety of situations in a huge country. Things came to a head during the Cultural Revolution, when the Gang of Four tried to push a policy of making the production brigade instead of the production team the basic accounting unit in a commune, even though conditions remained backward in the countryside and income uneven among the teams. They restricted or abolished the commune members' household sidelines and garden plots and the country markets in a campaign to "cut off the tails of capitalism" and banned efforts to diversify the economy as another capitalist tendency opposed to the practice of cultivating nothing but food grain, which they claimed to be the only socialist policy. In the

1. Chen Yun's speech at the Eighth Party Congress, in *Eighth National Congress of the Communist Party of China*, (Beijing: Foreign Languages Press, 1956), vol. 2, pp. 163, 165, 166, 167.

name of "combating material stimulants," they advocated equalitarianism and tried to abolish the system of "to each according to his
work," that is, the distribution of income on the basis of labor quotas
fulfilled and work points earned by the peasants. All this dampened
the initiative of the peasants and their collectives and handicapped
agricultural growth.

Farm production has varied in response to socioeconomic
changes in the countryside, as can be seen from Table 10.1. The big
growth rates of farm output value and grain output in 1952 were
due to two factors. First, only about 8 percent of the farmland was
affected by natural disasters during the year, the smallest figure registered in the history of the People's Republic. Second, through land
reform, peasants had received land and had been relieved of paying
35 million tons of grain in rent to the landlords, and so they showed
enormous enthusiasm in production. But the individual peasants,
with their meager economic strength and limited resources, could
not even cover such family expenses as those incurred in cases of
childbirth, old age, illness, and burials. It was naturally hard for
them to extend the scale of their production and fight natural disasters. Left as they were, they would have inevitably polarized into
rich and poor, and the growth of the productive forces would have
been restrained in the process. Statistics show that in Jingle County,
Shanxi Province, 880 peasant households, or 15.3 percent of the
5,758 households in 19 villages, sold their land. In Xijing Village,
Haocheng County, Hebei Province, only 47 percent of the poor
peasants and 43 percent of the farm laborers expanded production
after land reform, while 15 percent of the former and 29 percent of
the latter reduced their production scale.[2]

Clearly, forming cooperatives was the only way for the peasants
to achieve common prosperity and completely liberate the productive
forces in agriculture. Then why did the growth rate of farm output
value in 1953 and 1954—with 39.5 percent and 60.3 percent of the
peasant households already in mutual-aid teams and agricultural producers cooperatives—drop so significantly from the 1952 figure, from
15.2 percent to 3.1 percent and 3.4 percent? The answer lies mainly
in the fact that in those two years more than 20 percent of the farm-

2. See Su Xing, *The Socialist Transformation of Agriculture in China* (Beijing: People's
Publishing House, 1980), pp. 15, 48.

TABLE 10.1
CORRELATION BETWEEN FARM PRODUCTION
AND SOCIOECONOMIC CHANGES IN RURAL CHINA (IN PERCENTAGES)

Year	Households In Mutual-Aid Teams, Co-ops, or Communes	Those in Co-ops			Those in Mutual-Aid Teams	Those in Communes	Growth in Farm Output Value Over Previous Year	Growth in Grain Output
		In Advanced Co-ops	In Elementary Co-ops	Total				
1952	40.0		0.1	0.1	39.9		15.2	14.1
1953	39.5		0.2	0.2	39.3		3.1	1.8
1954	60.3		2.0	2.0	58.3		3.4	1.6
1955	64.9		14.2	14.2	50.7		7.6	8.5
1956	96.3	87.8	8.5	96.3			5.0	4.8
1957	97.5	96.2	1.3	97.5			3.6	1.2
1958	99.1					99.1	2.4	2.5
1959							−13.6	−15.0
1960							−12.6	−15.6
1961							−2.4	2.8
1962							6.2	8.5
1974							4.2	3.9
1975							4.6	3.4
1976							2.5	0.6
1977							1.7	−1.2

⎫ Years when the production team was made the basic accounting unit
⎬ in the system of three-level ownership in the commune

⎫ Years when farm production was affected by attempts at a transition
⎬ to a higher level of public ownership on a poor material basis

land suffered natural disasters, while the economic strength of the newly organized peasants was still limited. Between 1953 and 1977, the year 1955 saw the highest growth rate of farm output value (7.6 percent). In other words, production grew fastest in the period of mutual-aid teams and elementary cooperatives, with each co-op averaging 27 peasant households and passing out dividends according to labor contribution and land share. In 1956, when the co-ops became the advanced type, with each co-op embracing 159 households on the average and practicing distribution according to labor alone, the speed of growth declined sharply. Production plummeted in 1958, when people's communes, each with an average of 4,637 households, were generally set up in the countryside. Three years later a system of ownership of the means of production at three levels (commune, production brigade, and production team) was instituted, under which the production team, each with some 20 or 30 households or equivalent to an elementary co-op, was made the basic accounting unit. With this development, production began to recover, but it made insignificant headway because the commune and the production brigade could still take without reimbursement part of the earnings or gains of the production team. In the Cultural Revolution, the Gang of Four advocated making the production brigade and not the production team the basic accounting unit and went in for equalitarianism in distribution. This further impeded farm production. Clearly, while socialist transformation has been fully necessary for China's agriculture, it was wrong to have gone after large-scale collective farming to an extent beyond the level of the productive forces.

2. In the socialist transformation of the handicrafts industry, the emphasis put on concentrated production and unified management neglected the scattered and localized nature of the industry. The life of the people was affected as lack of competition in the market caused a drop of quality and variety in products, which of course ran counter to the purpose of socialist production. Also, before the elementary handicraft cooperatives were consolidated, the collective economy was greatly affected by two conversion drives in 1958–60. One drive was to convert the collective economy to the economy owned by the whole people, the other was to convert small collectives into large collectives. Specifically, cooperatives that were large and efficient, with more advanced technology and bigger profits, were turned into locally administered state enterprises, and small cooperatives were

upgraded as cooperative factories in which the profits were turned over to the higher authorities and the workers earned fixed wages instead of drawing dividends according to labor. In reality these factories were—and are—not much different from state-run enterprises because their wages, welfare benefits, and profits are uniformly controlled by the higher authorities. Although some readjustment was made after 1961, the general practice over the years has been to restrict or weaken the collective economy, and this has harmed the growth of the productive forces.

Statistics compiled by Beijing Municipality show the effects of this policy on the collective economy in the urban areas (see Table 10.2). The collectively owned industrial enterprises registered the highest growth rate of productivity during the First Five-Year Plan period (1953–57), when the socialist transformation of handicrafts had just been completed, the level of collectivization was still low, and the enterprises assumed sole responsibility for their own profits and losses and distributed earnings according to the amount of work done. The slower rate of growth in the subsequent years shows the effects of the two conversions on the development of the collective economy.

3. The socialist transformation of small tradesmen, peddlers, and independent handicrafts people proceeded far too hastily, especially in the later stage. In fact, the policy adopted during the Cultural Revolution was one of virtual annihilation. Before 1956, China's big cities were full of tailor shops, food stores, small tradespeople, peddlers, traveling repairmen, and pedicabs—many offering convenient services until midnight. They gradually disappeared in the blind effort to go after concentrated production and unified management. Service hours were shortened with fixed wages instead of earnings according to labor. And while business volume grew, the variety of goods on sale

TABLE 10.2
ANNUAL GROWTH RATE OF
PRODUCTIVITY IN COLLECTIVELY
OWNED INDUSTRIES

1953–57	1958–75	1976–78
16.3%	7.8%	3.2%

decreased. In Beijing the number of commercial and repair shops fell 80 percent from 1956 to 1978. A look at the vicissitudes in Shanghai will give an idea of the changes in individual economy in China's cities as a whole. According to statistics compiled in Shanghai, in the early 1950s individually operated businesses operated in more than 150 trades in roughly three categories: handicraft industry, 24 percent; repair and service trades, 40 percent; commerce, 36 percent. In 1956, the year when the socialist transformation reached a high tide, Shanghai had more than 200,000 individual producers and operators. After the consolidation and transformation in 1958, some of them joined advanced-type cooperative shops, vegetable markets, or teams, some shifted to work in state-run industry and commerce, and some went to work in the countryside. By 1960 there were only 14,000 self-employed laborers. A new batch of 70,000 individual producers and operators emerged in the three-year period of 1960–62, when the economy was in difficulty. But only 31,000 of these were given licenses, bringing the number of self-employed laborers to a little over 40,000. A clean-up movement in 1964 reduced the number to 34,000. The number further dwindled to 8,000 during the Cultural Revolution as some were absorbed by the collective economy and some moved out of the city. By the autumn of 1980 the number had grown to about 10,000.

As for China's cities in general, in 1953 there were 9 million individual producers and operators who paid taxes to the state, accounting for 16.6 percent of the national revenue. By 1978 their number had dwindled to 150,000, their taxes making up only 0.45 percent of the national revenue. Because the state economy was not strong enough to run all types of producing and service trades to cater to the needs of the people or to absorb all the newborn labor force, a strange phenomenon arose: much work was left unattended, while a huge number of people were jobless. The socialist transformation of the individual economy clearly has gone too far and too fast.

The growth of China's national economy since 1949 has been tremendous, but the country's productive forces are still backward and its economic development uneven. Furthermore, a uniform pattern was enforced all over the country in disregard of the differences in productive forces. In the remote, outlying regions in the Northwest and Southwest the level of productive forces is very low, falling several centuries behind that of the large cities in the Northeast and along the coast. Some regions were not long ago in the slash-and-burn stage of primitive communes, some were in slavery or serfdom. Marx says: "Social relations are closely bound up with productive forces. In acquiring new production forces men change their mode of production; in changing the way of earning their living, they change all their social relations. The hand-mill gives you society with the feudal lord; the steam-mill, society with the industrial capitalist."[3] The remote, outlying regions may get assistance from other places in their economic development, but they cannot overnight acquire productive forces with a high degree of socialization. Of course the transformation of the relations of production in these regions cannot possibly proceed at a rate equal to that in the coastal areas. Meanwhile, in the coastal areas with their high degree of socialized production, things vary from trade to trade, and the practice of concentrated production and unified management was not necessarily desirable for all trades. Failing to take notice of this, people blindly aimed at high speed in the socialist transformation of the means of production and imposed a high degree of public ownership and an ever larger scale of operation. Hence a train of defects.

NEW CHANGES IN ECONOMIC FORMS

After the downfall of the Gang of Four and particularly after the Third Plenary Session of the Eleventh Central Committee of the Party held at the end of 1978, Chinese theoreticians and personnel engaged in practical work came to agree on the achievements and short-comings of past economic work, seeing that the question of ownership was still open. Against this background, the Party has in the last few years adopted flexible policies in economic matters and started readjusting and reforming the structure of ownership. Today there is a state sector under ownership by the whole people, a collective sector, and an individual sector, plus a tiny sector of state capitalism. In particular, new links are being formed among these sectors.

To the best of our knowledge these new links are actually new forms of ownership. They are: (1) *jointly operated enterprises,* including enterprises jointly operated by units owned by the whole people

3. Karl Marx, *The Poverty of Philosophy* (Beijing: Foreign Languages Press, 1978), p. 103.

and collective units, enterprises operated by units owned by the whole people with private investment, enterprises operated by collective units with private investment, and joint ventures formed by collectively owned economic units; (2) *investment companies,* including stock companies run by the state, and companies with private investment; (3) *joint ventures with Chinese and foreign investment;* (4) *private capitalist enterprises,* including those run by overseas Chinese, Hong Kong, or Macao industrialists and businessmen as well as those run by foreign investors; and (5) *individual businesses.* These new forms of ownership range from a major shareholding construction company established by former industrialists and businessmen in Shanghai, to a self-employed woman in Beijing who hires several people to help her make brushes for industrial use. Further examples in each category:

• *Enterprises jointly operated by units owned by the whole people and collective units.* Generally established between state enterprises and rural communes or brigades, this form has shown unusually good economic results. Shanghai, for instance, set up sixty-five such enterprises between February 1979 and May 1980, covering handicrafts, light industry, textiles, metallurgical, meters and instruments, machinery, and power trades. In these firms both partners invest, exercise unified leadership and joint management, and share profits or losses —to the advantage of both parties. Enterprises owned by the whole people are willing to undertake this kind of joint operation because they wish to transfer old products and equipment to the joint enterprises so that they may upgrade their own products; to expand by building new factory buildings outside the limited space in the city proper; and to get away from the noise and pollution in the city. For their part, rural communes and brigades are eager to go into joint operation to utilize their surplus labor power and diversify their economy to increase income. An example of the success these joint enterprises can achieve is the shirt factories run by the Shanghai No. 5 and No. 2 shirt plants together with the Tangxing Commune in Jiading County and the Maqiao Commune in Shanghai County. The contracts were signed in April 1979, construction of both factories started in May, and they began producing shirts in September. By the end of that year, the two factories had turned out 670,000 shirts for export at a profit of 650,000 yuan, earning 1.6 million U.S. dollars. The profits for each factory accounted for 50 percent and 30 percent respectively of the investment for equipment; the share of profits for each commune amounted to 50 percent and 67 percent respectively of its initial investment.

• *Enterprises operated by units owned by the whole people with private investment.* These enterprises seek funds from their own staff. For instance, after failing to win enough orders in 1979, the Mutanjiang Mining Machinery Plant in Heilongjiang Province established a furniture-making company with shares bought by its own workers and staff members. Each share was worth 100 yuan, with an annual interest rate of 8 percent. Some 70 percent of the profits earned was used for the company's capital accumulation and extended reproduction, 25 percent was divided among the shareholders, and the remaining 5 percent was placed at the disposal of the company for emergency use. The company is led by a board of directors, who appoint the general manager. Annual rewards, each not exceeding 500 yuan, are given to the directors and the general manager according to the profits earned and their respective contributions. Fines, each not exceeding 300 yuan, are imposed on those who cause losses through dereliction. The manager and other principal officers, recruited by advertisement, draw wages corresponding to their positions. The manager is paid 125 yuan a month.

• *Enterprises run by collectively owned economic units with private investment* have developed into two kinds of organizations:

A. Urban collective enterprises draw funds from among their own workers and staff in order to expand production capacity. A steel-wood furniture factory in Harbin, Heilongjiang Province, which is a collective enterprise, faced a shortage of working capital as a result of fast-growing production. It needed 500,000 yuan in 1980, but had only one-third of it. According to banking regulations, the factory had to obtain another 80,000 yuan in order to be eligible for a loan of 250,000 yuan. So the factory issued shares, each worth 100 yuan, to be bought by its workers and staff. Shareholders were given a dividend according to the profits made at year's end.

B. Rural communes, brigades, or teams absorb funds from their own members to establish joint enterprises to diversify their economy and provide jobs for their surplus labor forces. Jinti Commune of Heze County, Shandong Province, began in 1979 to recruit funds from its production brigades and teams, functionaries, workers, and commune members to form a stock company. The shares, each worth 100 yuan, can be bought in cash or in the form of tools, houses, and so on. By the first half of 1980 the commune had collected 478,000 yuan and set up twelve enterprises, including a brick and tile kiln, a wood furniture factory, a carpet shop, a farm machinery repair shop, a construction team, and a transport team, which earned an aggregate of 340,000 yuan. As stipulated, 60 percent of the profits were distributed as dividends, 20 percent were used for extended reproduction, and 20 percent were set aside as public accumulation. The leading body of the stock company is the congress of shareholders under which a management committee takes charge of the day-to-day operations. Factory directors, technicians, and administrators earn fixed wages plus bonuses and are fined if they fail to fulfill production quotas.

• *Investment companies run by units owned by the whole people, by collectively owned units, or by individuals.* These usually take the form of integrated enterprises embracing agriculture, industry, and commerce or trading warehouses. Wuhan City is planning to erect a tall building for a trade center by issuing 1,000 to 1,500 shares, each worth 20,000 yuan, to be bought by any industrial or transport establishment, state-run commercial unit, supply and sales unit, or foreign trade unit, by any integrated enterprise, cooperative, collective unit, or individual. The investors are protected by law, and the shares, once bought, can be transferred or inherited.

• *Private investment companies,* which fall into three categories:

A. Those in which the investors do not take part in labor and no dividends are distributed among the shareholders. Former industrialists and businessmen in Shanghai pooled 57 million yuan in September 1979 to establish a Patriotic Construction Company. The investors, with at least 10,000 yuan from each, will be paid an interest every five years equivalent to the interest rate of the People's Bank. The company's main line of business is to build housing, provide funds for compensatory trade, and undertake other projects, construction or otherwise, conducive to China's modernization drive. Underway are a project to build 135,000 square meters of housing for sale and seventeen enterprises with a total investment of 800,000 yuan. The company employs some 800 people, including 700 urban young people who had been waiting for jobs for some time and 100 former industrialists and businessmen. All the profits will be used as the company's public accumulation fund after payment of state taxes and deduction of interest for the founding investors.

B. Those in which individuals pool funds to run factories, with shares bought by neighborhood committees, to provide job opportunities. Li Kesheng, a resident in Dahao Town, Shantou City, Guangdong Province, and fifty-eight others jointly opened a plastic goods factory in March 1980, offering shareholders an interest equivalent to bank rates. Using remittances from friends and relatives in Hong Kong and Macao, Li invested 40,000 yuan in the venture, and the others put in 20,000 yuan. Later the neighborhood committee added another 11,000 yuan. Providing work for a number of jobless young people, the factory accepts orders placed by domestic buyers and at the same time undertakes processing work for Hong Kong and Macao firms. In just five months it turned out 190,000 yuan's worth of products at a net profit of 40,000 yuan. The average wage of the workers is 60 yuan a month; the highest wage is 80 yuan.

C. Those in which jobless young people pool funds and get dividends on their shares. Sixty jobless young men and women in Jiamusi City, Heilongjiang Province, founded a stock company with each share valued at 50 yuan. With a capital of almost 20,000 yuan, the company makes clothes and kilowatt-hour meter components. It plans to go into the processing of wooden articles and commercial and service trades.

• *Joint ventures with Chinese and foreign investment and other forms of economic-technical cooperation with foreign countries.* In the interest of modernization, China follows the principle of light taxation and preferential treatment to attract foreign investment. The economic readjustment since 1979 has created new opportunities for business with other countries, not discouraged them.[4]

• *Individual businesses,* mainly in the fields of the retail trade, repairing, handicrafts, and the restaurant trade. By the end of May 1981 more than 700,000 such businesses had been established, regulated through a July 1981 State Council promulgation concerning nonagricultural individual businesses in urban areas. Each individual business, if necessary and approved by the administrative department for industry and commerce, may hire one or two helpers, craftsmen with special skills may take on two or three and at most no more than five apprentices. Contracts must be signed when helpers or apprentices are recruited, covering the rights and obligations of both sides as well

4. Developments in this area and the relationship between China's economic readjustment and her open-door policy are discussed in detail in Chapter 11.

as the duration and payment. The contracts must be checked by the local administrative department for industry and commerce.[5] Four types of individual businesses have emerged so far:

A. Businesses operated by the trades or handicrafts people themselves, some with the help of family members.

B. Businesses each with one or two apprentices. Three individually operated tailor shops in the East District of Beijing have taken on a total of four apprentices. The master-apprentice contracts are valid for six months, during which time the apprentice receives a monthly allowance of 24 yuan, works eight hours a day, and is off four or five days every month.

C. Some individual handicrafts people, besides working themselves, parcel out some processing work to other people. Wang Shuying, who lives in Beijing's Chongwen District, started a shop in November 1979 to manufacture various kinds of brushes for industrial use. Working in the shop, she is joined by her four children in their spare time. In addition, she pays three job-awaiting youths and a retired worker for their help in some of the work process.

D. Businesses with large means of production. Private fishing-boat building has made headway in the Houshan Production Brigade of Dabao Commune in Dianbai County, Guangdong Province, since individual members were allowed to build fishing boats in 1979. Before that time, from 1949 on, the collective economic units had built only seventeen motorboats and seventy wooden junks, a far cry from the need. Lack of boats forced local fishermen to take turns going out to sea. But in just one year after individuals were allowed to build fishing boats, seventeen motorboats and seventy wooden junks were constructed. With this rise in production, the fishermen's income has gone up too.

SOME THEORETICAL ISSUES IN DISPUTE

The introduction of new economic forms in China has created theoretical problems that are being carefully studied both by economists and by those involved in industry at all levels. Are these new forms an objective necessity or an expedient measure? How should they be

5. *People's Daily*, July 16, 1981.

controlled? What are the political implications? Any number of questions have arisen, and with them a wide range of views. Among these are:

1. Are the existing multiple forms of economy an objective necessity?

One view holds that, in the first place, China is still in the lower stage of transition from capitalism to communism and it will take a long time before economic relations can develop into a single economy in which the means of production is owned by the whole people. China's current stage of a relatively low level of productive forces automatically entails the coexistence of various economic sectors and different forms of management and operation. Also, the relations of production in any society are determined by the level of productive forces. The uneven economic development in China requires a corresponding multilevel economic structure ranging from the state sector to the private sector, a structure in which socialist public ownership is predominant. Finally, practical experience over the past three decades in China shows that depending on only two forms—the state sector and the collective sector—has satisfied neither the needs of the people nor the needs of social production. Therefore, varied forms of economy must be adopted to enliven the economy and boost economic development by supplementing the state sector and the collective sector.

An opposite view is that these new economic forms can be allowed to appear only as an expedient measure. With a backward economy, lack of construction funds, and a large number of jobless people, the state must use various channels to absorb private funds and technologies now in the hands of overseas Chinese, foreigners, and private citizens at home. But this is only a temporary measure. China is in the midst of an economic readjustment in which the state has adopted the policy of restructuring the economic management system to reshape the national economy, allowing for multisectors of economy and diverse forms of management and operation. This situation will rapidly change when the readjustment and reforms are completed and production has gone up. Besides, private investment in which individuals are allowed to invest their money and run enterprises questions the superiority of the socialist system.

2. What economic sectors should be developed?

One view holds that it is appropriate to develop individual economy—as one of the three sectors of the economy laid down in China's constitution—to supplement the economy of public ownership in the other two sectors, the economy owned by the whole people and the collective economy. However, if the country is to adhere to the socialist road, this development must be limited and controlled, because individual economy—a backward economic sector belonging to the category of small production—leads to capitalism and not to socialism. On the other hand, in the public-owned sector—both to enliven the economy and to prevent capitalism from running rampant—diverse forms of management and operation should be encouraged, such as cooperative teams and shops where the participants can draw extra dividends according to labor and shares.

Another view disagrees, maintaining that, as long as the economy under public ownership is dominant, state-capitalist economy, private capitalist economy, and individual economy should be allowed in principle to exist. Furthermore, as a matter of objective fact, these economic sectors already exist.

3. Should individuals be allowed to run private enterprises and hire laborers?

There are three basic views on this. The first holds that capitalism is incompatible with socialism. As a socialist country, China must never allow exploitation of labor or conversion of money into capital or labor power into commodity. The state's adopting a flexible economic policy does not mean giving a green light to the revival of capitalism in the area of ownership. True, China's constitution allows the existence of an individual economy, but one which does not exploit others. Permitting the hiring of hands and exploitation runs counter to the basic principles of scientific socialism. When China proposes to let some people get rich first, this means they will do so not by exploiting other people's labor but by adhering to socialist principles. Having followed the socialist road for three decades, China must never go backward merely because of this or that error made in past economic work. Further, policies must remain stable. Having long suffered from erroneous lines, China cannot afford another about-face just as its economy has begun to revive. Finally, domestic funds must be used in a way different from foreign funds. Under certain conditions—to help in construction and to introduce new technologies—it may be necessary to import and use foreign capital and funds from overseas Chinese and Hong Kong and Macao compatriots. But domestically it is not necessary to adopt the method of private investment in enterprises. Instead, investment shares or public bonds may be issued to be bought by individuals at interest rates higher than the savings bank rate.

The second view differs in that, while disallowing capitalism, it does allow for slight exploitation under the following argument. First, socialism is characterized by two things: public ownership of the means of production, and the institution of the principle "to each according to his work," which abolishes exploitation. But is it imperative to carry out these principles 100 percent? Not necessarily. Taking the country as a whole, as long as public ownership is predominant, a small number of individual economic units may be allowed to exist and grow. As long as the principle of "to each according to his work" is predominantly applied, limited exploitation may also be allowed. For example, the state laws may permit the hiring of a few hands under certain conditions. Also, although in principle the socialist system cannot allow the existence of capitalism or allow money or other resources to be converted into capital, from a long-term point of view the following types of capitalism should be allowed at the present stage to speed up economic development: (a) the import and utilization of foreign capital and overseas Chinese capital in given conditions; (b) national capitalism in special economic zones (like Taiwan); and (c) the taking on of a few hands or apprentices as permitted by state policy. Although capital exists to some extent in enterprises in the third category, it need not be defined as such under a flexible policy.

A third view holds that there is no harm in having a smattering of capitalism, allowing some exploitation and the hiring of a few workers. After all, China is a socialist country where the Communist Party exercises leadership, the state economy is predominant, and the economic units are guided by state policies and controlled by administrative departments for industry and commerce at various levels. So there is nothing formidable in having some capitalism; it will not alter the nature of China's socialist system. There are much idle labor power, many means of production, and many scattered funds at large in society. Pooled, they can form a mighty material force. Besides, the conditions are not ripe for the abolition of all private economy, which is still needed to supplement the socialist economy. Under these circumstances there is nothing wrong with having some capitalism within certain limits. And from the historical point of view of social development as a whole, capitalist economy is more advanced than individual economy. Since China allows individual economy to exist, why not capitalist economy? If foreigners and overseas Chinese are allowed to open factories, should not the capital of Chinese citizens be allowed to exist legally on their own soil? The funds, technical know-how, and managerial expertise of these people can be utilized, within the scope prescribed by the state, to serve socialist construction. Besides, the presence of some capitalism may even—as an antithesis to the state economy—impel the latter to improve its management and operation through competition. Finally, economics is closely related to politics. The presence of some capitalism is conducive to the realization of Taiwan's return to the motherland and to attracting investment by foreigners, overseas Chinese, and Hong Kong and Macao compatriots.

All in all, China is in a period of transition. The many new situations and problems in the economic field require both study and open discussion, so that policies may be worked out in conformity with reality and to ensure smooth progress in China's socialist construction under the guidance of the four basic principles: adherence to socialism, adherence to the people's democratic dictatorship, adherence to Marxism-Leninism and Mao Zedong Thought, and adherence to the leadership of the Communist Party.

11

Economic Readjustment and the Open-Door Policy

by Arnold Chao

DOES CHINA'S ECONOMIC READJUSTMENT MEAN a rise or fall in business with other countries? The answer has been given by China's latest foreign-trade figures. In 1979, the year when readjustment began, the import-export volume was valued at 45.56 billion yuan (29.39 billion U.S. dollars). In 1980 it rose to 56.3 billion yuan (37.79 billion U.S. dollars).[1] The 1981 figure, unavailable at this writing, is expected to be larger still. By now few people are saying that readjustment would mean less business with the outside world.

But where is the business, or where will it be? What kind of business does China desire in the period of readjustment, which will last at least four or five more years? What are some of the areas in which foreign investment is likely to be successful?

To answer these questions, we must discuss the nature of the country's open-door economic policy, the latest changes in her foreign-trade system, the economic-technical requirements in the period of readjustment, and the guidelines on trade and other forms of economic exchange with foreign countries.

---

1. The equivalents in U.S. dollars are worked out according to the average rate for exchange at the Bank of China in the year referred to, which was $1.00 to 1.55 yuan in 1979 and $1.00 to 1.49 yuan in 1980.

THE OPEN-DOOR POLICY IN ACTION

The open-door economic policy is a new development in China, both ideologically and practically.

The watchword of China's socialist construction has always been self-reliance. It goes without saying that a country as large as China must rely mainly on her own efforts to build a modern and prosperous economy, but for a long time self-reliance was misinterpreted as a policy of closing the door to the outside world. This was not a Marxist approach, but a reflection of the mentality of the peasants and other small producers, the dominant section of China's population for centuries, who were accustomed to a natural economy of self-sufficiency and were by nature resistant to a developed commodity economy, domestic or international. Of course, not even an advocate of a closed-door policy would object to any economic exchange with other countries. But that was seen as a matter of "exchanging what one has for what one has not," or filling the gaps in one's own production—something humanity has been doing since primitive times.

During 1952–78, China's exports came to only a little over 4 percent of its gross industrial and agricultural output value, as against 10 to 20 percent in the case of some developed countries. China accounted for about 0.6 percent of the total volume of world trade, a proportion even lower than exports taken up by some of the smaller developing countries.[2]

In 1980, China's exports made up only 0.9 percent of the total value of those of all countries of the world. In the same year, the Chinese government's domestic purchases for export came to 4 or 5 percent of the national industrial-agricultural production, while the world's export turnover was approximately 16 percent of the gross national product of all countries put together.[3]

The underdeveloped state of China's foreign trade was due primarily to the underdeveloped state of her economy, which limited the amount of merchandise available for export and consequently the amount China could afford to buy from other countries. It also had

2. Li Qiang (Minister of Foreign Trade until 1981), "Study and Expand Foreign Trade to Render Better Service to the Four Modernizations," *Guoji Mouyi Wenti* (Problems of International Trade), no. 1, 1980.

3. Speech by Chen Longzhu, member of the International Trade Research Institute of the Ministry of Foreign Trade, at the Symposium on China's Economy in Zurich, June 1981.

to do with the economic blockade and trade embargo which foreign powers imposed on the People's Republic. For many years, China could not have expanded her foreign trade freely even if she had wanted to. Apart from these factors, the idea of building up the country behind closed doors, the reluctance to borrow from foreign experience and know-how, and particularly the "Cultural Revolution" criticism of the utilization of foreign equipment and technology (not to say capital) as an expression of the "slavish comprador philosophy"—all part of the ultra-left guidelines on economic construction —had a serious restrictive influence on the growth of economic exchange with other countries.

The departure from these outmoded ideas, which started after the end of the Cultural Revolution in 1976, resulted in people taking a fresh look at the importance of international economic exchange for China's modernization. Economists pointed out that social production had long since been internationalized under capitalism, a process which would only go on under socialism. Instead of doing everything by itself, each nation must use what was being produced in other countries to its best advantage, and this was especially important for a modernizing socialist country like China, which would find many shortcuts to its objectives by a proper utilization of foreign equipment, technology, and capital. This new line of economic thinking formed the basis of China's open-door policy, and its official recognition was found in a statement made in June 1979 by Hua Guofeng, then premier of the State Council, at the National People's Congress: "Economic exchange between countries and the import of technology are [an] indispensable, major means by which countries develop their economy and technology. It is all the more necessary for developing countries to import advanced technology in a planned way in order to catch up with those economically developed."[4] In other words, economic exchange with foreign countries was far more than a means of filling the gaps in national production; it was seen as a powerful lever for China's modernization.

What happens to the principle of self-reliance? The latest interpretation of self-reliance is that, to achieve the purpose of moderniza-

---

4. Hua Guofeng, "Report on the Work of the Government," in *Main Documents of the Second Session of the Fifth National People's Congress of the People's Republic of China* (Beijing: Foreign Languages Press, 1979), p. 49.

tion, China must rely chiefly on her own resources and industrial foundation, her home market, and her domestic technical force, including scientists, engineers, and skilled workers. This is determined by the country's socialist system, the vastness of her territory, and the multitude of her people. But self-reliance does not mean closing the door to the outside world. Instead, it must be supplemented by a full utilization of foreign capital, equipment, technology, and managerial skill.

The National People's Congress session which heard the above statement adopted the Law of the People's Republic of China on Joint Ventures with Chinese and Foreign Investment, which was followed by the promulgation of a series of laws and regulations that have to do with foreign investment in China.[5]

To handle foreign investment, the China International Credit and Investment Corporation was established in the same year. It is headed by Rong Yiren, once a magnate of Shanghai's textile industry and the country's number one capitalist before the changeover to socialist ownership in 1956. On the staff are many of Rong's business associates from the old days. The foreign trade setup was decentralized for many government departments and localities to deal with foreign businessmen directly. This structural reform and its implications will be discussed in the next section.

Meanwhile, "special economic zones" for foreign investment were marked out in four cities in South China—Shenzhen, Zhuhai, and Shantou (Swatow) in Guangdong Province and Xiamen (Amoy) in Fujian Province. Much money was allocated for the building of the infrastructures there, including roads, wharves, and water and power supplies. Preferential rates were worked out for customs duties, land rent, and income tax to attract investors from overseas.

With all these preparations, China ventured into the business world outside, from which the country had been cut off for three decades. The business deals China has concluded with foreign countries since 1979 may be summarized as follows:

5. These include the Income Tax Law Concerning Joint Ventures with Chinese and Foreign Investment, the Personal Income Tax Law, a set of regulations for the implementation of these two laws, the Provisional Regulations on Foreign Exchange Control, the Regulations on the Registration of Joint Ventures with Chinese and Foreign Investment, the Regulations on Labor Management in these joint ventures, the Regulations on the Special Economic Zones in Guangdong Province, and the Regulations Concerning the Control of Resident Offices of Foreign Enterprises.

Joint ventures.[6] By the end of June 1981, the Chinese government had approved the establishment of twenty-eight joint ventures. Among these are eleven factories in the light and textile industries, two food factories, one winery, two factories making electrical appliances for everyday use, one electric elevator plant, one pig farm, one pharmaceutical plant, one equipment-leasing company, and eight tourist and service ventures. The regional breakdowns of the investors from the other side are: seventeen from Hong Kong, two from the United States, four from Japan, three from the Philippines, one from Switzerland, and one from France. Total investment amounts to 240 million U.S. dollars, of which 197 million are foreign investment, including direct investment by foreign firms and Chinese investment made from foreign loans.

Among those already in operation, the Beijing Airline Catering, Ltd., run jointly by the Beijing branch of the Civil Aviation Administration of China and businessmen from Hong Kong, prepares food on imported equipment and reports a rising amount of business and profit. The Sino-French Wine Corporation, operated by the industrial authorities of the city of Tianjin and the French Remy-Martin Corporation, is selling its wine abroad.

A joint venture is owned and operated by both parties, which share the profits as well as the risks. The Chinese side provides the site, the premises, and other resources, while the foreign side usually brings in the equipment, the know-how, and the cash. People from both sides sit on the board of directors, and the president is appointed by mutual agreement.

Cooperative enterprises. By the end of 1980, the Chinese government had approved the establishment of 330 cooperative enterprises, also known as contractual ventures. A cooperative enterprise differs from a joint venture in that it is owned and operated by one side, that is, the Chinese, and is usually an existing enterprise. An investor from another country or region may come to contribute whatever resources he wants to and draw his profit according to the terms of the contract. The two sides do not earn their profits on a single basis, nor do they take the same risks. The 330 cooperative enterprises are situated mostly in the "special economic zones" in Guangdong and Fujian, and the total investment from the other

---

6. The facts and figures on the various forms of economic cooperation with foreign countries have been verified with the Import-Export Commission of the State Council.

side, mainly from businessmen of Hong Kong and Macao, is valued at 500 million U.S. dollars.

Compensation trade. This is an arrangement under which the Chinese side produces goods with the equipment and technology supplied by foreign businessmen and pays off the value of such equipment and technology in installments by selling the goods to the suppliers. Over five hundred deals of this kind have been concluded, involving 200 million U.S. dollars of foreign investment. The undertakings are usually medium-size or small, from the making of textile machinery and fishing gear to the preparation of fried beans for export.

Foreign loans. [7] The Japanese Overseas Economic Cooperation Fund has offered to finance the construction of two ports, three railroads, and one electric power station. The amount of credit will be determined each year by the two parties in light of the progress of the projects. The loan for the year 1979–80 was 106 billion yen (about 400 million U.S. dollars); the interest rate is 3 percent. Repayment will begin in the eleventh year and will be completed in thirty years. The Japanese Export and Import Bank has offered a loan of 1.5 billion U.S. dollars for the development of energy resources, mainly the construction of coal mines and oil fields. The interest rate is 6.25 percent, and repayment will be made in installments over a period of fifteen years after each project goes into operation. A loan of 31.5 million U.S. dollars has been offered by the Belgian government for the purchase of electric power generating equipment. This interest-free loan will be repaid in fifty years. The International Monetary Fund[8] has agreed to a loan equivalent to 450 million U.S. dollars, to be used in professional training, agriculture, power generation, and the construction of ports and railroads. The Bank of China has signed buyer's credit agreements totaling 12 billion U.S. dollars with Britain, France, Italy, Canada, Sweden, Australia, the Federal Republic of Germany, Belgium, Norway, and Argentina, but because of restrictions on the loans and the small amount of equipment imported in the last few years, not much of the credit has been used.

7. The information in this category is based on a speech by Wei Yuming, vice-minister of the Import-Export Commission and the Foreign Investment Commission, at the European Economic Community–China Business Week in Brussels, March 31, 1981.

8. China is one of the founding members of the International Monetary Fund and the World Bank. The representation of the People's Republic of China in these two organizations was restored in 1980.

5. *Joint oil prospecting and exploitation.* The China Petroleum Company has signed contracts with Japanese and French oil companies for the joint prospecting and exploitation of oil in the Bohai (Pohai) Gulf and the Northern Gulf of the South China Sea. It has also started negotiations with American oil companies on joint undertakings in the Yinggehai Basin of the South China Sea. The Chinese authorities are also calling for bidders for projects in other offshore areas. When commercial production begins, a portion of the output and some operation fees will be set aside for China, and the remainder will be used to repay the investments from both sides with interest and go to the foreign companies as profit.

The above are only the beginning. In the field of joint ventures, for instance, negotiations have started on some three hundred projects with businessmen from thirty countries and regions.

CHANGES IN THE FOREIGN TRADE SYSTEM

Since the latter part of 1979, experiments have been carried out to decentralize the managerial system of China's foreign trade. There has not been, and will not be, any change in the state monopoly of foreign trade. In other words, no individual will be allowed to run an import-export firm, as in the case of a restaurant or a tailor shop. But state monopoly does not necessarily mean monopoly by authorities at the central level. A few years ago, foreign businessmen had to go through the corporations directly under the Ministry of Foreign Trade for all negotiations and transactions. Today they may deal with corporations under various ministries, local import-export companies, or even industrial and commercial enterprises that have been granted foreign-trade rights.

The previous highly centralized foreign-trade setup was historically justifiable, however. Immediately after the founding of the People's Republic, the severe blockade and embargo by foreign powers and the plight of the war-torn economy made it necessary for the government to take all foreign trade matters into its hands. For many years the People's Republic had few trade partners, and most of the business was done on an intergovernmental level. Concentration at the top met the needs at the time.

As foreign trade grew in volume and complexity, it became necessary to change this setup. The present reform has a double purpose: (a) to grant autonomy to various departments and localities so that the country's foreign trade potential can be tapped, and (b) to put producers of export goods in touch with the world market, so that the country will sell more and consequently increase its international purchasing power. The overall aim is better use of foreign trade as a means of promoting modernization.

The following changes have been made in China's foreign trade system:[9]

- The import-export corporations under the Ministry of Foreign Trade, which used to handle the bulk of the business with other countries, have changed their functions. Some still deal in a few important types of goods, others deal in none at all. Their present jobs are: (a) to organize and coordinate the business of their branch offices, which have been established recently in various localities; (b) to help establish or participate in joint ventures with investors from overseas; (c) to act as agents in import-export trade; and (d) to execute government trade agreements.
- The bulk of the business handled by import-export corporations has been taken over by their branch offices in the capitals of Heilongjiang, Jilin, Shanxi, Shaanxi, Inner Mongolia, Ningxia, Qinghai, Gansu, Xinjiang, Sichuan, Guizhou, Jiangxi, and Anhui. In principle, these branch offices export only local products.
- Foreign trade corporations have been set up in three municipalities (Shanghai, Tianjin, and Beijing), four provinces (Guangdong, Fujian, Liaoning, and Hebei), and one autonomous region (Guangxi). They are under the dual leadership of the local governments and the Ministry of Foreign Trade, but they usually refer matters to the former.
- Import-export corporations have been established under various central ministries as well as under the Chinese Academy of Sciences to form joint ventures with foreign investors or conduct co-production, compensatory trade, material-processing, and assembly work.

9. See Zhong Wen, "Reforming the Structure of China's Foreign Trade," *China's Foreign Trade*, no. 1, 1981.

- A number of corporations have been set up to contract construction projects abroad and provide technical and labor services to other countries.
- Transregional joint enterprises have been formed among different production departments for the export of a single item or several items.
- Some factories, mines, farms, and other enterprises at the grass roots may, with the approval of higher authorities, export their products through direct deals with foreign businessmen.

People who have been doing business with China for a long period of time may not be accustomed to the new practices, which nevertheless mean wider opportunities for them and for China itself.

THE GUIDELINES: PAST AND PRESENT

The ultra-left guidelines in China's socialist construction, discussed at length in previous chapters, also found expression in her foreign economic policies, particularly in the import policy of the People's Republic. The history of the country's importation of equipment and technology may be divided into three stages. In the 1950s, China imported a number of key projects from the Soviet Union and Eastern European countries, mainly the 156 projects provided by the Soviet Union. These projects played an important part in laying the initial foundation of China's industrialization. This was the first stage.

The second stage began in the early 1960s, when the country imported a limited number of whole plants from capitalist countries. Most of the imported items turned out to be good, but the process was interrupted by the Cultural Revolution, which began in 1966.

The third stage covers the period from the early 1970s to the present, during which foreign equipment and technology have been imported on a growing scale. Some of the imported items, including equipment for the production of chemical fertilizers, chemical fibers and plastics, steel-rolling equipment, and power generation plants, have gone into operation and are doing a good job enlarging production capacity and raising quality. In 1978, in an overzealous attempt to boost production, the import authorities purchased an excessive number of whole plants, most of which required cash payment and

CHINA'S ECONOMIC REFORMS

strained national finance. While learning from this mistake, the country's economic administrators do not think it is right to "stop eating for fear of choking." Because of the cutbacks in capital construction in the course of economic readjustment, the import of whole plants has basically come to an end, but more and more, single items of equipment are being purchased from abroad to update the country's industrial technology.

A critical review of the import policy in the past three decades reveals the following problems.[10] In the first place, import policy has been affected by a lopsided stress on heavy industry, particularly the steel industry, at the expense of light industry and agriculture. For this reason, the equipment and technology purchased for heavy industry took up too large a proportion, with those for the metallurgical industry accounting for 25 percent of the amount imported in the three decades from 1949 to 1979. By contrast, the light industries, including the textile industry, received 12 percent, communications and transport got only 0.5 percent, while almost nothing was spent on agriculture, which was called "the foundation of the national economy." Such an unbalanced import policy reflected an unbalanced economy and in turn aggravated its disproportions.

Second, while people talked about importing equipment and technology, what they had in mind was usually the former and not the latter, and there was often a craze for whole plants instead of a careful selection of certain crucial types of machinery. In the 1949–79 period, therefore, over 90 percent of the import money was spent on equipment, particularly whole plants, with little left for buying the know-how.

Third, in many cases China barely got its money's worth on the imported equipment. Sometimes the waste was caused by bureaucratic apathy, with the costly pieces lying idle and rusting away without anybody doing anything about it. More often the problem arose from rashness and bad planning. The hasty purchase of too many whole plants in 1978 had been preceded by similar, though less serious, cases. For instance, the output in some coal mines was raised several times through a combination of automatic coal-cutters, hydraulic supports,

10. For a full discussion of these problems, see the editorial in *People's Daily,* August 11, 1980, entitled "The Import Policy Must Serve the Readjustment of the National Economy," from which the relevant figures are quoted.

and scraper-chain conveyors, but the nation could not benefit from the increased production because there were not enough railroad freight cars to bring out the coal or enough wharves for exporting it. There were also cases where highly efficient open-hearth and blast furnaces for an iron and steel complex could not be put to use because of a lack of power supply. No equipment, however good, can work without the proper infrastructure, the lack of which has delayed the commissioning of some of China's most up-to-date projects.

It is estimated that on the average every U.S. dollar spent on imported equipment requires an investment of 4 yuan (more than 2 U.S. dollars) in ancillary equipment and the infrastructure at home.[11] In other words, such investment is more than double the amount needed for the purchase of foreign equipment and technology. Thus the effective way to use China's limited foreign exchange is to concentrate on key projects, complete with the infrastructure, instead of spreading it over too many undertakings.

The following guidelines have been suggested for any project financed with foreign funds:[12]

- Its products must be competitive on the international market.
- If the products are not for export or cannot be exported, they must at least serve as substitutes for imports, so that they will not cause an additional outlay in foreign exchange but enable the country to set aside a corresponding amount of foreign exchange to pay back the foreign funds used.
- The rate of profit earned on the project must be higher than the rate of interest on the foreign funds borrowed for its construction.

Does China need the most sophisticated types of equipment and technology? Not necessarily, because they may or may not be the best for China at present. In particular, it is important to guard against a blind quest for automation in disregard of the actual conditions in the country. Generally speaking, there should be introduced from abroad more technology and equipment that will require less investment,

11. Liu Lixin (vice-president of the People's Construction Bank of China), "On the Use of Foreign Funds," *Beijing Review*, no. 34, 1980.

12. Ibid.

absorb more of China's enormous manpower resources, and bring more monetary returns. Once the technology and equipment are brought into China, Chinese workers and technicians must study them carefully, use them properly, improve upon them, and develop something new. This is an oft-quoted belief of the late Premier Zhou Enlai.

Chinese importers are now trying to put into practice the above guidelines gleaned from thirty years' experience.

WHERE TO LOOK FOR BUSINESS IN CHINA

In the period of China's economic readjustment, business between China and other countries will increase, first because the developed countries facing a persistent "stagflation" need more outlets for their goods, services, and capital, and second, because some of these goods, services, and capital are needed by China to attain the aims of its modernization in general and the aims of its economic readjustment in particular.

China's basic policy on import-export trade is to import by the amount of export so as to balance her international payments and national budget. China wishes to import more for both modernization and readjustment, but in order to import more, the country must export more.

Old China was an exporter of farm and sideline produce, handicrafts, and industrial raw materials like tung oil and pig bristles. The cotton and silk China sold on the world market came back to the country in the form of manufactured goods. The situation has changed since the founding of the People's Republic in 1949, but today the country remains essentially an exporter of agricultural produce, light industrial and textile goods, and some minerals. She has also sold a small amount of industrial machinery abroad.

As China's rural economy improves in the course of readjustment, the export of farm produce, special local products, and animal by-products will increase, but not necessarily in terms of their proportion in the country's total export volume. On the other hand, much effort will be made to increase the export of minerals and chemicals. Utilizing the industrial capacity it has acquired since 1949, China will also try to update its machinery and electrical appliances and sell more of them on the world market.

As far as the imports are concerned, few whole plants will be purchased because of the cutbacks in capital construction. The large sums of money thus saved will be spent on key types of material, technology, and equipment needed for updating the existing enterprises, particularly in such fields as energy, building materials, and communications and transport. Equipment and technology for the production of various consumer goods will also be imported to meet the rising demand on the home market. Import priorities will be given to undertakings that increase the nation's export capacity.

In light of these policy emphases, some of the opportunities for foreign businessmen may be outlined as follows:

Technical renovation. China has nearly 400,000 enterprises in industry and communications. In the period of readjustment, production will be increased mainly not by building new enterprises but by improving the technology and management of the existing enterprises. Many of them will need some crucial equipment from abroad. Most of the imported equipment will go to enterprises in the light and textile industries, especially those producing export goods. To increase the competitiveness of the goods on the international market, it is necessary to improve their quality as well as their design and packaging, and better techniques are needed in all these respects. Some of the goods from China's heavy industry, such as machine tools, electric motors, pumps, meters and instruments, and electrical appliances for household use, have found a ready market in Third World countries. They may not be as sophisticated as those from the West, but they do good work and are much cheaper. Much know-how is needed to improve their marketability.

Coal mining and washing. Coal is designated as the principal source of energy in China because of the country's rich coal reserves and the limited petroleum output at present. China needs wider cooperation with foreign countries in coal mining and is ready to sign long-term contracts for export on terms satisfactory to both sides. For a better utilization of coal-heat energy, there is an urgent demand for technology in this field, including that of coal washing.

Oil exploitation. China is ready to receive bidders for talks on the prospecting and exploitation of the oil resources in her offshore areas. The product will be shared by the contracting parties on the basis of their respective investments.

Infrastructure. While there will generally be no further expansion of capital construction in the next four or five years, projects involving infrastructures are an exception. China can hardly increase her export capacity without enough roads, railroads, and harbors, and many of the existing harbors must be renovated so that they will acquire a greater cargo-handling capacity. Much investment is needed in these fields, but in China's present financial circumstances the country accepts only interest-free or low-interest loans. The same applies to the construction of power stations and the supply of power generation equipment, which are needed to enable existing enterprises and imported projects to operate at full capacity.

Processing and assembly. It is well known that countries like Japan and Singapore have built up their economies by processing foreign materials and assembling foreign parts for export in the postwar years. Since China is much larger, and since most of its land lies in the interior, the country cannot build its entire economy on processing industries or assembly manufacturing. But China can draw on the experience of such countries as Japan and Singapore and turn its extensive coastal areas into great exporters and foreign-exchange earners by developing such undertakings. Processing and assembling are already being done in the "special economic zones" in Guangdong and Fujian, but they can be done in many more areas. Coastal cities like Shanghai, Tianjin, Guangzhou, Dalian, Qingdao, Fuzhou, and a host of smaller cities, have a good industrial foundation, a large force of skilled workers, and many able managers and technicians. Export business along these lines will actually mean an export of manpower and technical skill, which is highly profitable for both China and the foreign contractors.

Tourism. This is a burgeoning industry in China. Visitors to the country, mostly tourists, totaled 4.2 million in 1979 and 5.7 million in 1980, bringing her an income of 696 million yuan (449.66 million U.S. dollars) and 920 million yuan (624.16 million U.S. dollars) respectively.[13] But these are very small figures for a country that has hundreds of historical sites and scenic spots. Growth is being limited by a shortage of facilities, including hotels, restaurants, recreational centers, and so on, many more of which should be built. While a few fancy facilities may be necessary, most of them should be simple and comfortable and cater to the majority.

13. The equivalents in U.S. dollars are worked out according to the average rates of exchange announced by the Bank of China in the years referred to.

Cooperation in all fields may take a variety of forms. In addition to regular buying and selling and the five forms outlined in the first part of this chapter, manufacturing may be undertaken on designs or models, supplied by clients or with materials provided by them; specialists may be brought to China to work on certain projects; and foreign firms may be contracted to conduct training programs for Chinese workers and technicians, either in China or abroad. The scope of cooperation may also be widened to include education, science and culture, and public health.

Epilogue: Prices in China

by Wang Zhenzhi and Wang Yongzhi

PRICING POLICIES SINCE 1949

The basic pricing policy of the People's Republic of China has always been one of price stability, which is considered necessary for socialist economic development and a secure, improving life for the people. Theoretically, the policy is founded on the basic law of the socialist economy—the law of meeting the rising needs of the people on the basis of rising production, as well as the law of a balanced development of the national economy, the law of value,[1] and the law of supply and demand. The specific guidelines are:

- Exchange of equal or almost equal values.
- Reasonable pricing on the basis of sound economic data, which takes into consideration the proper parities and differentials as well as the need to narrow the gap between industrial and farm prices.
- A steady improvement of price-control regulations.

Price stability is a long-term policy in China's socialist construction because it is essential for state economic planning and administration, for the exchange of products between industry and agriculture,

1. See Glossary.

220

for income distribution on the principle of "to each according to his work," and for the general well-being of the masses.

By price stability we mean the stability of the prices of basic necessities. In terms of retail prices, it means making allowances for fluctuations, both upward and downward, within a limit of around 2 percent every year. But this does not exclude readjustments of unsuitable prices, which should nevertheless be reset periodically and according to plan.

Thus price stability means a basic, relative stability. The policy has two aspects: basic stability and necessary readjustments. While emphasizing stability, one should not deny the need for readjustments, or else one would misinterpret the policy of stabilizing prices as a policy of freezing them. While recognizing the need for readjustments, one should not be misled by changes in the general retail price level to think that price stability is either unnecessary or impossible.

Back in 1956, Chen Yun, vice-chairman of the Central Committee of the Chinese Communist Party, pointed out that the pricing policy was being handled in a way that was not conducive to production. Speaking at the first session of the Party's Eighth National Congress, he noted that in their handling of prices some people were oversimplifying the stabilization of prices as a matter of unifying or even freezing them. He added that people should not be scared of the relatively high prices of certain types of goods which were being sold on the basis of their quality. The prices of such goods would drop as soon as more of them were produced, and the Party and the government were fully capable of rationalizing prices.

In the thirty-two years since 1949, the People's Republic has maintained the basic stability of prices. The Renminbi (People's Currency) is trusted by the people, and no one in China doubts its steady purchasing power. This is in contrast to the runaway inflation in old China over more than a decade up to 1949.

In March 1950, five months after the founding of the People's Republic, the Communist Party and the government launched a nationwide struggle against inflation. Two steps were taken. First, all prices were kept at their existing levels no matter how unreasonable they were. Second, the unreasonable prices were changed following stabilization. The economy and finance of the whole country were placed under unified government control. The amount of money in circulation was cut down through heavy purchases of goods by government offices, state enterprises, and the People's Liberation Army and through the issuance of national bonds, a streamlined tax system, and centralized control over cash money. Principal necessities like grain, cotton cloth, fuel coal, and table salt were procured by the government and marketed by the government at standard prices in all major cities without rationing. Capitalist speculation and profiteering were curbed. Prices began to drop immediately. A survey conducted in fifteen major cities showed a decline of 31.2 percent in wholesale prices during the period from March to June 1950. The inflation that had plagued China for a dozen years finally came to an end. In 1952 the nation's gross industrial and agricultural output value, as well as its grain and cotton production, exceeded the peaks before the start of the war with Japan in 1937. The national budget showed no deficit.

This was followed by the period of the First Five-Year Plan for national economic development (1953–57). The pricing policy in this period stressed keeping prices at stable levels, coupled with the readjustment of a few unreasonable prices, in the interest of the socialist transformation of agriculture, the handicraft industry, and capitalist industry and commerce. The measures adopted were:

- A national campaign to increase production and practice economy, which would make for a balance between supply and demand.
- State monopoly purchase and marketing of such essential means of subsistence as grain, cotton, cotton cloth, and edible oils, which would guarantee the supply of basic necessities to the urban and rural population.
- Basically fixed low prices for industrial goods which had a direct bearing on the people's living standard, and flexible, relatively high prices for luxuries.
- Rationalizing the sales prices of capitalist firms and state payment for processing work done by these firms.
- Narrowing the price differentials among various regions and between urban and rural areas, abolition of seasonal differences in the prices of grain, cotton, peanuts, pigs, cured tobacco, and many other types of goods, periodic readjustments in wholesale and retail prices, and effective control of the market.

These measures served to curb the hoarding of goods and speculation and profiteering by the capitalists and expedited the socialist
transformation of agriculture, the handicraft industry, and capitalist
industry and commerce. They kept market prices at stable levels and
facilitated the implementation of the First Five-Year Plan. The nation's retail price index in 1957 was 8.6 percent higher than in 1952,
representing a yearly increase of 1.7 percent. The same period saw an
annual increase of 10.9 percent in the gross output value of industry
and agriculture, of 8.9 percent in national income, of 7.4 percent in
the average wages of industrial and office workers, and of 5.1 percent
in peasant income. All this meant a relatively fast rise in the people's
living standard.

The good times of the First Five-Year Plan were followed by the
disastrous "Great Leap Forward" of 1958 which, coupled with natural adversities, caused serious difficulties to the nation during 1959–61.
Industrial and farm production dropped sharply. Many important
items of consumer goods were in short supply. State supplies lagged
far behind demand, while prices rose sharply on the free market. In
1960, the supply of consumer goods came to only 87.9 percent of
purchasing power. In 1961, prices on the free market averaged more
than three times the retail prices in state stores. The 1959–61 period
saw the sharpest rises in prices in the history of the People's Republic.
In 1962, the nation's retail price index was 25.8 percent higher than
in 1957, while the 1961 index grew by 16.2 percent over 1960.

In these circumstances, the Communist Party and the government shifted to a policy of "readjustment, consolidation, filling out,
and raising standards"[2] to put the economy back on its feet. It reinforced the agricultural front, revamped industry to provide more daily
necessities for the people, and adopted a series of measures with
respect to the distribution of goods and their prices:

- Strict adherence to the original price levels of eighteen categories of daily necessities accounting for 60 percent of the
spending of industrial and office workers, including grain, edible oils, cotton cloth, cotton textiles and knitwear, fuel coal,
basic pharmaceuticals, housing, water, and electricity. No fluc-
tuation whatever was permitted in these categories. Losses sus-

2. See Glossary.

tained by state industry and commerce because of higher state
purchasing prices for farm produce and higher production costs
were covered by the state budget.
- The main types of consumer goods were placed under a system
of planned distribution. Insufficiently supplied items were ra-
tioned among the population.
- High-priced foods were provided by restaurants, and high-
priced pastries and candies, knitwear, and so on, were offered in
state stores to withdraw money from the market.
- Centralized control of prices. Any change in the standard
prices set by the state must be authorized by the central authorities.

These measures ensured the basic stability of prices in the
economically most difficult years of the People's Republic. With a
general turn for the better in the economic situation in 1963–64, most
of the high prices dropped to the original levels, and rations were
abolished on many items of goods. The price differentials between
state stores and the free market returned to normal.

The task of economic readjustment was accomplished in 1965,
when the national retail price index dropped by 4.7 percent as compared with 1962, while prices on the free market dropped by 46
percent.

During the "Cultural Revolution" of 1966–76, the Party and the
government took much care to avoid a disruption of price stability in
this period of turmoil. On August 20 the Chinese Communist Party
Central Committee and the State Council announced the "Regulations on Further Practicing Economy in Making Revolution, Restricting the Purchasing Power of Collectives,[3] and Strengthening Control
over Funds, Supplies, and Prices." The regulations pointed out that
the authorities in all localities must pay attention to the stability of the
market and of prices. Although unsuitable prices and price differentials existed between one region and another and between urban and
rural areas, they should not be dealt with until the later stage of the
Cultural Revolution. Prices on the free market were to be placed
under strict control. Nobody would be allowed to buy or sell goods
subject to state monopoly purchase and marketing. Struggles should

3. The "collectives" here refer to government offices, state and collective enterprises,
schools, and so on, as distinguished from individuals.

be waged against attempts to disturb the market, and firm blows dealt to speculators and profiteers.

The announcement of these regulations was followed by a virtual freezing of prices. Practically no price readjustment took place during the Cultural Revolution.

By these efforts, the government was able to maintain the stability of prices on the main types of consumer goods. The amount of goods available was barely equal to purchasing power, with shortages appearing from time to time. The retail price index in 1976 showed a drop of 2.2 percent as compared with 1965. However, the chaos of the Cultural Revolution pushed the economy to the brink of collapse. The worsening economy could not but affect price stability. In actual practice, therefore, prices were raised in disguise, and those on the free market rose by an estimated 40 percent.

The Cultural Revolution came to an end with the arrest of the Gang of Four in October 1976. Since then, the government has carried out a policy of rationalizing prices step-by-step on the basis of maintaining general stability. In April 1979, state purchasing prices for eighteen major types of farm produce were raised substantially, including grain, cotton, and oil-bearing crops. In May of the same year, the pithead prices of coal were raised. In September 1979, the following decisions were made on the sales prices of consumer goods:

- No change would be effected in the sales prices of basic necessities like grain, edible oils, cotton cloth, sugar, and fuel coal for civilian use. Losses arising from the higher state purchasing prices for these goods would be financed by the state.
- From November 1, 1979, sales prices were raised on eight main items of nonstaple foods: pork, beef, mutton, poultry, eggs, aquatic products, vegetables, and milk, and on foods made from these products. At the same time, a nonstaple food subsidy of five yuan per month was granted to industrial and office workers in most areas, and a subsidy of eight yuan to those in livestock-breeding areas. The rises in the sales prices of nonstaple foods were to be effected simultaneously with wage increases.
- Rises in the prices of some consumer goods were to be balanced by drops in the prices of others.
- Beginning in the latter part of 1979, prices were to be floated on smaller quantities of farm and sideline produce, native specialty products, and miscellaneous goods, mostly handicraft prod-

ucts. The prices of these goods might be negotiated between buyer and seller on the basis of supply and demand, but without violent fluctuations.

What actually happened was that the prices of many items tended to rise. This was because the nation had not yet effected a basic turn for the better in an economy damaged by the Cultural Revolution, because the state budget was unbalanced, and because there were gaps between supply and demand. The retail price index in 1979, calculated on the basis of state prices, floating prices, and actual sales prices, showed a rise of 5.8 percent over December 1978. The figure includes a rise of 5.3 percent in state store prices.

Thus it became necessary to lay further stress on price stability. On April 8, 1980, the Chinese Communist Party Central Committee and the State Council issued a "Circular on Strengthening Price Control and Taking Firm Steps to Check Unauthorized and Disguised Price Increases." On December 7, 1980, the State Council issued a "Circular on Strict Control of Prices and on Supervision over Negotiated Prices." On January 8, 1982, the State Council issued a "Circular on Taking Firm Steps to Stabilize the Market and Prices," coupling it with a decision to lower the sales prices of homemade watches, television sets, semi-conductor radios, and woolen fabrics. The content of these announcements may be summarized as follows:

- There will be no increase in the state prices of industrial and farm products at the retail level.
- Negotiated prices may move downward, but not upward, and must not be applied beyond the categories of goods prescribed by the government.
- Important means of production subject to state procurement and allocation must be handled at state prices, which cannot be floated. This applies to goods produced above state quotas and those that the producers are entitled to sell through their own channels. The prices of important industrial consumer goods are to be handled likewise.
- No government department, central or local, is allowed to raise the prices of important farm and sideline products without authorization from the State Council, or to raise them in a disguised form. None of these products may be sold at negotiated prices

prior to the fulfillment of quotas for sales to the state. Ceilings are to be imposed on negotiated prices by the governments in the provinces, municipalities, and autonomous regions.

• No state institutions or army units are allowed to sell their surplus supplies at a profit.

• While the free market is to be guided by state policies, it should be further developed in the interest of invigorating the economy, stabilizing the market, and bettering the life of the people.

The nation's 1980 retail price index, which covers state prices and negotiated prices, shows a rise of 6 percent over 1979. This includes a rise of 8.1 percent in cities and of 4.4 percent in rural areas, of 7.1 percent in consumer goods, and of 1 percent in agricultural means of production. The 1981 retail price index, which likewise covers state prices and negotiated prices, shows a rise of 2 percent over 1980. State financial subsidies for the stabilization of prices amounted to 32 billion yuan in 1981. Of this amount, 22.80 billion yuan were spent as price subsidies for grain, cotton, and oil-bearing crops. The government subsidized the price of grain at 0.10 yuan per catty (1.10 pounds) and that of edible oils at 0.80 yuan per catty.

The 1979 retail price index shows a rise of 38.6 percent over 1950, averaging a yearly increase of 1.3 percent. The index of the cost of living of industrial and office workers rose 47.4 percent during the same period, averaging a yearly increase of 1.6 percent. (See Tables E.1 and E.2.)

More than thirty years of pricing experience in the People's Republic show that the following factors are essential for price stability in a socialist country like China:

• Growing production and rising labor productivity in both industry and agriculture, which lowers the cost of production and lays the basis of price stability.

• An improving economic pattern, a coordinated development of the various economic sectors, and balance between supply and purchasing power.

• Correct handling of the relationship between accumulation and consumption, an essentially balanced national budget, and the issuance of money for economic but not budgetary reasons, all of which are basic guarantees against inflation.

• Upholding the dominant position of state planning, which

TABLE E.1
RETAIL PRICE INDICES VS. WORKERS' COST-OF-LIVING INDICES
(COUNTED ON THE 1950 BASIS)

	Retail Price Index	Workers' Cost-of-Living Index
1952	111.8	115.5
1957	121.3	126.6
1965	134.6	139.0
1975	131.9	139.5
1979	138.6	147.4

TABLE E.2
BREAKDOWNS OF RETAIL PRICE INDICES IN STATE STORES
(COUNTED ON THE 1950 BASIS)

	1952	1957	1965	1975	1979
General index	112.1	121.4	132.3	128.4	130.9
Consumer goods	112.3	112.2	134.1	132.6	135.1
Foods	110.9	128.8	148.6	153.7	158.4
Clothing	111.9	111.7	113.6	112.7	112.3
Articles of daily use	118.2	116.2	130.4	126.2	127.1
Stationery and other cultural supplies	117.1	96.2	97.6	88.5	92.1
Pharmaceuticals	122.9	114.8	99.3	63.5	65.4
Fuels	135.7	150.3	160.1	154.0	154.4
Agricultural means of production	108.2	110.8	114.7	100.0	100.5

should nevertheless be supplemented by the functioning of the market mechanism, and the enforcement of price control wherever necessary.

PROBLEMS WITH CHINA'S PRICING SYSTEM

A number of problems have surfaced in China's pricing system over the years.

1. *Disparities between industrial and farm prices,* with the latter staying lower than the former for many years. Since Liberation, the state has raised its purchasing prices for farm produce on several

occasions. In particular, the substantial price increases effected in 1979 alleviated the disparities, and the peasants are generally happy with the new prices. But labor productivity is bound to rise in both industry and agriculture, which will lead to further disparities.

2. *Disparities among industrial prices.* In the past three decades little effort has been made to readjust the factory prices of industrial goods. In effect, this means that part of the value created by one industrial department is transferred to another through unequal exchange. The profit margin varies radically from one industry to another. The vast differences can be seen from an analysis of the 1979 final accounts of 60,000 industrial enterprises across the country, which belonged to 85 industries. Some 38 of these industries were operating at a profit margin anywhere from more than double the average to less than half the average. As to the other 47 industries, their profit margins varied to a maximum of four times. The wider profit margins were found in industries like watchmaking (61.1 percent), rubber processing (44.9 percent), bicycles (39.8 percent), dyestuffs (38.4 percent), daily utensils (30 percent), pharmaceuticals (33.1 percent), and cotton textiles (32.3 percent). The narrower profit margins were found in industries like chemical fertilizers (1.4 percent), iron mining (1.6 percent), coal mining (2.1 percent), shipbuilding (2.8 percent), chemical mining (3.2 percent), farm tools (3.1 percent), cement (4.4 percent), and farm machinery (5.1 percent).

3. *Disparities between the purchasing prices and sales prices of goods.* The main problem is that, in many cases, the sales price is not much higher than the purchasing price; it may even be lower. This means losses to state commerce. The sales prices of grain and edible oils, for example, should normally cover the expenses for purchasing, handling, storage, and marketing, plus tax and profit. But their sales prices are lower than the purchasing prices. This requires heavy subsidies from the state, which rose substantially in 1979. State subsidies for farm prices amounted to 7.8 billion yuan in 1978, some 14.6 billion in 1979, some 20.8 billion in 1980, and some 32.0 billion in 1981. The 1981 figure includes 22.8 billion yuan for grain, cotton, and edible oils, 2.8 billion for meats, fish, eggs, sugar, vegetables, and fuel coal, and 4.5 billion for chemical fertilizers, insecticides, diesel oil, electricity, and machinery for rural use.

The unsuitable prices, which reflect a radical departure of the prices of goods from their values, have affected economic development in the following respects:

• They contributed to the disproportions within industry. The price disparities dampen the initiative of people in industries with a narrow profit margin, resulting in the underdevelopment of these industries. On the other hand, they lead to an overgrowth of industries with a wide profit margin. Many types of machinery are overstocked because they are sold at prices far above their values and are therefore produced in excess of state quotas. Certain kinds of minerals and raw and processed materials are often produced in quantities below state targets because their prices are much lower than their values. This is one reason for the imbalances within industry.

• The price disparities make it difficult to appraise the performance of industrial departments and enterprises in terms of production, business operation, and investment returns. Thus one cannot depend on prices to draw economic parallels or conduct business accounting. Enterprises lack the initiative to improve their performance—those enjoying a wide profit margin are indifferent to their astonishing waste, while those suffering from a narrow profit margin make no effort to widen it, because they know it is impossible for them to catch up with the highly profitable enterprises and that their losses will be covered by the state. The variance of prices from values also makes it difficult to compare investment returns. Good returns may be due to the favorable prices on the products, and vice versa.

• The price disparities form an obstacle to a reform of the economic managerial system and to socialist competition. The problem has become all the more serious because experiments are being carried out to enlarge the decision-making powers of the enterprises, to collect taxes from them instead of transferring their profits to the state, and to make them responsible for their own profits and losses. Unfair prices give rise to an unfair distribution of profit earnings among different industries, trades, and enterprises. A reform of the pricing system is necessary for economic readjustment as well as managerial reform.

READJUSTMENT AND REFORM
OF THE PRICING SYSTEM

Prices are a sensitive question involving the entire economic situation. For this reason, while there has been much discussion on them, no major readjustment or reform has been carried out in recent years.

Opinions differ on a number of questions, but the general orientation seems to be clear, that is, the state will take the law of value into full account and try to make good use of it in setting prices in a socialist planned economy supplemented by the market mechanism.

The main questions involved in a readjustment and reform of prices are: (1) the basic forms of pricing, (2) state purchasing prices for farm produce, and (3) the factory prices of industrial goods.

1. There should be four basic forms of pricing:

a. *State prices*. The state should set uniform prices for goods and services vital to economic development and the people's livelihood. These may include the state purchasing prices for major farm produce, the factory prices of basic raw and processed materials and energy supplies, the factory prices of major types of consumer goods, and rates charged by railroads, civil aviation services, postal and telecommunication systems, and maritime and inland navigation systems. The prices may be set by the State Council or by the pricing authorities in the provinces, municipalities, and autonomous regions.

b. *Floating prices*. First, the state may impose a ceiling on these prices, or in other words, allow a downward but not upward movement of these prices, as it has already done in the case of mechanical appliances and electronic products. Second, it may allow fluctuations around standard prices within prescribed limits, as in the case of goods offered in many varieties and subject to fast changes in consumer preferences and market supply and demand. Third, minimum prices of a protective nature may be worked out, such as for state purchase of vegetables. The floating principle applies, within the prescribed scope of goods, to factory prices, wholesale and retail prices, and state purchasing prices.

c. *Negotiated prices*. Prices may be negotiated between buyer and seller on minor types of farm and sideline produce and on miscellaneous industrial goods, for which the state sets no standard prices. Major farm produce left over from state purchases may be bought by state commercial agencies at negotiated prices.

d. *Free market prices*. The free markets in rural and urban areas are a necessary supplement to the socialist economy. As long as the goods lie within government-prescribed categories, there should be no administrative interference with their prices, which should nevertheless be kept within certain limits by economic means, as by a supply of the same kinds of goods in state stores at reasonable prices.

2. Two questions are involved in the state purchasing prices for farm produce: (a) differential rent and (b) price parities among the various types of farm produce.

a. Land rent does not exist under the state and collective systems of landownership in China. "Differential rent," a term used in Marx's *Capital*, is borrowed here to mean the difference in returns from rich and poor soil. As far as weather conditions are concerned, state purchasing prices for farm produce should be based not on an unusually good year or an extremely bad one, but on a normal year. And since soil fertility makes much difference in the yield, the purchasing prices should be set so that they bring some profit to farm collectives that operate on poor soil at a high cost. This means, in effect, transferring part of the differential rent from high-yielding collectives to low-yielding ones. When we do this, the former would still earn more than the latter because of their higher per-acre yield.

b. Price parities among the various types of farm produce reflect the proportional relationships among their values. They serve as the basis of the prices of consumer goods, most of which are either farm produce or made from farm produce. The prices should be based mainly on the values of the products. Specifically, they should be based on a medium-level cost of production in a normal year plus the average profit. Price parities among farm products have a historical background, and we must study historical data to grasp the interrelationships.

In handling its purchasing prices for farm produce, the state must take into consideration both the interests of the farming population and its own financial resources. State purchasing prices were raised substantially in 1979, but sales prices have stayed at previous levels. This means a big financial burden on the state. Then there is the question of meeting the consumer needs of the peasants, which rise with the state purchasing prices for their products. If the supply of industrial goods to the countryside does not increase, the peasants will be unhappy because they cannot buy more in spite of their bigger earnings. Finally, one must not ignore the influence of the prices of major farm produce on market prices in general. Although the state can keep down the sales prices of major farm produce while raising purchasing prices, increases in the purchasing prices will still produce a chain reaction on the market because there is always a price ratio between major and minor types of farm produce, and rises in the prices of the former inevitably push up the prices of the latter. In the long run, it will be necessary to continue raising the purchasing prices for farm produce periodically, narrow the gaps between industrial and farm prices, and realize equal exchange between industry and agriculture. In view of the aforementioned circumstances, however, it seems advisable to keep the state purchasing prices for farm produce at the present levels for a few years and limit the scope of farm and sideline products to be marketed at negotiated prices.

3. Theoretically, the factory prices of industrial goods (the prices at the time they leave the factories) should be readjusted on the basis of the law of value. In other words, the prices of all goods should roughly correspond to their values except in a few cases where state policy requires a radical departure of price from value. By rough correspondence we mean a situation where all producers are assured of an average profit margin. If we go by this principle, there will have to be drastic increases and decreases in the present industrial prices, which are impossible. But it is necessary to formulate a rationalization plan and carry it out by stages along with growth in production.

The present system of economic management can hardly be changed without a readjustment of certain prices. In our opinion, readjustment may start with the factory prices of certain products as distinguished from their sales prices on the market. As far as the sales prices of consumer goods are concerned, they should generally not be raised without corresponding rises in wages. The prices of various products, however, present a different case. A readjustment of these prices means a redistribution of income among industrial enterprises or between industrial and commercial enterprises and normally does not lead to a decrease in state revenue. For this reason, it is possible to readjust factory prices without affecting sales prices. Tax rates may be changed to ensure roughly the same profit margin on products from industries with a similar technological and managerial level. It is well known, for example, that the profit margin is narrow in the coal industry and wide in the petroleum industry. Assuming that the average profit margin is 10 percent, we may let the coal industry have it by tax exemption and limit the petroleum industry to this rate by taxation. Without affecting the general price level, this will make possible a more equitable distribution of profit among industries and pave the way for a reform of the nation's system of economic management.

As to agricultural means of production, three contradictions are involved in their pricing. First, while their prices are generally a bit too high in terms of rural purchasing power, it is difficult to lower them because of the high production cost and narrow profit margin. Second, while more agricultural means of production are needed for the modernization of farming, they have for years been sold at a low profit rate or even at a loss. Third, a few big plants are making much profit and are in a position to lower the prices of their products, but the medium-size and small factories cannot do the same because they are earning little profit or are operating at a loss. In fact, the pricing authorities lowered the prices the moment they saw a rise in profit. This discouraged the producers of agricultural means of production and in turn affected the modernization of farming. In our opinion, the profit margin on agricultural means of production should be roughly equal to that on similar industrial goods, and the state should consider financial subsidies to people's communes, their subdivisions, and peasants for the purchase of such equipment.

Appendix: Tables on the Economic Development of the People's Republic of China, 1949–80

THE STATISTICAL DATA used in the following tables are compiled from data released by the State Statistical Bureau (SSB) of the People's Republic of China and data listed in *Jingji Nianjian* (Economic Yearbook), 1981, edited by Xue Muqiao and published by the journal *Jingji Guanli* (Economic Management) in 1981. Figures quoted in the Chinese press, which have been checked against SSB data, are used in some of the tables. Some tables have gaps because the relevant figures have not been officially released.

The term "current year's prices" means prices in the year referred to. "Constant prices" means prices in a specified year taken as the basis of calculation for a number of years, and the prices in two different years may be chosen for the calculation of monetary values in two different groups of years. "Comparable prices" means the prices of a single year taken as the basis of calculation for all the years listed in a table. For details, see the Glossary.

TABLE A.1
CHINA'S POPULATION (YEAR-END FIGURES IN THOUSANDS)

Year	Total Population*	Urban Population	Rural Population	Percent Urban Population in Total Population	Nonagricultural Population	Agricultural Population	Percent Agricultural Population in Total Population
1949†	541,670	57,650	484,020	10.6	94,410	447,260	82.6
1952†	574,820	71,630	503,190	12.5	82,910	491,910	85.6
1957	646,530	99,490	547,040	15.4	106,180	540,350	83.6
1976	932,670	113,420	819,250	12.2	140,670	792,000	84.9
1977	945,240	114,950	830,290	12.2	142,440	802,800	84.9
1978	958,090	119,940	838,150	12.5	147,800	810,290	84.6
1979	970,920	128,620	842,300	13.2	157,320	813,600	83.8
1980	982,550						

*Does not include the Chinese in Taiwan Province, the Chinese in Hong Kong and Macao, and overseas Chinese. The 1979 figure would have been 988.4 million if it were to include the 17.41 million in Taiwan and the 70,000 on Jinmen (Chinmen) and Mazu (Matsu) islands. The 1980 figure does not include them either.
†The figures for 1949 and 1952 are estimates. The figures for the urban population in these two years include the agricultural population in areas under the jurisdiction of cities and towns.

OUTPUT VALUE OF INDUSTRY AND AGRICULTURE (IN BILLIONS OF YUAN AT CONSTANT PRICES)

Year	Gross Output Value of Industry and Agriculture	Gross Output Value of Agriculture*	Gross Output Value of Industry	Gross Output Value of Light Industry	Gross Output Value of Heavy Industry
		(At 1952 Constant Prices)			
1949	46.6	32.6	14.0	10.3	3.7
1952	82.7	48.4	34.3	22.1	12.2
1957	124.1	53.7	70.4	37.4	33.0
		(At 1970 Constant Prices)			
1976	457.9	131.7	326.2	142.6	183.6
1977	506.7	133.9	372.8	163.0	209.8
1978	569.0	145.9	423.1	180.6	242.5
1979	617.5	158.4	459.1	198.0	261.1
1980	661.9	162.7	499.2	234.4	264.8

*The total output value of agriculture in each year is an initial figure and will remain as such until the final verification of the grain output.

237

TABLE A.3

Growth of Gross Output Value of Industry and Agriculture
(percent increase over the previous year)

Year	Gross Output Value of Industry and Agriculture	Gross Output Value of Agriculture	Gross Output Value of Industry	Gross Output Value of Light Industry	Gross Output Value of Heavy Industry
1950	23.4	17.8	36.4	30.1	54.1
1952	20.9	15.2	29.9	23.5	43.5
1957	7.9	3.6	11.5	5.7	18.4
1976	1.7	2.5 (0.8)	1.3 (2.0)	2.4	0.5
1977	10.7	1.7 (−0.5)	14.3 (14.6)	14.3	14.3
1978	12.3	8.9 (8.1)	13.5 (13.6)	10.8	15.6
1979	8.5	8.6 (7.5)	8.5 (8.8)	9.6	7.7
1980	7.2	2.7	8.7	18.4	1.4

NOTE: The figures in parentheses show what the growth rates would have been if the output value of industry run by communes and their subdivisions were deducted from the gross output value of agriculture and added to that of industry.

238

TABLE A.4
NATIONAL INCOME (IN BILLIONS OF YUAN IN TERMS OF THE CURRENT YEARS' PRICES)

Year	Total National Income	Industry	Agriculture	Building Trade	Transport	Commerce	Per Capita Amount (yuan)
1949	35.8	4.5	24.5	0.1	1.2	5.5	66
1952	58.9	11.5	34.0	2.1	2.5	8.8	104
1957	90.8	25.7	42.5	4.5	3.9	14.2	142
1976	242.7	105.1	99.5	11.9	9.2	17.0	260
1977	264.4	119.6	98.0				281
1978	301.1	140.6	107.2				314
1979	335.0						347
1980	363.0						369

239

TABLE A.5
RATES OF INCREASE IN NATIONAL INCOME
(PERCENT INCREASE OVER PREVIOUS YEAR IN TERMS OF COMPARABLE PRICES)

Year	Total National Income	Industry	Agriculture	Building Trade	Transport	Commerce
1950	19.0	33.3	17.1	400.0	16.7	9.1
1952	22.3	31.0	15.2	133.3	38.9	25.7
1957	4.5	11.6	3.1	−7.3	7.3	0
1976	−2.7	−5.3	0.6	3.7	−4.2	−6.0
1977	8.4	14.9	−0.9			
1978	12.4	17.3	6.1			
1979	7.0					
1980	7.0					

240

TABLE A.6
PROPORTIONS OF NATIONAL INCOME USED FOR CONSUMPTION AND ACCUMULATION
(IN BILLIONS OF YUAN IN TERMS OF CURRENT YEARS' PRICES)

Year	Total Spending	Consumption	Accumulation	Accumulation Rate (percent)
1952	60.7	47.7	13.0	21.4
1957	93.5	70.2	23.3	24.9
1975	245.1	162.1	83.0	33.9
1977				32.3
1978				36.5
1979	335.6	219.5	116.1	34.6
1980	363.0			32.6

TABLE A.7

GAINS IN NATIONAL INCOME EFFECTED BY THE USE OF EVERY 100 YUAN
FOR ACCUMULATION (IN TERMS OF CURRENT YEARS' PRICES)

Year	Total Accumulation (in billions of yuan)	Gain in National Income over Previous Year (in billions of yuan)	Gain in National Income Effected by Use of Every 100 Yuan for Accumulation (yuan)
1952	13.0	9.2	71
1957	23.3	6.0	26
1976		−7.6	
1977			
1978			
1979	116.1	35.9	31
1980	118.3	28.0	24

TABLE A.8 THE PLACE OF AGRICULTURE IN THE NATIONAL ECONOMY (PERCENTS)

	1949	1952	1957	1976	1977	1978	1979	1980
Proportion of agricultural work force in the country's total work force		83.5	81.2	76.8	75.7	73.8	73.8	
Proportion of gross output value of agriculture in gross output value of industry and agriculture	70.0	56.9	43.3	30.4	28.1	27.8	25.7	24.6
Proportion of net output value of agriculture in net output value of industry and agriculture	84.5	74.7	62.3	48.6	45.0	43.0		
Proportion of net output value of agriculture in national income	68.4	57.7	46.8	41.0	37.0	35.3		
Proportion of profits and taxes provided by agriculture in state revenue		20.2	12.8					
Proportion of output value of products made from farm produce in the output value of light industry		87.5	81.6	69.2	68.5	68.4		
Proportion of retail sales volume in rural areas in the national retail sales volume	60.2	54.6	49.7	52.7	52.8	53.1	54.7	
Proportion of export volume of agricultural and sideline products, raw and processed, in the total export volume		82.0	72.0	61.0	62.0	63.0	56.0	

The proportions of the gross and net output values of agriculture in the gross and net output values of industry and agriculture are calculated in terms of the current years' prices and are therefore different from the figures derived from constant prices.

243

TABLE A.9 OUTPUT OF MAJOR AGRICULTURAL PRODUCTS (IN THOUSAND TONS)

Year	1949	1952	1957	1976	1977	1978	1979	1980
Grain	113,200	163,900	195,050	286,300	282,750	304,750	332,120	318,220
Cotton	445	1,304	1,640	2,056	2,049	2,167	2,207	2,707
Edible oils (peanut, rapeseed, and sesame seed)	2,328	3,729	3,771	3,449	3,390	4,568	5,641	7,691
Jute and ambary hemp	37	306	301		861	1,088	1,089	1,098
Tea	41	83	112		252	268	277	304
Sugarcane	2,642	7,116	10,393		17,753	21,117	21,508	22,807
Sugar beets	191	479	1,501		2,456	2,702	3,106	6,305
Cured Tobacco	43	222	256				806	

Year	Draft Animals at Year-end (in thousands)*	Pigs at Year-end (in thousands)*	Meat Output (in thousands of tons)†	Output of Aquatic Products (in thousands of tons)
1949	60,020	57,750		450
1952	76,460	89,770	3,385	1,670
1957	83,820	145,900	3,985	3,120
1976	94,980	287,250		
1977	93,750	291,780		4,700
1978	93,890	301,290		4,660
1979	94,590	319,710	10,624	4,310
1980	95,246	305,431	12,055	4,497

*Prior to 1957, does not include those in Tibet.
†Includes only pork, beef, and mutton. All figures for the meat output listed here are estimates.

245

TABLE A.11
OUTPUT OF MAJOR INDUSTRIAL PRODUCTS

Year	1949	1952	1957	1976	1977	1978	1979	1980
Steel (thousand tons)	158	1,350	5,350	20,460	23,740	31,780	34,480	37,120
Pig iron (thousand tons)	250	1,930	5,940	22,330	25,050	34,790	36,730	38,020
Coal (million tons)	32	66	131	483	550	618	635	620
Electric power (million kwh)	4,300	7,300	19,300	203,100	223,400	256,600	282,000	300,600
Crude oil (million tons)	0.12	0.44	1.46	87.16	93.64	104.05	106.15	105.95
Natural gas (million cubic meters)	7	8	70				14,510	14,270
Timber (thousand cubic meters)	5,670	11,200	27,870	45,730	49,670	51,620	54,380	53,590
Cement (thousand tons)	660	2,860	6,860	46,700	55,650	65,240	73,830	79,860
Chemical fertilizers (thousand tons)*	6	39	151	5,244	7,238	8,693	10,653	12,320
Chemical pesticides (thousand tons)		2	65	391	457	533	537	537
Plastics (thousand tons)		2	13		524	679	793	898
Metal-cutting tools	1,600	13,700	28,000	157,000	198,700	183,200	139,600	134,000

Motor vehicles†			7,900	135,200	125,400	149,100	185,700	222,000
Tractors‡				73,700	99,300	113,500	125,500	98,000
Cotton yarn (thousand tons)§	327	656	844	1,960	2,230	2,382	2,635	2,930
Cotton cloth (million meters)	1,890	3,830	5,050	8,840	10,150	11,030	12,150	13,470
Chemical fibers (thousand tons)			0.2	146.1	189.8	284.6	326.3	314.0
Paper and paperboard (thousand tons)	110	370	910	3,410	3,770	4,390	4,930	5,350
Bicycles (in thousands)	14	80	806	6,680	7,430	8,540	10,095	13,020
Sewing machines (in thousands)		66	278	3,638	4,242	4,865	5,868	7,680
Wristwatches (in thousands)			0.4	9,496	11,040	13,510	17,070	22,160
Cigarettes (thousand crates)	1,600	2,650	4,460	9,820	12,110	11,820	13,030	15,200
Sugar (thousand tons)	200	450	860	1,650	1,820	2,270	2,500	2,570
Salt (million tons)	2.99	4.95	8.28	14.01	17.1	19.53	14.77	17.28
Synthetic detergent (thousand tons)				217	257	324	397	393

*The output of chemical fertilizers, including nitrogen, phosphorus, and potassium, is counted on the basis of 100 percent purity.
†Does not include chassis and cross-country motor vehicles.
‡Does not include those converted into bulldozers by enterprises.
§Prior to 1977, output is calculated on the basis of 181.44 kilograms of cotton per bale.

Table A.12

Basic Financial Indices of Enterprises Under Ownership by the Whole People Conducting Independent Accounting (in millions of yuan)

Year	1952	1957	1975	1979
Original value of fixed assets	14,920	33,660	242,830	346,670
Total capital	14,710	33,180	256,900	348,760
Net value of fixed assets	10,110	24,130	171,630	237,860
Fixed sum of working capital	4,600	9,050	85,270	110,900
Profits and taxes: total	3,740	11,510	58,270	86,440
Profits	2,830	7,950	36,340	56,280
Taxes	910	3,560	21,930	30,160
Sales revenue	11,060	39,510		
Total output value of industry (at 1970 constant prices)	19,950	46,600		

Note: Includes figures for industrial enterprises in nonindustrial trades. The term "enterprises conducting independent accounting" is used here in the sense of their financial relationship with the state. For example, if an iron and steel company is financially accountable to the state while its subdivisions (the iron mine, the steel plant, the rolling mill, etc.) are accountable to the company, only the former is considered an enterprise in this table.

TABLE A.13
FREIGHT VOLUME (IN THOUSANDS OF TONS)

| Year | Total Freight Volume | Railroad | Highway | Water Transport | | Oil and Gas Conveyed by Pipelines | Freight Volume of Civil Airplanes |
				Total	Ocean Shipping		
1949	160,970	55,870	79,630	25,430			24
1952	315,160	132,170	131,580	51,410	140		2
1957	803,560	274,210	375,050	154,380	600		8
1976	1,998,070	821,160	742,560	355,280	23,820	79,020	53
1977	2,213,170	927,110	808,330	388,610	25,530	89,070	53
1978	2,463,190	1,074,920	851,820	432,920	36,590	103,470	64
1979	2,456,300	1,094,950	815,560	432,290	42,490	113,420	80

TABLE A.14
INVESTMENT IN CAPITAL CONSTRUCTION (IN MILLIONS OF YUAN)

Year	Total Investment	Investment Through Allocations from State Budget	Investment Not Through Allocations from State Budget
1950	1,134	1,041	93
1952	4,356	3,711	645
1957	13,829	12,645	1,184
1976	35,952		
1977	36,441	29,439	7,002
1978	47,900	39,500	8,400
1979	49,988	39,497	10,491
1980	53,900	28,100	25,800

NOTE: For the differences between the two kinds of investment, see "State Investment and Self-provided Investment" in the Glossary.

TABLE A.15
INVESTMENT IN PRODUCTIVE AND NONPRODUCTIVE CONSTRUCTION (IN MILLIONS OF YUAN)

Year	Investment in Productive Construction	Investment in Nonproductive Construction	
		Total	Housing Construction
1952	2,914	1,442	448
1957	10,509	3,320	1,282
1976	30,595	5,357	2,193
1977	30,347	6,094	2,506
1978	39,624	8,331	3,754
1979	36,514	13,474	7,379
1980	35,736	18,164	10,780

TABLE A.16
INCREASES IN FIXED ASSETS

Year	Total Increase in Fixed Assets (in millions of yuan)	Percent New Fixed Assets Put to Use	Increases in Fixed Assets in Industry (in millions of yuan)	Percent New Industrial Fixed Assets Put to Use
1952	3,114	71.5		
1957	12,922	93.4	6,472	89.4
1976	21,183	58.9		
1977	25,985	71.4	15,555	71.6
1978	35,637	74.3	19,057	69.8
1979	41,827	83.7		
1980	42,664	79.1		

NOTE: The percentages of new fixed assets put to use refer to the ratio between the new fixed assets and total investment. The increases in fixed assets in industry are calculated by trades, not by the administrative affiliations of the industrial enterprises.

TABLE A.17
RETAIL SALES VOLUMES (IN MILLIONS OF YUAN)

Year	Total Retail Sales Volume	Consumer Goods	Agricultural Means of Production
1949	14,050	13,380	670
1952	27,680	26,270	1,410
1957	47,420	44,160	3,260
1976	133,940	109,900	24,040
1977	141,100	115,250	25,850
1978	152,750	123,380	29,370
1979	180,000	147,600	32,400
1980	214,000		

Year	In Millions of Yuan in *Reminbi*			In Millions of Dollars in U.S. Currency		
	Import and Export	Import	Export	Import and Export	Import	Export
1950	4,150	2,130	2,020	1,130	580	550
1952	6,460	3,750	2,710	1,940	1,120	820
1957	10,450	5,000	5,450	3,100	1,500	1,600
1976	26,410	12,930	13,480	13,430	6,580	6,850
1977	27,250	13,280	13,970	14,800	7,210	7,590
1978	35,500	18,740	16,760	20,640	10,890	9,750
1979	45,560	24,390	21,170	29,390	15,740	13,650
1980	56,300	29,100	27,200	37,790	19,530	18,260

NOTE: The equivalents in U.S. dollars are worked out according to the average ratio between the dollar and the yuan set by the Bank of China in each year. By this standard, the dollar was exchanged for 3.6 yuan in 1950, 2.227 yuan in 1952, 2.604 yuan in 1957, 1.97 yuan in 1976, 1.84 yuan in 1977, 1.72 yuan in 1978, 1.55 yuan in 1979, and 1.49 yuan in 1980.

TABLE A.19

STATE FINANCIAL REVENUE AND EXPENDITURE (IN MILLIONS OF YUAN)

| Year | Revenue | Expenditure | Balance | Increases over the Previous Year (percent) | |
				Revenue	Expenditure
1950	6,520	6,810	−290		
1952	18,370	17,600	770	38.0	43.7
1957	31,020	30,420	600	7.9	−0.5
1976	77,660	80,620	−2,960	−4.8	−1.8
1977	87,450	84,350	3,100	12.6	4.6
1978	112,110	111,090	1,020	28.2	31.7
1979	110,330	127,390	−17,070	−1.6	14.7
1980	106,990	119,090	−12,100	−3.0	−6.5

255

| Year | Total Labor Force | | Industrial and Office Workers | | | | Urban Individual Laborers | Rural Labor Force† |
	Number of People	Percent Total Population	Total	In Units Under Ownership by the Whole People*	In Units Under Collective Ownership			
1952	207,290	36.1	16,030	15,800	230		8,830	182,430
1957	237,710	36.8	31,010	24,510	6,500		1,040	205,660
1976	388,340	41.6	86,730	68,600	18,130		190	301,420
1977	393,770	41.7	91,120	71,960	19,160		150	302,500
1978	398,560	41.6	94,990	74,510	20,480		150	303,420
1979	405,810	41.8	99,670	76,930	22,740		320	305,820

*Includes those recruited in addition to the quotas under state plans. The number of such workers included in the 1976 figure is an estimate.
†Those temporarily employed elsewhere are not included in the 1978 and 1979 figures; they are included in the other years.

256

Table A.21
Number and Wages of Industrial and Office Workers in Units Under Ownership by the Whole People

Year	Total Number of Industrial and Office Workers at Year-end (in thousands)	Increase in Number over Previous Year (in thousands)	Percent Increase over Previous Year	Total Payroll (in millions of yuan)	Average Wage (yuan)
1949	8,000				
1952	15,800	2,980	23.2	6,800	446
1957	24,510	280	1.2	15,600	637
1976	68,600	4,340	6.8		605
1977	71,960	3,360	4.9	42,600	602
1978	74,510	2,550	3.5	46,900	644
1979	76,930	2,420	3.2	52,900	704
1980	80,190	3,260	4.2	62,800	803

TABLE A.22   NUMBER OF INDUSTRIAL AND OFFICE WORKERS IN INDUSTRIAL ENTERPRISES UNDER OWNERSHIP BY THE WHOLE PEOPLE, INCLUDING WAGES AND LABOR PRODUCTIVITY

Year	Number of Workers at Year-end (in thousands)	Increase over Previous Year (in thousands)	Total Payroll (in millions of yuan)	Average Wage (yuan)*	All-Personnel Labor Productivity (yuan)*	Percent Increase over Previous Year
1949	3,060				3,004	
1952	5,100	690	2,460	515	4,167	9.0
1957	7,480	310	5,070	690	6,336	−4.4
1976	28,660	1,750	17,750	634	9,134	−8.6
1977	30,130	1,470	18,700	632	9,873	8.1
1978	30,410	280	20,410	683	11,085	12.3
1979	31,090	680	23,020	758	11,792	6.4
1980					12,031	2.0

*The average wage and productivity in each year is worked out on the basis of the average number of workers and average rate of productivity in that year. For an explanation of the term "all-personnel labor productivity," see Glossary.

Table A.23   Enrollment at Schools and Colleges (in thousands)

	1949	1952	1957	1976	1977	1978	1979	1980
1. Enrollment								
Universities and Colleges	117	191	441	565	620	850	1,020	1,144
Secondary technical schools	229	636	778	690	680	880	1,198	1,243
Middle schools	1,039	2,490	6,281	58,360	67,790	65,480	59,055	55,081
Primary schools	24,390	51,100	64,280	150,060	146,180	146,240	146,630	146,270
2. Graduates								
Universities and colleges	21	32	56	149	194	165	85	
Secondary technical schools	72	68	146	339	340	232	181	
3. Newly admitted								
Universities and colleges	31	79	106	217	275	400	275	281
Secondary technical schools	98	351	123	348	366	447	491	

259

Table A.24
Scientists and Technicians in Units Under Ownership by the Whole People

	Unit	1952	1978	1979	1980
1. Total number of scientists and technicians	Thousand persons	425	4,345.1	4,700	5,296
Engineers and technicians	do	164	1,571.2		
Technicians in agriculture and forestry	do	15	294.2		
Medical and health workers	do	126.4	1,275.6		2,798
Scientific researchers	do	8	310.3		
Teachers at schools and colleges	do	111.6	893.8		
2. Breakdowns in percentages	percent	100	100		
Engineers and technicians	do	38.6	36.1		
Technicians in agriculture and forestry	do	3.5	6.8		
Medical and health workers	do	29.7	29.4		
Scientific researchers	do	1.9	7.1		
Teachers at schools and colleges	do	26.3	20.6		

3. Number of scientists and technicians among every ten thousand people	persons	7.4	45.4	
Engineers and technicians	do	2.9	16.4	
Technicians in agriculture and forestry	do	0.3	3.1	
Medical and health workers	do	2.2	13.3	
Scientific researchers	do	0.1	3.3	
Teachers at schools and colleges	do	1.9	9.3	
4. Number of scientists and technicians among every ten thousand industrial and office workers	do	269.0	583.2	660.4
Engineers and technicians	do	103.8	210.9	
Technicians in agriculture and forestry	do	9.5	39.5	
Medical and health workers	do	80.0	171.2	
Scientific researchers	do	5.1	41.6	
Teachers at schools and colleges	do	70.6	120.0	

TABLE A.25 HOSPITALS AND OTHER HEALTH ORGANIZATIONS, INCLUDING PROFESSIONAL MEDICAL AND HEALTH WORKERS

	1949	1952	1957	1976	1977	1978	1979	1980
Number of medical and health organizations	3,670	38,987	122,954	157,959	164,199	169,732	176,793	
Number of Hospitals	2,600	3,540	4,179	63,184	63,952	64,421	65,009	
Number of beds (in thousands)								
Total	80	160	295	1,687	1,777	1,856	1,932	1,982
In rural areas		39	74	1,024	1,089	1,140	1,192	
Number of Professional medical and health workers (in thousands)*								
Total	505	690	1,039	2,206	2,341	2,464	2,642	2,798
Practicing Chinese medicine	276	306	337	236	240	251	258	262
In rural areas		465	657	1,176	1,278	1,321	1,409	
Percent medical and health workers in rural areas		67.4	63.3	53.3	54.6	53.6	53.3	

*Does not include "barefoot doctors" and those who have other jobs.

A Glossary of Economic Terms Used in the People's Republic of China

THE FOLLOWING ECONOMIC TERMS are commonly used in the People's Republic of China. The equivalents in English are followed by Chinese characters and spellings in the Chinese phonetic alphabet. A few of the translations vary slightly from those used in the text of this book because of the need to keep them closer to the Chinese in the interest of those who wish to memorize the characters.

263

ACCUMULATION

积累 *(jilei)*.

That part of the net income from material production which is used for extended reproduction, nonproductive capital construction, and the building of material reserves. Accumulation is the source of extended reproduction, and its scale depends on the amount of society's surplus products. Excessive accumulation does not bring a speedy growth of the national economy, which cannot develop smoothly without a proper balance between accumulation and consumption.

ACCUMULATION FUND

积累基金 *(jilei jijin)*.

That part of the national income of a socialist country which is used for extended reproduction, nonproductive capital construction, and the building of material reserves. The accumulation fund is divided into (1) a fund for extended reproduction, used for capital construction in such fields of production as industry, agriculture, and transportation, and for increasing the working capital of the enterprises; (2) a fund for nonproductive capital construction, used for capital construction in such fields as culture and education, health, government administration, and national defense, as well as for nonproductive construction in productive sectors like industry and agriculture; and (3) a social reserve fund, used in case of natural disasters and other emergencies.

ACCUMULATION OF LABOR

劳动积累 *(laodong jilei)*.

In China the term refers specifically to the tremendous amount of labor put in by peasants during the construction of water conservancy and other farmland improvement projects sponsored by rural economic collectives. Because of a lack of funds, the manpower required for the building of such projects was contributed by production teams, which paid the participants from the annual collective income in terms of work points.

ADVANCED AGRICULTURAL PRODUCERS' COOPERATIVES

高级农业生产合作社 *(gaoji nongye shengchan henuoshe)*.

Socialist collective economic organizations of the Chinese peasants, also called advanced co-ops, at a higher degree of collectivization than the elementary agricultural producers' cooperatives. Land was owned collectively, with no dividends paid. Other principal means of production, such as draft animals and major farm implements, were pooled as collective property with compensation to the owners. The collective labor income was divided among members according to their work after deductions for state tax and the co-op's public accumulation and welfare funds.

AGRICULTURAL AND SIDELINE PRODUCTS

农副产品 *(nongfuchanpin)*.

The general term for the products from agriculture, forestry, and fishery provided by state and collective enterprises and by individuals in China's rural areas, including grain, cotton, edible oils, sugar, fruit, and aquatic products.

AGRICULTURAL COOPERATION MOVEMENT

农业合作化运动 *(nongye hezuohua yundong)*.

A movement to change the small peasant economy into a socialist collective economy. Immediately after the completion of land reform in 1952, agricultural cooperation started on the principle of voluntary participation and mutual benefit. In 1956, China basically completed the socialist transformation of agriculture, with 96.3 percent of the peasant households in agricultural cooperatives.

ALL-PERSONNEL LABOR PRODUCTIVITY

全员劳动生产率 *(quanyuan laodong shengchanlü)*.

An important indicator of the economic performance of an enterprise, this refers to the ratio between its gross output value and the average number of its workers and staff members within a given period of time. The latter includes not only those directly engaged in production but also all administrative and managerial personnel, kitchen and dining room workers, medical doctors and assistants, kindergarten teachers, and so on. Thus:

$$\text{all-personnel labor productivity} = \frac{\text{gross output value (yuan)}}{\substack{\text{average number of} \\ \text{workers and staff members} \\ \text{(persons)}}}$$

ALLOCATION (PROCUREMENT AND ALLOCATION)

调拨 *(diaobo)*.

A system of supply by which the socialist state collects important products and distributes them directly without going through the channel of the market.

AVERAGE PRODUCTION COST

平均生产成本 *(pingjun shengchan chengben)*.

The average value of the production cost and the material resources consumed, plus payment for laborers, used by different enterprises to produce a certain line of goods.

AVERAGE PROFIT RATE OF FUNDS

平均资金利润率 *(pingjun zijin lirunlü)*.

The ratio between the total amount of profit earned and the total amount of funds expended in all industries and trades. The rate is a general indicator of economic performance.

BASIC ACCOUNTING UNIT

基本核算单位 *(jiben hesuan danwei)*.

The basic unit in a people's commune which carries out production and income distribution by conducting independent accounting. At present the basic accounting unit in a people's commune is usually the production team and, in a few cases, the production brigade.

BONUS AND DIVIDEND FUNDS

奖励分红基金 *(jianglifenhong jijin).*

Funds set aside by a socialist enterprise, according to state regulations, for rewarding its workers and staff. An enterprise which makes a profit may keep a certain percentage of its profit to set up funds for the development of production, for the welfare of the workers and staff, and for the distribution of bonuses and dividends, and these funds increase with the profit of the enterprise. The workers and staff members receive bonuses every month and get dividends at year-end.

BONUS SYSTEM

奖励制度 *(jiangli zhidu).*

A system practiced by socialist enterprises to give workers and staff material incentives. It is also important in implementing the principle of "to each according to his work." Bonuses are given as rewards to those who overfulfill their tasks and make special contributions. The bonus system was abolished for a time under the influence of ultra-left ideas, but it has been reintroduced since the collapse of the Gang of Four in 1976.

CAPITAL CONSTRUCTION

基本建设 *(jiben jianshe).*

Activities for building up fixed assets in various departments of a socialist national economy. They include the construction of factories, mines, railroads, bridges, water conservancy works, shops, housing, hospitals, schools, and the procurement of machinery, equipment, vehicles, and ships.

CAPITAL CONSTRUCTION OF FARMLAND WATER CONSERVANCY WORKS

农田水利基本建设 *(nongtian shuili jiben jianshe).*

This includes the building of reservoirs, irrigation and drainage canals, flood control works, and the sinking of wells to develop agricultural production.

CENTRAL AND REGIONAL SYSTEMS OF MANAGEMENT (LITERALLY: THE VERTICAL STRIPS AND THE SQUARES)

条条块块 *(tiaotiao kuaikuai).*

The central system of management means management of enterprises by central ministries and their provincial and municipal equivalents. The regional system of management mainly follows the demarcation lines between administrative regions. In China there has been for years a vacillation between the two systems, both of which have shortcomings: the central system tends to cut off connections among economic departments, the regional system connections among regions. The solution is giving enterprises more power to handle their own affairs, developing cooperation among enterprises on the principle of economic rationality, and forming all kinds of economic associations of enterprises under state guidance.

CENTRALIZATION AND DECENTRALIZATION

中央集权和地方分权 *(zhongyang jiquan he difang fenquan).*

Referring to the managerial system of the national economy, centralization means the unified administration of all economic activities by the central government. Since this system gives little autonomy to the localities, it has been an obstacle to encouraging the development of local economy in line with local conditions. In the reform of the managerial system, it is expected that this problem can be solved by the localities being given a certain amount of autonomy and therefore more incentive under the guidance of a centralized plan.

CERAMIC RICE BOWL

瓷饭碗 *(ci fanwan).*

The ceramic rice bowl refers to the practice by which municipal or district authorities take responsibility for the profits and losses of collectively owned enterprises. Developed under the influence of "Left" guidelines, this is an imitation of the practice with enterprises owned by the whole people. It must be changed to make the collectives independent accounting units and to inspire the enthusiasm of their workers and staff. Although a ceramic rice bowl is not as durable as an "iron rice bowl," it is also quite secure.

CIRCULATION CHANNELS

流通渠道 *(liutong qudao).*

Channels for the exchange of goods through the medium of money. China's circulation channels are state commerce, cooperative shops, and free markets in both rural and urban areas.

CLOSING, SUSPENSION, AND MERGING OF ENTERPRISES AND THE SHIFTING OF THEIR LINES OF PRODUCTION

关、停、并、转 *(guan, ting, bing, zhuan).*

These are the four measures adopted in the period of economic readjustment beginning in 1979 for enterprises which turn out inferior products at a high cost and through much waste, which have long been running at a loss, or which are not producing according to social demand. A few of these enterprises are being closed down, while most of them are required to stop production for revamping, to merge with other enterprises, or to shift their lines of production.

COMMODITY

商品 *(shangpin).*

A commodity is a product of labor brought to the market for exchange. It has two properties: a use value (it is something that can satisfy a human want, such as food and clothing) and a value (it contains a certain amount of human labor). The amount of value of a commodity becomes manifest only when it is exchanged for another commodity and is expressed in terms of money or another kind of commodity.

Things that have no use value are not commodities. Things that have a use value but are not products of human labor, such as sunlight and air, are again not commodities. Things that have a use value and are the products of human labor but are not intended for exchange, like the grain grown by a peasant for his own use, are not commodities either. Commodities are only those products of labor which have a use value and are sold in the market.

COMMODITY GRAIN BASES

商品粮基地 *(shangpinliang jidi)*.

Areas which provide large quantities of marketable grain. The Central Committee of the Communist Party of China and the State Council have set goals—based on a general nationwide increase in the output of grain—to expedite the development of commodity grain bases in the following areas during the period from 1976 to 1985: Heilongjiang Province, the central part of Jilin Province, the Poyang Lake area in Jiangxi Province, the Dongting Lake area in Hunan Province, the Jianghan (Yangtze and Han rivers) Plain in Hubei Province, the northern part of Jiangsu Province, the northern part of Anhui Province, the Changjiang (Yangtze) Delta, the Zhunjiang (Pearl River) Delta, the Gansu Corridor, and the Hetao (Yellow River Bend) area in the inner Mongolia autonomous region and the Ningxia Hui autonomous region.

COMMODITY RATE

商品率 *(shangpinglü)*.

This refers specifically to the ratio between the agricultural produce sold to the state by the collective economic organizations of the rural people's communes and the state farms and their total produce. Agricultural tax paid in kind is also counted as commodity. The commodity rate of grain produced by rural collectives in China is around 15 percent, while that of the country's total agricultural produce is about 30 percent.

COMMUNE-, BRIGADE-, AND TEAM-RUN INDUSTRIES

社队工业 *(shedui Gongye)*.

This refers to small-scale industrial and transportation enterprises, such as coal mines, brickyards, farm tool factories, and food processing factories, run by rural people's communes, the production brigades, or teams. Collectively owned with commune members as most of the workers, these enterprises use local material and financial and human resources for undertakings closely related to agricultural production. They absorb much of the surplus manpower in the countryside, enliven rural economy, increase the income of the commune members, promote the development of agriculture, and add to state revenue.

COMMUNIST WIND

共产风 *(gongchanfeng)*.

A trend anticipating an early transition from socialism to communism, which arose during the "Great Leap Forward" in 1958. It negated commodity production and exchange and the principle of "to each according to his work." This idea led to some prevailing practices which harmed China's socialist construction, such as equalitarian distribution, free food handouts, appropriation of manpower and materials without compensation, and premature transition from "small collectives" to "big collectives" and from collective ownership to ownership by the whole people. The Central Committee of the Chinese Communist Party corrected these mistakes during the early 1960s.

COMPARABLE PRICES

可比价格 *(kebi jiage)*.

This is usually the name for "constant prices" when the constant prices of a single year, not those of two or more years, are used for comparing economic figures of a series of years.

COMPENSATED APPROPRIATION OF STATE FUNDS

资金有偿占用制 *(zijin youchang zhanyong zhi)*.

A system by which an enterprise periodically pays a fee for its appropriation of state funds in the form of fixed assets and working capital. A measure taken in the present reform of the system of economic management, it is designed to eliminate waste in the administration and use of state funds by changing the present practice by which an enterprise bears no economic responsibility in its use of state funds for production and business operations.

COMPETITION

竞争 *(jingzheng)*.

Competition, a product of commodity economy, refers mainly to the struggle between different producers over the purchase and sale of products for their own economic interests.

Competition pervades a capitalist society because of the highly developed commodity economy there.

In China, people have struggled to confront the theoretical problem of whether competition exists under socialism.

As envisaged by Marx and Engels, socialism is a society that has neither commodity production nor competition, having been created by socialist revolution in a country marked by a high degree of capitalistic development. Marx and Engels even came to the conclusion that competition is incompatible with socialism. Stalin was of the opinion that what exists in a socialist society can only be emulation (or contest) aimed at mutual help and common progress, but not competition characterized by the success of the superior elements and the failure of the inferior ones. Influenced by this concept, Chinese economists for a long time recognized only socialist emulation but not socialist competition, which nevertheless has always existed in real economic life.

After the end of the Cultural Revolution, Chinese theoreticians gradually came to realize, amid the drive for the four modernizations, that since commodity production and commodity exchange continue to exist in a socialist country and since the enterprises in a socialist country are relatively independent commodity producers, competition is inevitable. Competition is now considered an important prerequisite to using the market mechanism as a means of regulating the economy and something which, if handled properly, can serve as a driving force in improving management and service and in raising labor productivity. In a socialist society where the principal means of production are publicly owned and social production is basically organized through a unified plan, competition can serve to promote production while its negative effects can be prevented. Based on this understanding, the State Council of the People's Republic officially recognized for the first time the existence and positive function of competition when it announced, on October 17, 1980, its "Provisional Regulations on Developing and Protecting Socialist Competition."

CONSTANT PRICES

不变价格 *(bupian jiage).*

Also called "fixed prices" (固定价格 , *guding jiage*), these are the average prices in a certain year adopted as the basis for comparing economic figures of different years—such as figures on gross output value, national income, scales of construction and production, and growth rates. In the People's Republic, the state designates the years from which constant prices may be chosen to eliminate the price factor in computation. So far only the prices of 1952, 1957, and 1970 have been used as constant prices.

CONSUMPTION FUND

消费基金 *(xiaofei jijin)*.

The national income minus accumulation. It consists of a fund for state administration, a fund for culture, education, and public health, a fund for social insurance (including social welfare and social relief), and a fund for the remuneration of producers (workers' wages).

CONTRACTING JOBS AND OUTPUT QUOTAS (TO INDIVIDUALS OR GROUPS) AND PAYING (THEM) ACCORDING TO THE OUTPUT

包工包产，联产计酬 *(baogong baochan, lianchan jichou)*.

A form of the system of responsibility in agricultural production whereby the production team contracts land and farm jobs to individuals or groups of individuals and pays them in an agreed number of work points for an agreed amount of output. The work points are increased for extra output and reduced for failure to meet the target. Sometimes neither the work points nor the output is fixed, and the total output goes to the contractor or contractors after deductions for the state agricultural tax, the public accumulation, and reimbursement of the production cost covered by the team.

CONTRACTING OUTPUT QUOTAS TO INDIVIDUAL HOUSEHOLDS (WITH THE PRODUCTION TEAM CONDUCTING UNIFIED ACCOUNTING)

包产到户 *(baochan daohu)*.

A practice in agricultural production criticized as a capitalist tendency both before and during the Cultural Revolution, this has become an important form of the system of responsibility in agricultural production. While maintaining collective ownership of land and water conservancy works, the production team contracts all its farmland to individual households for separate cultivation. The contracted part of the output goes to the production team for unified distribution among the membership, and the rest is either shared between the team and the contractor or granted to the latter as a bonus.

CONTRACTING OUTPUT QUOTAS TO INDIVIDUAL HOUSEHOLDS (WITHOUT
THE PRODUCTION TEAM CONDUCTING UNIFIED ACCOUNTING)

包干到户 *(baogan dauhu).*

A form of the system of responsibility in agricultural production with
a pronounced character of individual operation. While the production team
maintains collective ownership of land and other basic means of production,
it divides the land and the general run of farm tools among individual
households. By contract, each household has to bring in specified crops in
specified amounts for payment of the state agricultural tax and as contributions to the team's public accumulation and welfare funds. Apart from this,
it may grow anything and handle all the rest of the output in any way it wants
to. By such a practice the production team no longer conducts unified accounting and income distribution among its membership.

CONTRACTING OUTPUT QUOTAS TO WORK GROUPS

包产到作业组 *(baochan dao zuoyezu).*

A form of the system of responsibility in agricultural production. By this
system the production team divides its labor force into several work groups
and contracts a certain amount of land to each. The team management and
the group agree on the targeted output, the pay for it in terms of work points,
the expenses required, and so on. After the crop is brought in, the group
receives the stipulated number of work points for the targeted output. Any
extra output is given to the work group as a bonus, either in full or in part,
according to the agreement. The production team reduces the work points
if the group fails to fulfill the agreed output quota.

CONTRACTING SEASONAL JOBS AND REGISTERING WORK POINTS ON THE
BASIS OF STANDARD QUOTAS

小段包工、定额记工分 *(xiaoduan baogong, ding'e jigongfen).*

A form of the newly developed system of responsibility in China's farm
production. The management of a production team announces the payment,
in terms of work points, for a job in a given farm season on the basis of the
average labor time, skill, and intensity required for it, sets the quality norms,
and contracts it to one or several peasants. The contractor or contractors earn
more work points by accomplishing more farm jobs within a given period of
time. The practice has raised peasant enthusiasm and work efficiency.

CONTRACT SYSTEM ON REVENUE AND EXPENDITURE

财政收支包干 *(caizheng shouzhi baogan).*

A new system of state finance introduced in 1980 which follows the principle of dividing the items of revenue and expenditure between the central and local authorities and making each responsible for the collection and payment of some items. The 1979 final accounts of each local government were used as the basis for the division of financial responsibility between it and the central government, which would remain unchanged for five years. The system gives more incentive to local governments in handling financial matters because it allows them to keep their extra revenue and their savings on expenditure. But they have to balance their budgets by their own means in case of a drop in income or overspending, and only in unusual circumstances may they ask for aid from the central government. The system offers more liberal and favorable terms to regions inhabited by national minorities.

COOPERATIVE SECTOR OF THE ECONOMY

合作社经济 *(hezuoshe jingji).*

A form of economy under collective ownership, this sector was transformed from individual ownership. Cooperative members own the cooperatives' means of production and take part in productive labor. After deductions for taxes, production costs, and public accumulation and welfare funds, the income is distributed among members according to the amount of labor they have contributed. In the elementary stage, apart from payment for work, cooperatives also hand out part of their annual income in proportion to the members' contributions of means of production, mainly land.

COUNTRY MARKET TRADE

农村集市贸易 *(nongcun jishi maoyi).*

Country market trade (also called the free market) is a form of commodity exchange among peasants or between peasants and city inhabitants under state administration. Commodities permitted for sale in these markets include agricultural and sideline products, special local products and handicrafts, most of which are yields from private plots or products of household sideline production. Prices are negotiable between buyer and seller.

CURRENT YEAR'S PRICES

当年价格 *(dangnian jiage)*.

Also called "prevailing prices" (现行价格 , *xianxing jiage*), these represent the actual price levels in a year. Use of such price figures in planning and statistics helps give people a concrete picture of production and business operations in a certain year.

DAN

担 *(dan)*.

A Chinese unit of weight used for agricultural produce, which equals 100 *jin* (catties) or 50 kilograms. For example, a *dan* of cotton weighs 50 kilograms.

DEVELOPING ONE'S STRONG POINTS, AVOIDING ONE'S WEAKNESSES, AND WINNING A FAVORABLE POSITION

扬长避短，发挥优势 *(yangchang biduan fahui youshi)*.

This refers to the need for a nation, a region, an economic department, or an enterprise to utilize its favorable natural, economic, and technological conditions and avoid the unfavorable ones in its economic development. The economic pattern and lines of production should be based on an analysis of these conditions.

DIFFERENCES BETWEEN TOWN AND COUNTRY

城乡差别 *(chengxiang chabie)*.

The vast difference between urban and rural areas, left over by history, in production level, income, and living standards, which can only be narrowed gradually under socialism.

DISTRIBUTION ACCORDING TO WORK

按劳分配 *(anlao fenpei)*.

The socialist principle for the distribution of income among laborers. In a socialist society, where the means of production are public property, the total product is distributed (in the form of consumer goods) among laborers according to the quantity and quality of their work after necessary deductions for society.

ECONOMIC ASSOCIATIONS

经济联合体 *(jingji lianheti).*

Associations established in recent years between enterprises, between different regions, between urban and rural areas, or between producers, marketing agencies, and research institutions on the principle of giving full play to the respective advantages of the participants and conducting cooperation on the basis of specialization. These associations may cut across different systems of ownership, economic departments, and administrative regions to form joint ventures or carry out joint business operations, the transfer of technology, and compensation trade. By the end of 1980 there were 3,300 such associations in China.

ECONOMIC BASE AND SUPERSTRUCTURE

经济基础和上层建筑 *(jingjijichu he shangcenjianzhu).*

In Marxist terminology, economic base refers to the totality of relations of production, relations which people enter into in the process of material production, and superstructure refers to the legal and political structure as well as the various forms of social consciousness arising from such an economic base. Marxism holds that while the superstructure is determined by the economic base, it nevertheless exerts much influence on the base.

ECONOMIC MEANS

经济办法 *(jingji banfa).*

These offer an antithesis to the administrative means of managing the economy and running enterprises. From a macroeconomic point of view, the economic means include pricing, taxes, bank loans and interests, and so on, which may be used as levers to adjust economic life and the major proportions of the economy. From a microeconomic point of view, that is, from the angle of running an enterprise, the economic means refer to the ways it shares its profits with the state, the source and distribution of payment for labor, the bonus system, and so on, all of which may be used to influence its economic performance.

ECONOMIC PATTERN (ECONOMIC STRUCTURE)

经济结构 *(jingji jiegou).*

An economic pattern or structure may generally be looked at from two standpoints: (1) the pattern or structure of ownership of means of production, such as the ratio between state-owned, collectively owned, and individual enterprises; and (2) the pattern or structure of the various branches of the national economy, including (a) the ratio between agriculture, light industry, and heavy industry, the internal ratio of each, and the ratio between industrial and agricultural production, communication and transportation, and commerce and the service trades; (b) the pattern of distribution, including the ratio between the consumption fund and the accumulation fund, and the distribution of each; (c) the pattern of exchange, including the pattern of commodity circulation, the price pattern, and the pattern of imports and exports; (d) the pattern of consumption, that is, the spending on different kinds of consumption; and (e) the technological pattern, that is, the ratio between automation, semi-automation, mechanization, semi-mechanization, and manual labor. The term may be applied to the national economy as a whole, to a certain department of the national economy, to the economy of a certain region, and to an individual enterprise.

ECONOMIC SECTOR UNDER STATE-PRIVATE (PUBLIC-PRIVATE) OPERATION

公私合营经济 *(gongsi heying jingji).*

In the 1950s private capitalist enterprises in China were turned into state-owned enterprises. The former capitalists were paid fixed interest proportionate to the amount of their capital, which severed their link with the economic performance of the enterprises. This constituted a form of state-capitalist economy.

EIGHT ECONOMIC-TECHNICAL NORMS

八项经济技术指标 *(baxiang jingji jishu zhibiao).*

These include (1) output, (2) variety of goods, (3) quality of goods, (4) rate of consumption of raw and processed materials, (5) labor productivity, (6) costs of goods, (7) profit earnings, and (8) the amount of working capital appropriated. They serve as the basis for judging the performance of an enterprise, showing how far it has fulfilled state targets.

ELEMENTARY AGRICULTURAL PRODUCERS' COOPERATIVES

初级农业生产合作社 *(chuji nongye shengchan hezuoshe).*

Called elementary co-ops for short, these were semi-socialist collective economic organizations formed on a voluntary basis by Chinese peasants in the early 1950s to develop agricultural production. The members pooled their land, draft animals, and farm implements for use in collective labor and drew income from the co-op on the basis of their labor contributions and shares in the means of production. Most of them were upgraded as fully socialist advanced co-ops in 1956.

ELEMENTS OF THE PRODUCTIVE FORCES

生产力诸要素 *(shengchanli zhu yaosu).*

The elements making up the productive forces—mainly the laborer, the tools (or means) of labor, and the objects of labor.

ENERGY PATTERN (ENERGY STRUCTURE)

能源结构 *(nengyuan jiegou).*

The energy makeup of a country. Coal has long been the principal source of energy in China, a situation that has not changed in spite of the increased production of oil and natural gas since the 1960s. In 1979, for example, the makeup of China's civil consumption of energy consisted of 80 percent coal, 10 percent electricity, 6 percent oil, and 4 percent gas.

ENLARGING THE DECISION-MAKING POWERS OF ENTERPRISES

扩大企业自主权 *(kuoda qiye zizhuquan).*

This is one of the main aspects of the present economic reform in China. Under the existing system of economic management, an enterprise has no right to handle its own affairs and can only take orders from higher authorities. This practice has been found to hamper enterprise initiative. Enlarging the powers of enterprises to make their own decisions means giving them more managerial powers, including powers in planning, production, capital construction, technology, procurement of supplies, finance, and the handling of the labor force.

ENTERPRISE

企业 *(qiye)*.

An economic unit engaged in production, circulation, or the provision of services. Enterprises in the People's Republic are classified, from different standpoints, into (1) large, medium-size, and small enterprises; (2) enterprises run by central authorities and those run by local authorities (provincial, municipal, and county enterprises), by people's communes and their subdivisions, and by street communities; (3) enterprises in industry, agriculture, the building trade, transportation, commerce, banking, and the service trades; and (4) enterprises under ownership by the whole people (state ownership), under collective ownership, under individual ownership, and under state capitalism.

ENTERPRISE FUND

企业基金 *(qiye jijin)*.

A fund derived by an enterprise from its profit, equivalent to a certain percentage of its payroll. It is generally used for collective welfare, farm and sideline undertakings, bonuses, and technical renovation. The percentage derived from the profit varies with the enterprise's performance in meeting state targets, and no such fund is granted in case of failure to attain some of the main targets, such as output, variety, quality, profit, and the provision of goods under contracts. The practice has proved useful in improving management and increasing worker enthusiasm.

EXTENDED REPRODUCTION

扩大再生产 *(kuoda zaishengchan)*.

Production carried out on an expanded scale. For the purpose of extended reproduction, society has to produce both the means of production and the means of subsistence required for the extension of the scale of production in addition to replenishing the regular amount of material means consumed in production from year to year.

FEUDAL ECONOMY

封建经济 *(fengjian jingji).*

Also called "landlord economy," in which landlords use their private landownership to appropriate rent from peasants without compensation.

FEUDAL LANDLORD CLASS

封建地主阶级 *(fengjian dizhu jieji).*

A class of people who own land, do not participate in labor or participate only in labor of a supplementary nature, and live by exploiting the peasants. In China the feudal landlord class, the ruling class in feudal society, was abolished in the course of the land reform during the Chinese People's War of Liberation (1945–49) and in the early 1950s.

FINAL PRODUCTS

最终产品 *(zuizhong chanping).*

As distinguished from intermediate products, these are the directly usable products which require no further processing. However, Chinese economists differ on the scope of final products. Some of them consider all means of consumption and part of the means of production, such as machinery and equipment, to be final products, while others limit them to products for consumption by individuals or communities.

FIVE-YEAR PLANS (FYPS)

五年计划 *(wunian jihua).*

The Five-Year Plans carried out by the government of the People's Republic of China for national economic development were as follows: First FYP (1953–57), Second FYP (1958–62), Third FYP (1966–70), Fourth FYP (1971–75), and Fifth FYP (1976–80). The years 1963–65 are referred to as a period of economic readjustment, which actually started in 1961. The Sixth FYP (1981–85) is now under way.

FIXED ASSETS

固定资产 *(guding zichan).*

This refers to means of labor belonging to enterprises and other economic organizations that can be used for a fairly long period of time without losing their material forms: factory buildings, machinery and equipment, transportation vehicles, and so on. Fixed assets are divided into productive and nonproductive assets. In Chinese bookkeeping practice, fixed assets are only those which have a use value lasting one year or more and a stipulated per unit value.

FLOATING PRICES

浮动价格 *(fudong jiage).*

A form of planned pricing by the socialist state, which permits the prices of some products to rise or fall within a certain range according to market supply and demand. The prices of some products, however, are permitted to float only downward. For example, the prices of some electronic components were floated downward in China as of August 1, 1979.

FOUR MODERNIZATIONS

四化 *(si hua).*

The modernization of agriculture, industry, national defense, and science and technology.

FUND FOR THE DEVELOPMENT OF PRODUCTION

生产发展基金 *(shengchan fazhan jijin).*

A fund established by a socialist enterprise under state regulations for the expansion of production. By these regulations, the enterprise retains a certain percentage of its profit earnings while handing over the rest to the state and sets aside a certain percentage of the retained earnings to establish the fund. Thus the size of the fund depends on the amount of profit. The fund must be used for major overhauls of the existing equipment before it can be spent on measures of technical renovation, including the purchase of new equipment and technology.

GIVING PRIORITY TO THE DEVELOPMENT OF HEAVY INDUSTRY AND TAK-
ING STEEL AS THE KEY LINK

优先发展重工业，以钢为纲 *(youxian fazhan zhonggongye, yigangweigang).*

The policy of economic development followed in China for many years, especially from 1958 onward. Supporters of this policy believed that the growth of the iron and steel industry would spur the growth of the coal, power, and other industries. The policy is being changed as more and more people recognize its one-sidedness.

"GREAT LEAP FORWARD"

大跃进 *(dayaojin).*

The rash movement launched in 1958 to achieve a super speed of national economic development. It called for increasing steel output from the 1957 figure of 5.35 million tons to 10.70 million tons within the year, and a doubling of grain output in many areas. Other industries and trades faced similar requirements. The unrealistic goals resulted in shoddy work and enormous loss and waste. The "Great Leap Forward" became an advance at great risks, an ultra-left mistake. Beginning in 1962, the lessons of the "Great Leap Forward" were initially reviewed, but for many years the mistake was not thoroughly corrected.

HANDICRAFT COOPERATIVES AND HANDICRAFT GROUPS

手工业合作社（组） *(shougongye hezuoshe, shougongye hezuozu).*

These refer to the forms of organization by which individual handicraft workers underwent socialist transformation in the early and mid-1950s. Handicraft cooperatives or groups practiced independent accounting based on the collective ownership of the means of production and were responsible for their own profits and losses. The income of a cooperative or group was distributed, after deductions for state tax and for accumulation and public welfare, in wages and dividends on labor contributions among its members.

HEAVY INDUSTRY

重工业 *(zhonggongye)*.

The general term for such industrial departments as the fuel, metallurgical, machine-building, power, building materials, and chemical industries that are engaged mainly in the production of the means of production (roughly equivalent to the capital goods in the West). Most heavy industrial products are used to meet production needs, but a small portion, such as electricity and coal, is also for everyday use.

HIGHLY CENTRALIZED SYSTEM OPERATED CHIEFLY BY ADMINISTRATIVE MEANS

高度集中，以行政管理为主的体制 *(gaodu jizhong, yixingzheng guanli weizhu de tizhi)*.

The system of economic management followed in China at present. It stresses unified leadership by the central authorities and economic management chiefly along administrative lines. The production and business operations of the enterprises are governed by mandatory state targets. Their products are purchased and marketed on a monopoly basis by state agencies in charge of commerce and the allocation of supplies. The state procures and distributes the supplies needed by the enterprises, takes over their income and pays for their expenses, sets the prices of goods, and handles the distribution of the labor force.

HIGHER PRICES FOR PURCHASES BEYOND STATE QUOTAS

超购加价 *(chaogou jiajia)*.

The prices paid for state purchases of agricultural and sideline products sold by production teams and peasants beyond the set quotas. The increased rates have been followed since summer grain was brought to the market in 1979.

HOUSEHOLD SIDELINE PRODUCTION

家庭副业 *(jiating fuye)*.

This applies to individual production undertaken by the urban and rural people in their spare time or by the nonworking members of the families in rural people's communes. These undertakings include the cultivation of private plots, the growing of fruit trees and bamboo in courtyards, the raising of livestock and poultry, household handicrafts like weaving and knitting, tailoring and sewing, as well as the gathering of fruits and berries, fishing, hunting, breeding of silkworms, and beekeeping.

HUSBAND-AND-WIFE SHOP (HUSBAND-AND-WIFE BOSS SHOP)

夫妻老婆店，夫妻老板店　　*(fuqi laopodian* or *fuqi laobandian).*

A small shop, service center, or processing shop where the workers include husband and wife only, or their children too. They are at once the owners, managers, salespeople, and attendants.

IDEAS OF A NATURAL ECONOMY

自然经济思想 *(ziran jingji sixiang).*

This refers to the economic ideas of self-sufficiency. Because of an underdeveloped commodity economy, the overwhelming majority of peasants in pre-Liberation China lived in a state of economic self-sufficiency or semi-self-sufficiency, which accounted for the prevalence of the ideas of a natural economy. Such ideas have found expression in socialist construction since Liberation, and some of the manifestations are a neglect of the social division of labor and cooperation, an aversion to commodity exchange, and a craze for self-sufficiency in a department, locality, or enterprise, combined with a reluctance to depend on others for certain resources or products. These ideas and the resulting practices do not suit the needs of large-scale socialized production.

INCOME FROM THE COLLECTIVE

从集体分得的收入 *(cong jiti fende de shouru).*

The incomes of members of a rural people's commune come from two sources: from their production team and from the private plots and household sideline productions (pig-raising, vegetable-growing, weaving and knitting) of their families. The income from the collective is generally the major source of income, distributed by the production team according to the quantity and quality of labor contributed by each commune member.

INDIVIDUAL ECONOMY

个体经济 *(geti jingji).*

The economy of individual peasants, independent handicraft workers, small businessmen, and peddlers, who own a limited amount of means of production and earn their living through their own labor. Their businesses are scattered and usually based in individual households. Back in 1956, most of such individuals were organized in cooperatives and other collective enterprises. During the Cultural Revolution nearly all the rest were absorbed into state or collective enterprises. Individual economy is now being restored to some extent under government protection and guidance to serve as a supplement to the economy under public ownership.

INDUSTRIAL LAYOUT

工业布局 *(gongye buju).*

The national or regional layout or distribution of industry. The industrial layout of old China was irrational in that the majority of the industries were in the coastal provinces or cities while hardly any modern industry could be found in the vast interior. The situation has been changed through thirty years of socialist construction.

INTEGRATION OF GOVERNMENT ADMINISTRATION WITH COMMUNE MANAGEMENT

政社合— *(zhengsheheyi).*

People's communes in China's rural areas are both organizations of political power and economic entities at the grass-roots level. In the current discussions on reforming the system of economic management, many of China's economic researchers and administrators have advocated separating the two, seeing this as a change conducive to running the economy by economic instead of administrative means. Some experiments in this vein are being carried out.

INTEGRATION OF GOVERNMENT ADMINISTRATION WITH ENTERPRISE MANAGEMENT OR WITH COMMUNE MANAGEMENT

政企不分，政社不分　*(zhengqi bufen, zhengshe bufen).*

The integration of government administration with enterprise management refers to the present system, under which the operations of an enterprise under ownership by the whole people are directed by government organizations, leaving little autonomy to the enterprise.

The integration of government administration with commune management refers to the present system under which a rural people's commune functions both as an economic entity and as a grass-roots governmental organization, again putting government organizations in direct control of the management of a collective.

Both systems affect independent management in an economic entity and hamper the drive and enthusiasm of its membership. From a long-term point of view, government administration will have to be separated from enterprise or commune management.

INTERMEDIATE PRODUCTS

中间产品 *(zhongjian chanpin).*

Products like timber, cotton yarn, and steel billets, needed for the manufacture of final products.

IRON RICE BOWL

铁饭碗 *(tie fanwan).*

In China every laborer taken on by an enterprise owned by the whole people has the security of knowing that he has a monthly paid and lifelong job, irrespective of performance or contribution. While job security is a good thing, this practice also discourages initiative among workers and staff members. In a broader sense, the "iron rice bowl" refers to the state taking full responsibility for all its enterprises irrespective of their performance—a major obstacle to economic progress.

ISSUANCE OF MONEY FOR FINANCIAL PURPOSES (FOR BUDGETARY REASONS)

财政性货币发行 *(caizhengxing huobi faxing).*

The issuing of extra money in case of a state budget deficit.

KEEPING ECONOMIC ACCOUNTS

算经济帐 *(suan jingji zhang).*

A reference to the need to conduct business accounting and evaluate economic results in socialist production and construction. Emphasis on the need was criticized under the influence of ultra-left thinking by those who favored "keeping political accounts" (stressing political considerations).

KEEPING POLITICAL ACCOUNTS

算政治帐 *(suan zhengzhi zhang).*

Used in contrast to "keeping economic accounts," the term refers to evaluating national economic development by political needs and not by economic results, a practice which caused great losses to China's economy.

LABOR PRODUCTIVITY

劳动生产率 *(laodong shengchanlü).*

The output value or the net output value per laborer:

$$\text{labor productivity} = \frac{\text{year's gross output value}}{\text{number of laborers}}$$

or

$$\text{labor productivity} = \frac{\text{year's national income (net output value)}}{\text{number of laborers}}$$

LAND REFORM

土地改革 *(tudi gaige).*

A revolutionary movement in which the peasants, led by the Chinese Communist Party, abolished feudal landownership and realized Dr. Sun Yat-sen's slogan of "land to the tiller." Land reform was carried out in

China's liberated areas during the War of Liberation (1945–49). After the founding of the People's Republic in 1949, the Central People's Government issued the Land Reform Law of the People's Republic of China, which was followed by a land reform throughout the country. During the movement, 700 million *mu* (117 million acres) of land were distributed to 300 million peasants, who were thus freed from payment of 35 million tons of grain in rent to the landlords each year. The movement thoroughly destroyed the feudal system of exploitation.

"LARGE AND ALL-INCLUSIVE" AND "SMALL BUT ALL-INCLUSIVE" ECONOMIC UNITS

"大而全","小而全" 的经济单位 *("daerquan," "xiaoerquan" de jingji danwei).*

A reference to the big and small enterprises of a self-sufficient nature that have appeared in China because of a lack of industrial cooperation based on specialization. Each of these enterprises completes all the main production processes by itself and consequently suffers from low efficiency and poor economic performance. This situation is being changed through the establishment of specialized companies and the readjustment of the lines of production on the principle of specialization and cooperation.

"LARGER SIZE AND A HIGHER DEGREE OF PUBLIC OWNERSHIP"

"一大二公" *(yi da er gong).*

This summarizes the characteristics of the rural people's communes set up in 1958. "Larger in size" means a people's commune is much larger than the previous agricultural producers' cooperative. For example, the average number of households in the original cooperative was only 159, while that in a people's commune in 1958 was 4,637, over twenty-eight times as many. "A higher degree of public ownership" means that a people's commune, compared to a cooperative, has some elements of ownership by the whole people as well as collective ownership at the commune level. Experience over the past twenty years and more has proved that the people's communes with "a larger size and a higher degree of public ownership" promoted in 1958 were not in keeping with the level of productive forces in China's countryside and represented a premature advance and a "Left" error.

LAW OF VALUE

价值规律 *(jiazhi guilu)*.

The law of value means that the value of a commodity is determined by the socially necessary labor time required to produce it and that the exchange of commodities must be based on an exchange of equal amounts of value. Socially necessary labor time refers to the labor time needed to produce a certain kind of use value under the normal conditions of social production at a given time, at an average degree of labor skill and intensity.

The law of value is the basic law of a commodity economy and operates wherever commodity production exists.

Under the capitalist system, the law of value spontaneously regulates the production and circulation of commodities irrespective of the will of the producer. While the law of value continues to function in a socialist society because of the continued existence of commodity production, it no longer plays a spontaneous role as in a capitalist society. Instead, it is often consciously utilized by the state for the benefit of socialist construction.

While organizing and administering the socialist economy according to plan, the socialist state should act according to the objective economic laws, including the law of value, establish a rational price system, properly regulate the supply and demand of various commodities, and see to a reasonable distribution of human and material resources among the various departments of production. While strictly enforcing a planned regulation of the national economy as a whole, it should also regulate the economy through the market mechanism with respect to the activities of the enterprises, so that they can gear production to social demand and improve their economic performance.

"LEFT" (ULTRA-LEFT) EXPERIENCE OF DAZHAI

大寨的左倾 "经验" *(dazhai de zuoqing jingyan)*.

The ultra-left practices developed by the Dazhai production brigade in Xiyang County, Shanxi Province, after it was publicized as a pacesetter on the agricultural front. It banned the cultivation of private plots by members as well as their household sidelines; introduced "political work points" (work points granted according to one's political attitude) and negated the principle of "to each according to his work" in income distribution; and frequently launched criticism and struggle by exaggerating differences within the ranks of the people as a matter of conflict with the class enemy.

"LEFT" (ULTRA-LEFT) MISTAKE

左倾错误 *(zuoqing cuowu).*

A mistake characterized by rashness, adventurism, or an overzealous attempt to achieve success. Ideologically, it is interpreted as a utopian departure from objective reality at a given stage of development, from the lives and aspirations of the great majority of people.

LIGHT INDUSTRY

轻工业 *(qinggongye).*

The general term used for the industrial departments that make consumer goods, such as the textile, foodstuffs, leather, paper, clock, and watch-making industries, as well as industries producing articles used in the fields of culture, art, education, and sports. Most light industrial products meet consumer needs, but some products, such as textiles and paper, are also for industrial use.

LONG-OVERDUE IMPROVEMENTS IN PEOPLE'S LIVELIHOOD

生活方面的欠帐   *(shenghuo fangmian de qianzhang).*

The phrase, which literally means "debts owed (to the people) with respect to (their) livelihood," refers to the fact that improvements in people's livelihood were delayed during the Cultural Revolution of 1966–76. Under ultra-left guidelines, the state set aside too much money for accumulation, reduced the allocations for people's consumption, effected no rise in the average wage level, and built little housing. The government started to solve these problems after the collapse of the Gang of Four in 1976.

MACROECONOMICS

宏观经济 *(hongguan jingji).*

Activities involving the entire national economy, including the orientation and speed of development of the national economy, changes in the industrial pattern, the distribution of the national income between accumulation and consumption, the total amount of investment, major capital investments, the general price level, the pricing of major products, and so on.

MANDATORY PLAN TARGETS

指令性计划指标 *(zhilingxing jihua zhibiao).*

The economic-technical targets which the socialist state requires its enterprises to fulfill, including targets for output, quality, profit, and so on.

MARKET MECHANISM

市场机制 *(shichang jizhi).*

The process or mode by which enterprises and individuals carry out economic activities on the basis of information provided by the market. The market mechanism is capable of balancing production and demand by its automatic regulation of what is produced or purchased by enterprises and individuals and how much.

MEANS OF PRODUCTION

生产资料 *(shengchan ziliao).*

This refers to the means and object of labor, including production tools, machinery and equipment, factory buildings, land, and raw materials.

MEANS OF SUBSISTENCE

生活资料 *(shenghuo ziliao).*

Products for consumption in people's everyday life, such as food, clothing, radio and television sets, and bicycles.

MEDIUM-TERM AND LONG-TERM PLANS

中长期计划 *(zhongchangqi jihua).*

Plans for the development of the national economy covering more than one year, such as a five-year or ten-year plan.

MERGING OF FACTORIES AND COOPERATIVES FOR THE PURPOSE OF TRANSITION TO HIGHER FORMS OF PUBLIC OWNERSHIP

联厂并社，升级过渡 *(lianchang bingshe, shengji guodu).*

This refers to the policy (now considered erroneous) carried out in 1958 and thereafter toward the handicraft cooperatives which pushed them into larger sizes and to higher degrees of public ownership. Under this "Left" policy, the handicraft cooperatives or groups were merged into cooperative factories and the collectively owned enterprises were changed to larger ones and finally to enterprises under ownership by the whole people. Members of these collectively owned enterprises were denied the right to draw dividends on the basis of their labor contributions. These enterprises were also required to adopt the managerial system of those owned by the whole people. All this damaged productivity. The policy gradually lost its influence following the issuance of the "Thirty-Five Articles Concerning the Handicraft Industry" in 1961.

METAPHYSICS

形而上学 *(xinger shangxue).*

As opposed to dialectics, metaphysics views natural and social phenomena, including economic phenomena, as unconnected, static, and unchangeable.

MICROECONOMICS

微观经济 *(weiguan jingji).*

The economic activities within an enterprise, including the line and amount of production, the choice and source of raw materials, sales prospects, overhauls, small-scale investment, payment of wages, makeup of the personnel, and so on.

MIDDLE PEASANTS

中农 *(zhongnong).*

The section of peasantry lying between rich peasants and poor peasants before the socialist transformation in the countryside. Being the rural petty-bourgeoisie, they owned land and a fair number of farm tools and derived their income totally or mainly from their own labor. Generally speaking, they did not exploit others or sell their labor power.

MULTILAYER RELATIONS OF PRODUCTION

多层次的生产关系 *(duo cengci de shengchan guanxi).*

The different layers of relations of production arising from different levels of development of productive forces in a society. In China, apart from the dominant socialist relations of production representing a relatively higher level of productivity, there are other types of relations of production, such as the individual economy representing a lower level of productivity.

MULTIPLE ECONOMIC SECTORS

多种经济成份 *(duozhong jingji chengfen).*

The various economic sectors, instead of one, existing in a socialist country. In China the economic sectors under ownership by the whole people and collective ownership are accompanied by individual economy and state-capitalist economy.

NATIONAL INCOME

国民收入 *(guomin shouru).*

The total produced by workers in a country over a period of time, usually a year. In the sense of value, it means the total output value produced minus the value of the means of production consumed in the process of production. In a material sense it means the total output (including means of production and means of subsistence) produced minus the means of production expended.

NATURAL ADVANTAGES

自然优势 *(ziran youshi).*

The advantages of the environment and resources in a locality over other localities. China's Hainan Island, for example, is a superior place for growing tropical crops; the soil and climate of Jiangsu, Shandong, and Hebei provinces are suitable for cotton planting; the sandy soil of Shandong Province is good for growing peanuts; and Shanxi Province is ideal for the development of the coal industry because of its rich coal seams.

NEGOTIATED PURCHASE

议购 *(yigou).*

Purchase of farm and sideline products conducted by state commercial agencies through negotiation with producers. The products are either not covered by state plans or are sold by producers after fulfilling state purchase quotas. Prices for negotiated purchases are generally higher than those for regular state purchases.

NONPRODUCTIVE ACCUMULATION

非生产性积累 *(fei shengchanxing jilei).*

The accumulation of fixed assets built up through nonproductive construction, such as housing, schools, hospitals, cultural facilities, and office buildings.

NONPRODUCTIVE CONSTRUCTION ("THE FLESH")

非生产性建设（"肉"）   *(fei shengchanxing jianshe or "rou").*

Capital construction of facilities for people's livelihood, including housing, schools, hospitals, theaters, cultural centers, office buildings, buildings for people's organizations, and so on.

OVERALL BALANCE

综合平衡 *(zonghe pingheng).*

The basic approach to the management of the national economy through state planning. It covers the balance of the state budget, of bank credits, of supply and demand, and of international payments.

OVERSUPPLIED PRODUCTS

长线产品 *(changxian chanpin).*

Products that have been oversupplied for a relatively long period of time.

PATTERN (STRUCTURE) OF AGRICULTURAL PRODUCTION

农业生产结构 *(nongye shengchan jiegou).*

This refers mainly to the lineup of products and the regional makeup in agriculture, which includes farming, forestry, animal husbandry, sideline production, and fishery. Farming is again divided into grain-crop farming and cash-crop farming. The proportions between these different sectors constitute the pattern or structure of agricultural production.

PATTERN (STRUCTURE) OF CIRCULATION

流通结构 *(liutong jiegou).*

The various forms of circulation in a society. The two dominant forms of circulation in China today are state-run commerce and commerce run by the supply and marketing cooperatives. These are supplemented by some country market (free market) trade and commercial undertakings by individuals.

PATTERN (STRUCTURE) OF COMMODITIES

商品结构 *(shangpin jiegou).*

The makeup of commodities, as shown in the proportion of daily necessities in the total volume of retail sales; the proportion between the means of production and consumer goods in import commodities; and the proportions of industrial and mineral products, agricultural and sideline produce, processed goods, and so on, in export commodities.

PATTERN (STRUCTURE) OF CONSUMPTION

消费结构 *(xiaofei jiegou).*

This refers generally to comparative consumer spending—or to the percentages of money spent by people on food, clothing, shelter, transportation, and other basic necessities of life. For example, food makes up 50 percent of consumer spending in China. Food can also be further divided into staple and nonstaple food. Sometimes the term refers to both individual and social spending on consumption.

PATTERN (STRUCTURE) OF HEAVY INDUSTRY

重工业结构 *(zhonggongye jiegou).*

The ratio between the various industries—such as the raw materials, processing, energy, machine-building, and communications and transportation industries—that make up heavy industry. One of the problems in the pattern of China's heavy industry is a lopsided development of the processing industries in separation from the development of the raw materials industries, and an insufficient development of the energy industries and communications and transportation. Readjustment of the pattern of heavy industry is one of the tasks of the current economic readjustment.

PATTERN (STRUCTURE) OF INVESTMENT

投资结构 *(touzi jiegou).*

The makeup of capital construction investment, including the investment ratio between productive and nonproductive construction; between agriculture, light industry, and heavy industry; between the various departments of the national economy; and between the different localities. China's pattern of investment is being changed in the current economic readjustment to speed up the development of agriculture and production of consumer goods.

PATTERN (STRUCTURE) OF OWNERSHIP

所有制结构 *(suoyouzhi jiegou).*

Corresponding to the pattern of relations of production, this refers to the different kinds of ownership in a society. Apart from the dominant systems of ownership by the whole people and by collectives, China also has a smattering of individual ownership and state capitalism.

THE PATTERN (STRUCTURE) OF PRODUCTION DETERMINES THE PATTERN
(STRUCTURE) OF DISTRIBUTION

生产结构决定分配结构 *(sheng chan jiegou jueding fenpei jiegou).*

This is a principle of Marxist economics. From a macroeconomic point
of view, if the production of the means of production develops much faster
than the production of the means of subsistence, the percentage of accumulation consisting mainly of the means of production in the national income
inevitably increases, and the percentage of consumption has to decrease. On
the other hand, the pattern of distribution also reacts on the pattern of
production. Thus a change in the pattern of distribution serves as an important means of readjusting the proportions of production. A cut in the investment in capital construction (for accumulation, for example) can save raw
materials, fuel, and transportation facilities for a faster development of the
production of consumer goods.

PATTERN (STRUCTURE) OF PRODUCTIVE FORCES

生产力结构 *(shengchanli jiegou).*

The pattern (structure) of social productive forces may be viewed from
different angles: the industrial pattern (the types of industries carrying on
social production); the technological pattern (the types of technology used
in social production); the pattern of products (the major types of products);
and the regional pattern (the geographical distribution of productive capacities).

PATTERN (STRUCTURE) OF RELATIONS OF PRODUCTION

生产关系结构 *(shengchan guanxi jiegou).*

The different types of relations of production in a society. The dominant
type in China is the socialist relations of production, including those based
on ownership by the whole people and those based on collective ownership.
In addition, there are also the relations peculiar to individual economy and
state capitalism, which have been preserved on a small scale.

PAYMENT ACCORDING TO LABOR CONTRIBUTIONS

按劳分红 *(anlao fenhong)*.

A form of income distribution in the economic sector under collective ownership. After deducting for taxes, production costs, and public accumulation and welfare funds, a collective distributes income among its members according to work points earned for the quantity and quality of labor rather than by a fixed wage scale.

PAYMENT OF TAX IN PLACE OF THE HANDING OVER OF PROFIT (BY AN ENTERPRISE), (ITS) INDEPENDENT ACCOUNTING, (AND ITS) RESPONSIBILITY FOR (ITS) PROFITS AND LOSSES

以税代利，独立核算，自负盈亏   *(yishui daili, duli hesuan, zifu yingkui)*.

In this experimental reform of China's system of economic management, an enterprise may pay tax to the state instead of turning over all its profits to the latter, and thus conduct independent accounting and assume sole responsibility for its profits and losses. This is an attempt to change the present situation in which the state bears all financial responsibility for an enterprise, which accounts for the phenomenon of everybody "eating from the same big pot." The reform aims at strengthening the economic responsibility of each enterprise and establishing a closer connection between its economic performance and the interests of its members.

PAYMENT ON LAND SHARES

土地参加分红 *(tudi canjia fenhong)*.

A form of income distribution in the elementary agricultural producers' cooperatives during the 1950s. Peasants who joined the cooperatives pooled their land as shares in public property. After deducting the agricultural tax, production costs, and public accumulation and welfare funds, a cooperative would divide the rest of its income into two parts to be distributed among members, one part distributed on the basis of the labor the members contributed, the other part on the basis of the quantity and quality of the land they had pooled plus the draft animals and farm tools they had put in.

PERIOD OF ECONOMIC READJUSTMENT IN THE 1960s

六十年代调整时期 *(liushi niandai tiaozheng shiqi).*

To correct serious imbalances in the national economy, the Party Central Committee put forward the policy of readjustment, consolidation, filling out, and raising standards. It decided to cut back on the output quotas of heavy industry and the scale of capital construction. To replenish rural labor force, it sent back to the countryside 20 million workers out of the 25 million recruited from there during the 1958 "Great Leap Forward." The economy began to take a turn for the better in 1962. The period between 1961 and 1965 came to be known as a "readjustment period" in new China's economic history.

PILOT ENTERPRISES (ENTERPRISES IN THE NATURE OF "EXPERIMENTAL PLOTS")

"试验田"性质的企业 *("shiyantian" xingzhide qiye).*

Enterprises where experiments are being carried out in the reform of the system of economic management, such as exercising greater power in decision-making, and assuming financial responsibility for profits and losses. They are likened to "experimental plots," where new farming techniques are tried out in the countryside.

PLANNED ECONOMY

计划经济 *(jihua jingji).*

Planned economy, a basic feature of socialist society, is a system of economic management based on public ownership of the means of production. Considering objective economic laws and the special features of the country, the socialist state works out the proportionate relationships between various branches of the national economy and sees to a rational distribution of production forces to meet the rising requirements of the people.

PLANNED PROCUREMENT AND ALLOCATION

计划调拨 *(jihua diaobo).*

The distribution and transfer of supplies among enterprises, or between enterprises and state agencies in charge of supplies, under unified state planning.

POOR PEASANT

贫农 *(pinnong).*

The poor peasants were the rural semi-proletariat in old China. They owned a few farm implements and little or no land. As a rule, they were exploited by landlords from whom they had to rent land. Often they had to work as hired laborers to supplement their income, and they were also exploited by usurers.

PRICE DIFFERENCES IN THE EXCHANGE OF AGRICULTURAL AND INDUSTRIAL PRODUCTS

工农产品交换的差价 *(gongnong chanpin jiaohuande chajia).*

The irrational price parities between industrial products (which are priced too high) and agricultural produce (which are priced too low) in the exchange of the one for the other.

PRICE SUBSIDY FOR NONSTAPLE FOOD

副食品价格补贴　*(fushipin jiage butie).*

The State Council, at the suggestion of the Third Plenary Session of the Eleventh Central Committee of the Communist Party of China, decided to raise the purchasing prices of some agricultural and sideline products beginning in 1979 and to raise correspondingly the selling prices of some nonstaple foods (meat, eggs, milk, etc.). This was done to rationalize gradually the price parities between industrial and agricultural products, improve the peasants' standard of living, and encourage production in agriculture. To prevent a drop in the living standard of the urban population, the State Council also decided to give each industrial or office worker, beginning in November 1979, a price subsidy of five yuan per month, in addition to the monthly salary.

PRINCIPAL PROPORTIONS (RELATIONSHIPS OF PRINCIPAL PROPORTIONS)

主要比例关系 *(zhuyao bili guanxi).*

The proportions between the two major departments of the national economy (production of the means of production and production of the means of consumption), between agriculture, light industry, and heavy industry, and between accumulation and consumption.

PRIVATE PLOT

自留地 *(ziliudi)*.

The small plot of land distributed to a peasant for private cultivation after the collectivization of agriculture. Originally set at no more than 5 percent of the per capita average of cultivated land in a given collective, the private plot allotment has gone up in recent years to 15 percent under flexible policies. In terms of ownership, the private plot belongs to the collective but may be used permanently by the commune peasant and his family, who own its products. The cultivation of private plots is a household sideline occupation which provides supplementary income for commune members. In the mountainous or pastoral areas, the commune members also have private livestock.

PRODUCTION BRIGADE

生产大队 *(shengchan dadui)*.

The intermediate organization in a three-level rural people's commune. A brigade usually comprises several production teams. The brigade management committee, under the leadership of the people's commune committee, takes care of the brigade's production and construction, the procurement of supplies, and the marketing of goods, some credit business, and enterprises of the brigades. In a small number of communes, the brigade and not the production team serves as the basic accounting unit.

PRODUCTION TEAM

生产队 *(shengchan dui)*.

The basic organization in a three-level rural people's commune. With some thirty families, a production team conducts independent accounting, assumes responsibility for its profits and losses, and handles production and income distribution. It has the right to manage its land, forests, meadows, water resources, farm implements, and machinery. It is usually the basic accounting unit in a people's commune.

PRODUCTIVE ACCUMULATION

生产性积累 *(shengchanxing jilei).*

The accumulation of fixed assets built up through productive construction, such as the factory buildings, warehouses, machinery and equipment, railroads, highways, ports, and docks.

PRODUCTIVE CONSTRUCTION ("THE BONES")

生产性建设（ "骨头" ）   *(shengchanxing jianshe or "gutou").*

Capital construction in which investments are made in factory buildings and machinery and equipment. Fixed assets built up in the sphere of circulation (transportation, commerce, etc.), such as railroads, highways, ports, docks, motor vehicles, ships, warehouses, and other equipment, also come under this category according to Chinese government stipulations.

PRODUCTIVE FORCES

生产力 *(shengchanli).*

Also called "social productive forces" or "material forces of production," productive forces refer to man's ability to conquer or control nature, to produce the material means of life. Reflecting the relationship between man and nature, productive forces consist of the means of labor, the objects of labor, and the laborers engaged in the production of the material means of life. They form one aspect of the mode of social production, the other aspect being the relations of production.

PROFIT RETENTION SYSTEM

利润留成制度 *(lirun liucheng zhidu).*

A system whereby a state enterprise retains part of its profit earnings instead of turning over practically all of them to the state. Until late 1978, the funds and expenses of all state enterprises for trial-producing new products, carrying on scientific research, training workers and technicians, and allotting collective well-being funds and bonuses were allocated by higher authorities or registered as production costs paid by the latter in fixed quotas. Now these funds and expenses are paid, in the case of some state enterprises, from the profits they are entitled to keep for their own use.

This practice links the interests of the enterprises with their business performance and strengthens their sense of economic responsibility. It is basic to the current experiments in allowing enterprises more power in handling their affairs.

PROPORTIONATE DEVELOPMENT OF THE NATIONAL ECONOMY

国民经济按比例发展 *(guomin jingji an bilifazhan).*

The proportionate development of the national economy (which refers to all the economic activities of a nation, including production, distribution, exchange, and consumption, and to all its economic departments, including industry, agriculture, commerce, communications and transportation, and so on) means that the various departments and links of the national economy should be developed in proportion to one another. For this purpose, it is crucial to ensure a balanced distribution of the means of production and the labor force among these departments and links. Any social production based on a division of labor requires a proportionate distribution of the means of production and the labor force among different departments of the national economy. Failure to achieve such a balanced distribution would result in a disproportionate development of social production and a waste of human, material, and financial resources.

Under capitalism, where the means of production are owned by the capitalists, the lines and amounts of production are determined by market prices and profitability; consequently, a proportionate distribution of the means of production and the labor force among various departments and links of the national economy is realized through the spontaneous operation of the law of value, that is, through competition, the anarchic state of production, and periodic economic crises.

Under socialism, where the means of production are publicly owned and the economy is a planned one, the state can work out plans suitable to the economic development of the various departments, make use of the market mechanism to achieve a rational distribution of the means of production and the labor force among these departments, and ensure a proportionate development of the national economy, avoiding the blindness and spontaneity found in capitalistic development. Thus a planned and proportionate development of the national economy can only be realized under socialism.

PROVISIONAL MUTUAL-AIM TEAM

临时互助组 *(lingshi huzhuzu).*

A collective labor organization, containing rudiments of socialism, formed by individual peasants in the early 1950s to help each other during busy seasons.

PUBLIC OWNERSHIP OF THE MEANS OF PRODUCTION

生产资料公有制 *(shengchanziliao gongyouzhi).*

Under socialism the two basic forms of public ownership of the means of production are ownership by the whole people and collective ownership. The means of production under ownership by the whole people belong to the proletarian state, the representative of the working people as a whole, and are controlled and used by enterprises. The means of production under collective ownership belong to workers' collectives, large or small, and are controlled by these collectives.

RATION SYSTEM

配给制 *(peijizhi).*

Equal distribution of goods in limited quotas at times when the supply of these goods cannot fully satisfy consumers' needs.

READJUSTMENT, CONSOLIDATION, FILLING OUT, AND RAISING STANDARDS

调整、巩固、充实、提高 *(tiaozhen, gonggu, chongshi, tigao).*

The policy adopted by the Central Committee of the Chinese Communist Party in 1961 to correct the ultra-left mistakes committed during the "Great Leap Forward" in 1958.

Readjustment means remedying the imbalances in the national economy by cutting down the overextended scale of capital construction and giving more attention to agricultural development.

Consolidation means consolidating the gains in national economic development.

Filling out means enabling some of the enterprises set up during the "Great Leap Forward" to start working by giving them a little more investment for building the infrastructure and buying ancillary equipment.

Raising standards means improving the quality of products, managerial skill,, and economic results.

REGISTRATION OF WORK POINTS BY WORK DAYS COMBINED WITH PERIODIC APPRAISAL

按时计工分加评议 *(anshi jigongfen jia pingyi).*

A system of labor management and income distribution practiced in China's rural people's communes for a long period of time. By this system, the basic number of work points for each work day contributed by a peasant is fixed according to his physical condition and labor skill and may be modified through periodic discussions among workmates, with reference to the difficulty of the work and the conscientiousness of the worker. The total number of work points registered under the name of a peasant in a year serves as the basis of his annual income from the collective. This practice is being replaced by the various forms of the system of responsibility in farm production.

REGULATION THROUGH PLANNING

计划调节 *(jihua tiaojie).*

The basic way by which the socialist state administers the national economy. Through its planning, the state seeks a balanced development of the economy by working out its major proportions (those between agriculture, light industry, and heavy industry, and those between consumption and accumulation) and by arranging the production and exchange of products vital to national economic life. In China, regulation of the economy through state planning is being supplemented by utilization of the market mechanism.

REGULATION (OF THE ECONOMY) THROUGH THE MARKET UNDER THE GUIDANCE OF (STATE) PLANS

计划指导下的市场调节 *(jihua zhidao xia de shichang tiaojie).*

The regulation or adjustment of part of the economic activities of enterprises and individuals by utilizing the market mechanism in a planned economy. The practice gives enterprises and individuals some options in making their own decisions, while the state directs their economic activities into the orbit of a planned national economic development by using such economic levers as supply and demand, pricing, cost, profit, credit and interest, and taxation. Chinese economic researchers and administrators differ in their understanding of the concept, and the practice is only beginning.

RELATIONSHIP AMONG AGRICULTURE, LIGHT INDUSTRY, AND HEAVY INDUSTRY

农、轻、重关系 *(nongqingzhong guanxi).*

Relationship by which agriculture, light industry, and heavy industry support and condition one another. The proportions among them are the most important ones in the national economy.

RELATIONS OF PRODUCTION

生产关系 *(shengchan guanxi).*

The relations formed by people as they work to turn out material products. Since production is a social undertaking that cannot be carried out by a single individual, people must enter into certain kinds of relationships with one another and exchange their activities if they want to go in for production. The relations of production in a socialist country are characterized by public ownership of the means of production and the absence of exploitation.

REPRODUCTION

再生产 *(zaishengchan).*

The continuous cycle of production in any society.

RESPONSIBILITY FOR ONE'S PROFITS AND LOSSES

自负盈亏 *(zifu yingkui).*

A system under which an economic organization assumes full responsibility for its profits and losses, linking its economic performance with the interests of the workers and staff. This principle applies differently to state enterprises and collective ones. In a collective enterprise, since the means of production are owned by the collective, the accumulation fund of the enterprise and the personal income of the members vary with the results of its undertakings apart from payment of state tax. In a state enterprise, since the means of production belong to the whole people, the profits or losses depend on contributions to the state. The greater the contributions, the more profit it may retain for the expansion of production, collective welfare, and workers' bonus. A state enterprise is economically accountable to the state in case of losses.

ROAD OF COLLECTIVIZATION

集体化道路 *(jitihua daolu)*.

The course by which individual peasants and handicraft workers form cooperatives to conduct collective production and strive for common prosperity. The process was basically completed in late 1956 and early 1957.

RURAL PEOPLE'S COMMUNE

农村人民公社 *(nongcun renmin gongshe)*.

A socialist economic organization under collective ownership by rural working people. The people's communes were set up in 1958 through the amalgamation of advanced agricultural producers' cooperatives. at present, most communes are based on a three-level ownership of the means of production: ownership by the commune, the production brigades, and the production teams, with the production teams as the basic accounting units. The economic organizations at all three levels have the right to handle their own production, and they follow the principles of "from each according to his ability, to each according to his work," mutual benefit and voluntariness, and exchange of equal values. Commune members may cultivate small private plots for their own needs and engage in household sidelines. The communes are also government administrative organizations at the grass-roots level in rural China.

SCIENTIFIC SOCIALISM

科学社会主义 *(kexue shehuizhuyi)*.

The socialism defined by Karl Marx and Friederich Engels, as distinguished from the schools of feudal and petty bourgeois socialism. It is characterized by public ownership of the means of production and the principle of "to each according to his work" in the sphere of distribution.

SELF-SUFFICIENT SMALL PEASANT ECONOMY

自给自足的小农经济   *(zigeizizude xiaonongjingji).*

The economy of the owner-peasants (small holders), where each household is a production unit and the scale of production is very small. The products satisfy household needs and are generally not for sale.

SERIOUS IMBALANCES (DISPROPORTIONS) IN THE NATIONAL ECONOMY

国民经济比例关系严重失调   *(guominjingji biliguanxi yanzhongshitiao).*

The serious imbalances in China's economy refer mainly to (1) the overextended scale of capital construction and excessive rate of accumulation, which made it difficult to raise the people's living standard and strained the nation's financial and material resources; (2) the high growth rate of heavy industry and the slow growth rates of light industry and agriculture, accompanied by an irrational industrial pattern; and (3) the fast growth of the processing industries within heavy industry, unmatched by the supply of raw materials, fuel, and power and the imbalance between extraction and drilling or tunneling in the energy industries.

SHARING THE ENTIRE PROFIT

全额利润分成   *(quan'e lirun fencheng).*

A system developed in the current economic reform by which an enterprise shares the entire amount of its profit earnings with the state on the condition of fulfillment of all state targets. Part of the profit goes to the state treasury, while a certain percentage is kept by the enterprise to establish a production expansion fund, a collective welfare fund, and a workers' bonus fund.

SHARING THE EXTRA PROFIT

超额利润分成   *(chao'e lirun fencheng).*

A system developed in the current economic reform by which an enterprise gets part of its earnings over and above the profit norm set by the state. On the condition of fulfilling all state targets, it turns over part of this extra profit to state finance and keeps the rest for its own use as a production expansion fund, a collective welfare fund, and a workers' bonus fund.

SIMPLE REPRODUCTION

简单再生产 *(jiandan zaizhengchan)*.

The cycle of production carried out on the original scale by which no accumulation is created and the same want is satisfied through the provision of the same amount of products from year to year.

SMALL PRODUCER

小生产者 *(xiaoshengchanzhe)*.

A producer who owns his means of production individually and takes part in labor. The term usually refers to individual peasants or handicraft workers. Most small producers in China have taken the road of cooperation in the course of socialist transformation.

SOCIALIST ECONOMY

社会主义经济 *(shehuizhuyi jingji)*.

An economy based on public ownership of the means of production and on the principle of "to each according to his work." It consists of an economic sector under ownership by the whole people and an economic sector under collective ownership.

SOCIALIST PUBLIC OWNERSHIP, SOCIALIST OWNERSHIP

社会主义公有制，社会主义所有制 *(shehuizhuyi gongyouzhi, shehuizhuyi suoyouzhi)*.

The public ownership of the means of production by the working people. The principal form of such public ownership is ownership of the means of production by the entire working people. Another form of public ownership is ownership of a certain part of society's means of production by a group of working people or a collective. Socialist public ownership precludes the possibility of any social group's using its ownership of the means of production to exploit the labor of another group and determines the distribution of social products according to work—more goes to those who work more, less to those who work less, and nothing to those who refuse to work.

SOCIALIST TRANSFORMATION

社会主义改造 *(shehuizhuyi gaizao).*

This refers to the historical task, basically fulfilled by late 1956 and early 1957, to change to socialist ownership the three private sectors of the economy: the individual economy in agriculture, the individual economy in the handicrafts, and capitalist industry and commerce. In the course of this transformation, the peasants and handicraft workers gradually joined agricultural producers' cooperatives and handicraft cooperatives. Capitalist industrial and commercial enterprises were changed, by a state policy of redemption, to enterprises owned by the whole people through the medium of state capitalism.

STATE-CAPITALIST ECONOMY

国家资本主义经济 *(guojia zibenzhuyi jingji).*

The capitalist sector of the economy with state participation or under state leadership. It refers generally to joint state-private enterprises and joint ventures formed by state authorities with foreign businesses.

STATE ECONOMY

国营经济 *(guoying jingji).*

The economic sector consisting of enterprises owned and operated by the socialist state, which are also referred to as enterprises under ownership by the whole people.

STATE FARM

国营农场 *(guoying nongchang).*

An agricultural enterprise under ownership by the whole people. The socialist state owns all the means of production on the farm, such as land, machinery, farm tools, draft animals, and buildings for use in production, and controls all the products. The workers and staff members get paid in wages. The state farm plays an important role in trying out and spreading modern agricultural techniques and managerial skill. There were 2,093 state farms in China by the end of 1980.

STATE INVESTMENT AND SELF-PROVIDED INVESTMENT

国家投资和自筹投资 *(guojia touzi he zichou touzi)*.

As two different types of investment in China's capital construction, the former refers to investment by allocations from the state budget, while the latter comes from a variety of other sources—it may be provided by local authorities, enterprises, people's communes, and other economic collectives. According to state regulations, the second type of investment may be derived by plan from budgetary surpluses of local governments and funds for use at their discretion; surtaxes on industry, commerce, and public utilities; the rent income on public housing; and funds recently established by some state enterprises from the profit earnings they have been allowed to retain.

STATE MONOPOLY PURCHASING PRICE FOR GRAIN

粮食统购价格 *(liangshi tonggou jiage)*.

In China the state exercises a monopoly, through its purchasing plan, over the purchase and marketing of principal agricultural produce like grain, edible oils, and cotton. The purchasing prices for agricultural produce are based on historical and current price parities between industrial and agricultural products. While setting these prices, the state also takes into consideration such factors as the cost of agricultural production, the income level of the peasants, state accumulation, effects on the cost of industrial production, and the stability of market prices. Since Liberation, China has made several adjustments in the pricing of agricultural products to reduce the unreasonable price parities between industrial and agricultural products left over by history. In 1957 the prices of agricultural produce were raised by 20.2 percent, compared to those of 1952, while the retail prices for industrial products during the same period went up only 2.2 percent. Beginning with the summer harvest in 1979, the purchasing prices for grain were raised by 20.0 percent and those for purchases beyond state quotas were set at 50.0 percent over the increased prices. These measures have stimulated agricultural production.

STRENGTHENING THE PARTY IDEOLOGICALLY AND ORGANIZATIONALLY

党的思想建设和组织建设 *(dangde sixiangjianshe he zuzhijianshe)*.

The ideological education conducted by the Chinese Communist Party among its members, the consolidation of its organizations, and the recruitment of new members.

STYLE OF "GOVERNMENT INDUSTRY" AND "GOVERNMENT COMMERCE"

"官工"、"官商"作风 *("guangong," "guanshang" zuofeng)*.

An expression which compares the drawbacks of China's current system of industrial and commercial management to those of the handicraft and commercial undertakings of the feudal courts in Chinese history. Due to an emphasis on administrative ways of management, the present industrial-commercial system suffers from a low efficiency and much waste, a phenomenon comparable to the poor performance of court-run businesses in old times.

SUMMER GRAIN

夏粮   *(xialiang)*.

Grain crops harvested in summer, such as wheat in North China and early rice in South China.

SUPPLY SYSTEM (SUPPLY SYSTEM IN THE DISTRIBUTION OF FUNDS)

供给制（资金供给制）   *(gonggeizhi, zijin gonggeizhi)*.

The supply system refers to a system practiced during the revolutionary wars in China and in the early days after Liberation by which all people working for the Party, government, and the army and their dependents were provided with the basic necessities of life free of charge. The supply system in the distribution of funds refers to the practice whereby the funds needed by various departments, localities, and enterprises for production and construction purposes are given gratis by the state. This system often leads to squabbles over investments, a careless use of funds, and a neglect of the results.

SYSTEM OF OVERALL LEADERSHIP BY THE FACTORY DIRECTOR

厂长负责制 *(changzhang fuzezhi)*.

The system under which the director (manager) of an enterprise is its overall leader, exercising unified leadership over production, administration, and management. The director is also the representative of the enterprise as a legal person, being fully accountable for all matters of production and technology. At present most Chinese enterprises follow a system under which the director takes charge of day-to-day affairs under the leadership of the factory Communist Party committee. But as soon as the workers' congress becomes the organ of power for democratic management, the director must carry out all resolutions adopted by the congress.

SYSTEM OF RESPONSIBILITY IN AGRICULTURAL PRODUCTION

农业生产责任制 *(nongye shengchan zerenzhi)*.

A system of labor management and evaluation which links the results of labor with the amount of payment in collectivized agricultural production. Practiced over the past two or three years with satisfactory results, the system takes two forms: payment based on the accomplishment of a certain job, and payment based on the final output, that is, the harvest. Under the conditions of public ownership of the means of production, the system takes into account the characteristics of agricultural production, makes clear the peasants' economic responsibilities to their collectives, and enhances their incentive for production.

SYSTEM OF THREE-LEVEL OWNERSHIP IN A PEOPLE'S COMMUNE

人民公社三级所有制 *(renmingongshe sanjisuoyouzhi)*.

The people's commune, with production brigades and production teams as its subdivisions, constitutes a system of ownership of the means of production at three levels: the commune level, the production brigade level, and the production team level. The production team is generally the basic accounting unit, enjoying the right of autonomy over its farmland, forest, and grassland and its draft animals and farm tools. The team takes care of its own operations and distributes income among its peasant members. The people's commune or production brigades may organize joint undertakings among production teams when necessary, such as building reservoirs or power stations. Meanwhile, industries like brick and tile plants, canneries, and farm tools repair factories can also be run by the people's communes or production brigades.

The people's commune is both an economic organization and an agency of the state at the grass roots. Thus it is easily subjected to administrative intervention by higher authorities, and the commune and the brigades have often appropriated without compensation the manpower and material resources of production teams. These practices have damaged the production teams' right to handle their own affairs. China's theoreticians have suggested reform of this economic organization. The new system of linking payment to output quotas instituted in rural areas implies a readjustment and reform in the commune organization.

"TAILS OF CAPITALISM"

"资本主义尾巴" *(ziben zhuyi weiba).*

Forms of individual economic operation which are supplementary to socialist economy, including the peasants' private plots and household sidelines, the herdsmen's private livestock, the free markets in urban and rural areas, and individual businesses in cities. Denounced as "tails of capitalism" during the Cultural Revolution, all of them were restricted or abolished by administrative means.

TAKING GRAIN AS THE KEY LINK

以粮为纲 *(yi liang wei gang).*

This has been the policy behind the development of agricultural production since the late 1950s. It means that agricultural production should center on grain as the key to the development of other crops as well as of forestry, animal husbandry, sideline production, and fishery. In the implementation of this policy over the past twenty years, however, there has been a lopsided emphasis on the production of grain at the expense of cash crops and other agricultural pursuits. Opinions differ among Chinese economists on the validity of this policy. Some argue that the policy in itself is incorrect, others hold that it is a correct policy which has been distorted in practice.

TAPPING THE POTENTIAL (OF AN ENTERPRISE), EFFECTING (ITS TECHNICAL) RENOVATION AND TRANSFORMATION

挖潜、革新、改造 *(waqian, gexin, gaizao, often abbreviated as "wa ge gai").*

This refers to tapping the potential of the productivity of an existing enterprise by changing its outmoded production techniques and equipment. The aim is to raise the technical level and labor productivity for the purpose of extended reproduction without too much investment.

TECHNICAL PATTERN (TECHNICAL MAKEUP)

技术结构　 *(jishu jiegou).*

The proportions of different kinds of technology used in a country's economy, such as automation, semi-automation, mechanization, semi-mechanization, and manual operation. Some Chinese economists hold that China should, in existing conditions, develop technologies of an intermediate level which can be easily applied with the best economic results, instead of striving blindly to acquire the most up-to-date technologies.

TENDENCY TOWARD A RETURN TO INDIVIDUAL FARMING (TENDENCY TO-WARD GOING IT ALONE)

单干风 *(dangan feng).*

This originally referred to the vacillation of some peasants and cadres in the period of the collectivization of agriculture and their desire to return to individual farming. From 1958 onward, however, proper requests by peasants and cadres to carry out a system of responsibility in production, such as contracting production quotas to individual households, were often criticized as a tendency toward individual farming. This "Left" mistake was corrected after the Third Plenary Session of the Eleventh Central Committee of the Chinese Communist Party in December 1978.

THIRD PLENARY SESSION OF THE ELEVENTH CENTRAL COMMITTEE OF THE CHINESE COMMUNIST PARTY

党的十一届三中全会　 *(dangde shiyijie sanzhongquanhui).*

Held in Beijing, December 18–22, 1978, this plenary session shifted the Chinese Communist Party's focus of work to socialist modernization from 1979 onward. The session also decided on the guiding principles of "emancipating the mind," "seeking truth from facts," and "uniting as one in looking forward to the future," as well as correcting "Left" errors of the past.

THIRTY-FIVE ARTICLES ON THE HANDICRAFTS

手工业三十五条   *(shougongye sanshiwutiao).*

This refers to "Some Policy Regulations on the Handicrafts in the Urban and Rural Areas (Draft)," issued by the Central Committee of the Chinese Communist Party in June 1961. This document aimed at rectifying the "Left" mistakes committed in connection with the handicraft cooperatives from 1958 onward. The regulations deal with the system of ownership of the handicrafts, the sizes of handicraft enterprises, the distribution of their earnings, the wage scale and welfare system, arrangements for production, procurement of supplies and marketing, and the pricing of products.

THREE CATEGORIES OF SUPPLIES

三类物资   *(sanlei wuzi).*

Beginning in the 1950s, all commodities in China have been classified into three categories according to the principle of unified planning and management at different levels.

Commodities vital to the national economy and the people's livelihood, such as grain, edible oil, cotton, cloth, and coal, fall into the first category. These are procured and marketed by state commerce on a monopoly basis. The State Council plans quotas for the procurement and distribution of these commodities and entrusts its ministries and commissions to control them separately.

Commodities of great importance to the national economy and the people's livelihood, such as pigs, eggs, sewing machines, and bicycles, fall into the second category. Central ministries and commissions take charge of the procurement, allocation, and import and export quotas of these goods.

All other commodities fall into the third category, covering a wide range of varieties involving a complexity of production and marketing conditions. Their procurement and distribution are left to the provinces, municipalities, and autonomous regions.

This supply system has proved necessary for a planned and balanced development of the national economy, but it also entails an excessively rigid grip on commodities, which hampers the functioning of the market mechanism and the initiative of enterprises. Studies on reforming the system are under way.

TO EAT FROM THE SAME BIG POT

吃大锅饭 *(chi daguofan).*

This analogy refers to the present system of economic management by which the state treats alike and takes care of all enterprises owned by the whole people regardless of their gains or losses. Under this system, the production plan of an enterprise is handed down by government planning departments, its supplies are allocated by higher authorities, and its labor force is assigned by government labor departments. All profits earned by the enterprise are turned over to the state, and all losses are covered by it. Thus the whole country is likened to a huge pot from which food is provided for all. This derogatory term implies that the managerial system must be changed if it is to bring out the enthusiasm of the enterprises, their staff members, and the workers.

TOTAL (GROSS) OUTPUT VALUE

总产值 *(zongchanzhi).*

The value of the total social product in monetary form. It shows the total result of the economic activities of production units of various branches of the national economy during a given period of time.

TREASURY BONDS

国库券 *(guokujuan).*

A kind of government bonds issued within China since January 1981. They are redeemable, at an annual interest rate of 4 percent, from the sixth year after issuance. Treasury bonds differ from the national economic construction bonds issued in the 1950s in that they are sold mainly to state-owned or collectively owned enterprises and local governments at various levels, whereas the latter were sold to individuals. The issuance of treasury bonds is an attempt to balance state revenue and expenditure, stabilize market prices, and collect idle money to meet urgent needs in national construction.

TWO DEPARTMENTS (OF SOCIAL PRODUCTION)

两大部类 *(liangda bulei)*.

The production of social products is divided into two departments according to their final uses. Department I turns out the means of production (capital goods) to be consumed in the course of production. Department II produces the means of subsistence (consumer goods) to be consumed in people's everyday life.

UNDERSUPPLIED PRODUCTS

短线产品 *(duanxian chanpin)*.

Products which have been in short supply for a long time.

UNIFIED CONTROL OVER INCOME AND EXPENDITURE

统收统支 *(tongshou tongzhi)*.

Under the existing system of economic management in China, enterprises under ownership by the whole people (state enterprises) turn over all their income to the state and receive state allocations to cover all their expenses.

UNPAID APPROPRIATION

平调 *(pingdiao)*.

A "Left" tendency in agricultural collectivization from 1958 onward when large-scale projects were undertaken through the uncompensated appropriation of manpower and materials belonging to different collectives, mainly production teams. This line of action discouraged the peasants. The Party Central Committee started to correct the mistake in 1959, and the resources were returned to their rightful owners wherever possible.

USE, RESTRICTION, AND TRANSFORMATION

利用、限制、改造 *(liyong, xianzhi, gaizao)*.

The Constitution of the People's Republic of China adopted by the First National People's Congress in 1954 stipulated that state policy toward capitalist industry and commerce was to use, restrict, and transform them. This meant making use of those aspects of capitalist industry and commerce which were beneficial to the national welfare and the people's livelihood while restricting their negative aspects and encouraging and guiding their transformation into various forms of state-capitalist economy. In this way, capitalist ownership was gradually replaced with ownership by the whole people.

WAGE SCALES

工资级别 *(gongzi jibie).*

A unified wage system, based on the principle of "to each according to his work," by which wages are graded according to different kinds of labor skill, labor intensity, and working conditions. The current wage scale for industrial workers consists of eight grades; the scale for office workers, including leading cadres, has twenty-six grades.

WAGE ZONES

地区工资类别 *(diqu gongzi leibie).*

Geographical zones designated in China for variations in the payment of wages. While the state sets a single wage scale for cadres and another one for industrial workers throughout the country, it takes into consideration the differences in natural and economic conditions, price levels, and traditional living standards among various areas, and allows the standard wages to be modified by regional subsidies. The wage scale set in 1953 was accompanied by a division of the country into ten wage zones, each separated by a 3 percent difference in pay.

WELFARE FUND

福利基金 *(fuli jijin).*

The part of the national income used for collective welfare and social welfare. The collective welfare fund comes from the initial distribution of the national income—the process in which sums are set aside for collective welfare from the costs and profits of enterprises. The social welfare fund comes from a redistribution of the national income—the process in which allocations are made from the state budget for the welfare of society as a whole.

WELL-SUPPLIED PRODUCTS

中线产品　　*(zhongxian chanpin).*

Products which are supplied according to demand, reflecting a proper coordination between production and marketing.

WIND OF BOASTING AND EXAGGERATION

浮夸风　*(fukuafeng).*

This "wind" or tendency emerged from the unrealistic practices of the "Great Leap Forward" in 1958. Characterized by boasting, exaggeration, reporting of false production figures, and a blind emphasis on high targets, it was accompanied by arbitrary, uninformed direction of economic activities.

WORKERS' CONGRESS

职工代表大会　　*(zhigong daibiaodahui).*

The organ of power which enables the workers and staff of an enterprise to take part in decision-making and management and to supervise cadres. It has the right to examine and adopt resolutions on work reports submitted by the factory director, production and construction plans, budgets and final accounts, and all major issues concerning business and management. It also has the right to discuss and decide on the use of funds for labor protection, worker and staff welfare, and bonuses, as well as to map out regulations for the enterprise, supervise cadres, and elect administrative leaders.

The congress, whose delegates are elected by the workers, meets regularly. When the congress is not in session, the enterprise's trade union acts as its agent.

WORK POINTS

工分 *(gongfen).*

Units by which rural economic collectives record the amounts of labor put in by their members and work out their remuneration. The number of work points to be paid for a certain job every work day depends on the skill of the worker, the intensity required, and the importance of the undertaking. Each worker gets his pay according to the total number of work points he has earned in a year. The value of each work point varies from one collective to another and depends largely on the year's collective income.

YEAR-ROUND MUTUAL-AID TEAM

常年互助组   *(changnian huzhuzu)*

A collective labor organization, containing rudiments of socialism, formed by individual peasants during the early 1950s to help one another by exchanging labor year-round.

About the Contributors, Editors, and Translators

(In Order of Appearance)

Lin Wei (林韦)

Born in 1916, joined the Eighth Route Army in 1937. He has been a member of the Editorial Board and Director of the Department of Marxist Theory of *People's Daily* and subsequently Director of the Research Department of the State Capital Construction Commission. He is now a Deputy Chief Editor of *Social Sciences in China,* the journal of the Chinese Academy of Social Sciences. Among his many published articles are "The Confusion Created by Yao Wenyuan on the Question of Bourgeois Right" (*Guangming Daily,* April 12, 1977) and "Uphold Historical Materialism on the Question of Relationship Between Economics and Politics" (*Guangming Daily,* May 1, 1980).

Arnold Chao (Zhao Yihe, 赵一鹤)

Born in 1923, received his B.A. in history from the University of Nanking in 1946 and his M.A. in journalism from the University of Wisconsin in 1950. He is a member of the Editorial Board and Director of the English-Language Department of the Foreign Languages Press, Beijing.

Zhang Zhuoyuan (张卓元)

Born in 1933, graduated in economics from the Central-South China Institute of Finance and Economics in Wuhan in 1954 and joined the research staff of the Institute of Economics of the Chinese Academy of Sciences upon graduation. He is Associate Research Fellow of the same institute, now under the Chinese Academy of Social Sciences, and Associate Editor of *Jingji Yanjiu* (Economic Research). He is one of the authors of *The Relationship Between Planning and the Market in China's Socialist Economy* (Jilin People's Publishing House, 1980), a co-author of *The Pattern of Production in Socialist Economy* (in collaboration with He Jianzhang [Heilongjiang People's Publishing House, 1981]), "Methods of Investigation and Computation of the Cost of Farm Produce" (*Jingji Yanjiu*, no. 8, 1961), and "The Relationship Between Labor Productivity and the Formation of Value and Price" (*Jingji Yanjiu*, no. 1, 1964).

Zhou Shulian (周叔莲)

Born in 1929, graduated in economics from Fudan University in Shanghai in 1953 and is now Associate Research Fellow, a member of the Academic Council, and Vice-Director of the Institute of Industrial Economics under the Chinese Academy of Social Sciences. He is the author of *Profit and the Management of a Socialist Enterprise* (People's Publishing House, 1979) and one of the authors of *Socialist Economic Construction and Marxist Political Economy* (China Social Sciences Publishing House, forthcoming).

Wang Haibo (汪海波)

Born in 1930, graduated in economics from Fudan University in Shanghai in 1953 and completed graduate studies in political economy at China People's University in Beijing in 1956. He is now Director of the Department of Synthetic Studies of the Institute of Industrial Economics under the Chinese Academy of Social Sciences and a Council Member of the China Society of Enterprise Management. Among his works are *An Initial Inquiry into the Economic Problems of Socialism* (Hunan People's Publishing House, 1979), *Mental and Manual Labor Under Socialism* (Guangdong People's Publishing House, 1980), and *The Relations of Production in Immediate Production Under Socialism* (Hunan People's Publishing House, 1981).

Zhang Yulin (张雨林)

Born in 1924, graduated in biology from Northwest University in 1949. He once served as deputy chief editor of *Hunan Nongmin Bao* (Peasants' Daily of Hunan) and is now an editor of *Social Sciences in China*.

Xiao Liang （晓亮）

Born in 1928, joined the revolution in 1941. He is Director of the Department of Economics of *Social Sciences in China,* Editor of *Jingjixue Zhoubao* (Economics Weekly), and Associate Research Fellow of the Institute of Economics under the Chinese Academy of Social Sciences. Among his articles are "The Working Class and the Bourgeoisie," "The Purpose of Raising Labor Productivity," "On the Economic Laws in China's Period of Transition," "Questions of Economic Cooperation Under Socialism," "Science and Technology Constitute a Productive Force," "Economic Management by Economic Means," and "An Inquiry into the Theories of Management."

Fang Sheng （方生 ）

Born in 1925, completed his graduate work in political economy at China People's University in Beijing in 1952 and is now Associate Professor of Economics at the same university. Among his articles are "The Socialist Industrialization in the U.S.S.R.," "Socialism and the Personal Interests of the Worker," "Consumption in a Socialist Society," "On Socialist State Ownership," "Taking an All-Round View of the Policy of Utilizing Economic Advantages," "The Importance of Economic Forecasts," and "Comments on the Relationship Between Agriculture, Light Industry, and Heavy Industry."

He Jianzhang （何建章 ）

Born in 1925, graduated in political science from Fudan University in Shanghai in 1949 and completed graduate studies in political economy at China People's University in Beijing in 1956. He is Research Fellow, Vice-Chairman of the Academic Council, and Vice-Director of the Institute of Economics under the State Planning Commission, and a member of the Academic Council of the Institute of Economics under the Chinese Academy of Social Sciences. Among his articles are "Production Prices in a Socialist Economy" (*Jingji Yanjiu,* no. 5, 1964), "Problems in the Management of a Planned Economy Under the System of Ownership by the Whole People and the Orientation of Reforms" (*Jingji Yanjiu,* no. 5, 1979), and "The Integration of the Regulation of the Economy Through Planning and Its Regulation Through the Market" (*Jingji Yanjiu,* no. 5, 1980).

Zhang Wenmin (张问敏)

Born in 1937, is an Assistant Research Fellow of the Institute of Economics under the Chinese Academy of Social Sciences and an editor of *Jingji Yanjiu.* He is the author of *An Inquiry into the Theory of Distribution According to Work* (Jilin People's Publishing House, 1981).

Wang Zhenzhi (王振之)

Born in 1928, graduated in industrial management from Jiangnan University, Wuxi, in 1949. He is an Associate Research Fellow of the Chinese Academy of Social Sciences and Director of the Department of Cost Prices of the Institute of Finance, Commerce, and Supplies, and is co-author of *A Study of Prices Under Socialism* (China Social Sciences Publishing House, 1982).

Wang Yongzhi (王永治)

Born in 1937, graduated in economics from Beijing University in 1960. He is an instructor and Chairman of the Faculty of Economic Management in the Department of Economics of the same university, and is co-author of *A Study of Prices Under Socialism.*

Hu Genkang (胡根康)

Born in 1937, graduated in English from the Beijing Institute of Foreign Languages in 1958 and is now a news editor of the Xinhua News Agency. He translated the Introduction and Chapters 2, 6, 7, 8, 9, and 10 of this book, as well as part of Chapter 1.

B. W. Liu (Liu Bingwen,   刘炳文)

Born in 1931, graduated with a degree in English from the Beijing Institute of Foreign Languages in 1954 and is now a feature writer of the Xinhua News Agency. He translated Chapters 3, 4, and 5 of this book, as well as part of Chapter 1.

Xing Wenjun (邢文军)

Born in 1944, graduated in English from the Beijing Institute of Foreign Languages in 1967, completed graduate studies in English-language journalism at the graduate school of the Chinese Academy of Social Sciences in 1981, and is teaching English in the Chinese People's Liberation Army. He translated part of the Glossary.

Xie Zhenqing (谢振清)

Born in 1937, graduated in English from the University of Nanjing in 1962 and is an editor of the English edition of *Social Sciences in China*. He translated the tables on the Economic Development of the People's Republic of China and part of the Glossary, and he compiled the index.

Fang Zhiyun (方芷筠)

Born in 1931, graduated in English from Beijing University in 1954 and is a translator of the monthly journal *China Reconstructs*. She translated part of the Glossary.

Sara Grimes

Born in 1941, received her B.A. in English literature at Cornell University in 1964 and her M.S. at the Graduate School of Journalism of Columbia University in 1966. She was a reporter and editor of the *Philadelphia Bulletin* from 1966 to 1976 and has been Associate Professor of Journalism at the University of Massachusetts since 1976. She is currently on leave from the university and is serving as a specialist in the English Language Department of the Foreign Languages Press, Beijing. She edited the English texts of Chapters 6, 7, 8, and 10, as well as part of the Glossary.

Melissa Ennen

Born in 1953, received her B.A. in economics and Chinese studies from Wellesley College in 1975 and her M.A. in political economy from Goddard College in 1977. She was a member of the *Dollars and Sense* collective and came to China in 1978 to teach macroeconomics at the Beijing Foreign Trade Institute. Since 1981 she has been a specialist with the English edition of *Social Sciences in China.* She edited the English texts of Chapters 4 and 9.

Judy Polumbaum

Born in 1953, received her B.A. in East Asian studies from McGill University in Canada in 1976 and her M.S. from the Graduate School of Journalism of Columbia University in 1977. She is currently serving as a specialist on the English-language *China Daily,* published in Beijing. She edited part of the translation of the Glossary.

Zhao Jingxing (赵京兴)

Born in 1950, and Gao Liang 高梁, born in 1947, are both editorial assistants in the Department of Economics of *Social Sciences in China.* They wrote parts of the Glossary.

Subject Index

Accumulation, 29; adjustment of the ratio between consumption and, 57–58; drop in the rate of, in 1979–80, 36; for productive and nonproductive purposes, 54–55; high rate of, in 1958–78, 29–30; lower the rate of, 65; unbalanced consumption and, 57

Advantages of various localities, giving full play to, 65

Agriculture: agricultural bases specializing in forestry, animal husbandry, and fishery, 142; cooperative movement, 126–27, elementary and advanced producers' cooperatives, 126, the establishment of people's communes, 127, mutual-aim teams, 126; ecological imbalance, 138; farming mechanization, 45; farmland capital construction, 45–46; lags far behind industry, 48–49; land reform, 125; class polarization after, 190; necessity of the transition to socialism, 125–26; policies for the development of, Decisions of the Central Committee of the Chinese Communist Party on Some Questions Concerning the Accelleration of Agricultural Development (Draft), 130, lopsided stress on the policy of "taking the grain as the key link," 48–49, "take grain as the key link," ensuring an all-round development with appropriate emphasis on certain lines of

production, 140–41; readjusting the relations of production, 128–37; readjusting the rural economy, the principles of, 129–30, problems of readjustment, 143–46; reforming the planning system for, 141; rich resources, 139–40; socialist transformation of, 187, characterized by a blind effort to seek a large-scale of collectivization and a higher level of public ownership, 189–92, a drop in the output of some agricultural subsidiary occupations caused by speedy socialist transformation, 188–89; system of responsibility in production, 123, 136–37, contracting output quotas to individual households, 134–36; three categories of farm collectives, 129

Agriculture, light industry, and heavy industry: disproportions among, 31; relationship among, 57

Anarchy in production under capitalism, 119

Apprentice: contracts signed between individual businessmen and apprentices, 199–200; the master and apprentice in China, 176–77

Arts and crafts: glass grapes blown by Chang Family—an individual handicraftsman, 181; individual economy promotes the expansion of, 181

Associations: based on specialization and

Index compiled by Xie Zhenqing